Live Long & Prosper

Live Long & Prosper

Keys to a Longer, Healthier, Productive Life

Thomas J. Lobl, PhD
Stan Schatt, PhD

BUSINESS EXPERT PRESS

Leader in applied, concise business books

First published in 2025 by
Business Expert Press, LLC
222 East 46th Street, New York, NY 10017
www.businessexpertpress.com

ISBN-13: 978-1-63742-892-4 (paperback)
ISBN-13: 978-1-63742-893-1 (e-book)

Business Career Development Collection

First edition: 2025

10 9 8 7 6 5 4 3 2 1

EU SAFETY REPRESENTATIVE
Mare Nostrum Group B.V.
Mauritskade 21D
1091 GC Amsterdam
The Netherlands
gpsr@mare-nostrum.co.uk

For Michele, my true love, past, present and future

For Jane, love of my life and best friend

Description

Live Long and Prosper is the only guide you need to learn:

- How to keep your brain healthy as you age.
- The secrets of supercentenarians, those people living over 110 years of age.
- The latest research on the best advice for eating, sleeping, and exercising.
- How to hack your body for optimal results.
- How scientists now have the ability to increase large dogs' longevity.

Live Long and Prosper provides the very latest research on new drug therapies, stem cell use, and gene editing, as well as the latest lab tests to catch problems early, the best relief for stress, and a complete list of healthy habits to develop. It explains the importance of your gut bacteria in your health and the best use of wearable devices as you age.

Scientists have discovered how to rejuvenate cells of aging lab animals. Will humans be next?

Contents

Preface

It is truly an exciting time to be alive. Scientific and medical discoveries as well as the growing use of electronics in medicine are leading to innovations that will impact people's health spans and lifespans. We are excited to share these medical innovations with you to show you why medical research is in the process of making it possible to live long and prosper. In the following chapters, we will share the latest research on how it is possible to live fully (health span) into old age (lifespan) without being bedridden and too ill to enjoy life.

These terms, *health span* and *longevity* or *lifespan*, have a number of different meanings in common usage. For the purposes of this book, we will focus on how they apply to readers of this book and not to some abstract government definition of its entire population in comparison to other countries' populations. Still, these comparisons can be useful. For example, blacks have higher rates of high blood pressure and are 30 percent more likely to die from heart disease. Blacks and Hispanics have higher rates of strokes, and, in particular, African American men are twice as likely to die from stroke than whites.[1,2] It is just for these reasons, these kinds of statistics are important and useful for the nation to reduce disparities in access, medical insurance coverage, and, if appropriate, increase the number of providers in underserved communities.[3]

Studies of time further suggest that the life expectancy gap is increasing, at least here in the United States. Life expectancy of women in the 90th percentile of earners rose by 6.4 years, from 84.1 to 90.5 between 1970 and 1990. There was no improvement in the life expectancy of low earners. Expressed in another way, the difference in life expectancy between the 10th percentile and the 90th income percentile increased from a little over 3.5 years to more than 10 years during this period. Similarly, the gap in life expectancy between men in the 10th and 90th income percentile increased from 5 to 12 years.[4] There's nothing particularly mysterious about the life expectancy gap. Lower-income people in ill health, who are at risk of dying relatively young, face limits on the quality and amount of food available to them. By contrast, the higher-income people live in better and safer neighborhoods, can eat more nutritious diets, and can obtain access to first-rate health care. People who have higher incomes, moreover, tend to have more schooling, which means they may also have better information about the benefits of exercise and good diet.[5] These income-based differences in life expectancy can also be seen across communities. For example, Virginia's Fairfax County, one of the richest counties in the country, and West Virginia's McDowell County, one of the poorest, are separated by just 350 miles; however, in Fairfax, "men have an average life expectancy of 82 years and women, 85, about the same as in Sweden." By contrast, the average male and female life expectancy in McDowell County is 64 and 73 years, respectively, about the same as people living in Iraq.[6]

These statistics clearly show that people's health span and longevity are closely linked to access to good medical care throughout life. These examples also show that remaining active and socially connected is also important for longevity. In the coming chapters, we will focus on these and more topics to explain and illustrate how this affects health span and longevity for individuals and not just in aggregate national statistics. It is truly an exciting time to be alive and participate in the advances in medicine that will improve longevity.

CHAPTER 1

Old Age Then and Now

There is no reason why you can't remain productive, be healthy, and prosper into old age. Old age? Until the advent of modern medicine and improved sanitation, the odds of humans living to a ripe old age were poor. Steven Johnson's *Extra Life: A Short History of Living Longer* reveals how dramatically human life expectancy has improved. He points out that life expectancy at birth for a British child in 1668 was only 30 years while a baby born in Britain today can expect to live 80 years on average.[1]

The most common cause of death for people in the United States has changed as scientific breakthroughs have eliminated many of the leading causes of death in the nineteenth century. Tuberculosis, diphtheria, and influenza have been replaced by cancer, heart disease, and strokes.[2]

While a few animals live far longer than humans, most have far shorter lives. In general, large mammals tend to outlive smaller mammals, probably because their size gives them a competitive advantage in their fight for survival. The exception seems to be dogs. When it comes to these particular animals, smaller breeds generally live far longer than their larger counterparts. Researchers are currently working on developing a pill to help larger dogs live longer with a secondary, longer-term goal of finding the "magic bullet" that will help humans live longer. Of course, one difference is that among the entire animal kingdom only humans worry about longevity.[3]

Dying of Old Age

Our Neanderthal cousins rarely lived past 40 years. One almost complete skeleton of a male reveals a man who lived between 40 and 55 years. The bones reflected his relative old age for his time with degenerative lesions in his spine associated with osteoarthritis, bone fractures, and severe dental problems along with an infected lung. Imagine the severe pain this person lived with as he aged. So, while he enjoyed longevity relative to others of his time, he certainly had a very short health span, the period in his life when he enjoyed reasonably good health.[4,5] Throughout recorded history and until fairly recently, it was common to refer to "Old Age" as a common cause of death for an elderly person. Today, old age is not generally accepted as a cause of death by the medical community. The standard cause of death on a death certificate today when an elderly person dies is to identify one of the more common causes of death in the elderly, such as heart disease, cancer, diabetes, dementia, and so on.[6]

Life expectancy tables going back centuries reveal that these numbers are distorted and lowered until the twentieth century by the enormous proportion of deaths in childbirth by as much as 25 percent or more for women bearing children.[7] So, while on average people today live well into their seventies, there are so many mitigating factors. Just as medieval serfs who toiled in the fields were unlikely to live as long as their masters who lived in castles, people today with the wherewithal to pay for quality food as well as shelter are likely to outlive those with food insecurity and poor living and working conditions. In fact, a *Washington Post* study revealed that the gap in longevity between upper and lower classes in the United States is wider now than it was in the 1980s.[8] In this book, we cover the latest cutting-edge research on how you can improve the odds of increasing your lifespan as well as your health span by adopting healthy habits. From a vitality perspective, the longer you can be healthy enough to be productive, the better. In other words, living a longer but healthier life is the goal.

Health Span

A person's health span is "that portion of their life spent in good health free of chronic diseases and the disabilities of aging."[9] Nobody wants to contemplate living their last 20 years of their life bedridden or in constant pain.

Calculating Healthy Life Expectancy (HLE)

Researchers have come up with a way of calculating Health-Adjusted Life Expectancy (HALE). HALE is "the average number of years a person can expect to spend in full health, not hampered by disabling illnesses or injuries."[10] Using what is known as Sullivan's Index, it is possible to subtract probable duration of disabilities from life expectancy to come up with the remaining years of good health. In the United States, the average life expectancy is 84.1 years, and the average HALE is 78.9 years. Women enjoy good health on average two years more. HALE also differs by race. Interestingly enough, people in certain states such as Vermont, Hawaii, Connecticut, and Minnesota known to be more health-conscious enjoy much higher HALE numbers than those people living in Mississippi, West Virginia, and Alabama (the lowest). Not surprising, obesity is associated with lower HALE numbers.

The Blue Zones

Researchers studying longevity discovered that the Barbagia region of Sardinia had the world's highest concentration of male centenarians. They were unable to conclude whether it was the particular environment in which these people lived or genetic factors that contributed to this longevity. To determine which villages showed the highest concentration of centenarians, the researchers used blue ink to mark these areas on maps.[11]

Drawing on this research on "blue zones," author Dan Buettner and the National Geographic Society assembled a crew that included medical researchers, anthropologists, demographers, and epidemiologists to comb the world looking for similar locations where people lived far longer than the norm. After lengthy research they identified Ikaria, Greece, the Nicoya Peninsula of Costa Rico, Loma Linda, California—home to many Seventh Day Adventists, and Okinawa, Japan. The Japanese location had the longest-lived population in the world of women over 70 years of age. The result of this research was a National Geographic video series where Buettner visited these sites and talked with the elderly population. What is striking is just how vital these people are. They obviously are enjoying their lengthy health spans.

What can we learn from this blue zone research? Buettner and his researchers interviewed inhabitants of these "blue zones" at length. They came to the conclusion that while genes obviously played some part in their longevity, there were several other characteristics and lifestyle habits blue zone inhabitants shared. Buettner identified what he called "Power 9"—the nine lifestyle habits these healthy, longest-lived people shared.[12]

1. While these people did not formally exercise at a gym, their daily lifestyle included a lot of movement. They tended to do work by hand and not use mechanical tools in their gardening and other activity. They walked to visit friends rather than drive.

2. These people shared a sense of purpose. Buettner concluded that knowing one's sense of purpose is "worth seven years of extra life expectancy." That doesn't necessarily mean a religious sense of purpose though.

3. The ability to handle stress successfully. While the Okinawans pause to remember their ancestors every day, the Seventh Day Adventists pray and the Ikarians nap.

4. Eating sensibly. None of these long-lived people were overweight. In fact, the Okinawans believed in an 80/20 rule associated with a 2,500-year-old Confucian mantra that reminded them that they should stop eating while they were only 80 percent full.

5. Diet. These people tended to eat a mostly plant-based diet with meat (serving size 3 to 4 ounces) only eaten around five times per month.

6. Alcohol in moderation. Surprisingly, moderate alcohol drinkers outlive nondrinkers. These long-lived people tend to have one to two drinks per day with friends.

7. Faith-based groups. These long-lived people for the most part belonged to some faith-based community. Buettner states that research shows that "attending faith-based services four times per month will add 4–14 years of life expectancy."

8. Family is very important. This group of people put their family first and tended to live with extended family members, including grandparents. Buettner's research suggests that committing "to a life partner…can add up to 3 years of life expectancy."

9. Social circles. Buettner points to research that "smoking, obesity happiness, and even loneliness is contagious."

We will return to the concept of blue zones later in this book when we discuss what healthy habits can be gleaned from this research as well as medical research on long-lived experimental animals (see Chapters 7, 12, and 16). It is clear from all kinds of studies on longevity that while genes play a significant role on life expectancy, how people live also plays a major role in longevity as well as in extended health spans.

Supercentenarians

While the world is seeing more and more people living to the age of 100 (centenarians), a new subset group of supercentenarians (those people living longer than 110 years) is emerging. The Gerontology Research Group that monitors and validates the age of people who claim to be supercentenarians estimates that there are approximately 60 to 70 such people in the United States and 250 to 300 such people worldwide.[13] What is fascinating is that recent research on a group of 32 supercentenarians revealed that most of them still were in remarkably good health. In fact, 41 percent of those aged 110 to 119 years required little or no help in their daily lives. Because a sample of 105 centenarians revealed that 88 percent of them were functionally independent at a mean age of 92, researchers concluded that compression of disability up to age 100 probably is required for these people to live beyond 110 years. While 25 percent of supercentenarians had cancer at one time or another, all were cured.[14]

Most researchers assume that there has to be some genetic component to supercentenarians' longevity. The first researchers to examine genetic changes in supercentenarians used whole genome sequencing to examine this select group to see if their genes can reveal the secrets resulting in their extended lives. The results were nonconclusive since while some genetic differences from the general populace were found, they were not statistically significant.[15]

During the subsequent years, it has become far easier and less expensive to conduct genetic testing. A study six years later (2020) on 81 supercentenarians aged 105 to 110 years of age yielded more positive results. While the population was limited to Italians, a specific gene identified as *STK17A* was found to be statistically significant in the group tested. This particular gene is identified with the repair of DNA (and genetic) damage. This suggests that being able to repair such damage contributes significantly to these people's longevity.[16]

Biological Age Versus Physical Age

Steve Horvath, a professor of human genetics and biostatistics at UCLA, came up with a way of measuring the genetic changes in people's bodies to determine their biological rather than their chronological age. Based on research on thousands of subjects, Horvath developed a kind of "clock" that used algorithms to measure the genetic changes, or DNA damage, to determine biological age.[17]

It should come as no surprise then that people not only age in different ways and at different speeds, but the various parts of their bodies also age at different speeds. Recent research reveals that one in five healthy adults 50 years or older is an "extreme ager," a person with at least one organ aging much faster than those of their peers. By examining organ-specific proteins, the researchers estimated an age gap between an organ's biological age and its chronological age. Depending on the specific organ, the researchers determined that the person with such an "aged" organ had an increased disease and mortality risk over the next 15 years.[18]

What Are the Physical Age Limits for Humans?

Since we already have a small number of people living beyond 110 years, are there practical limitations on how long humans can live? Researchers examined demographics and concluded that while life expectancy continues to rise, the limit on how long people live seems to hold at somewhere around 122 years of age. There are a number of reasons for this limit. As the researchers point out, medical intervention in the form of surgery is generally not available for people over a certain age. Doctors won't recommend heart surgery on someone over 100 years old, for example. The researchers point to advances in certain drugs such as rapamycin that appear to have positive impact on aging at least in animal research as a hopeful sign.[19] The conclusion from this research is that we don't know yet if there is a practical age limit.

A Passion or an Obsession?

There is a group of biohackers who don't want to wait for medical science to come up with solutions to living longer and choose to experiment on themselves. The most famous example is a multimillionaire by the name of Bryan Johnson. He has chosen to turn his body into a laboratory to examine how the very latest research on longevity can be used to help him live longer and lower his biological age. Johnson takes 111 pills a day, consumes pounds of vegetables prepared in a blender, and monitors several parts of his body, including his penis. He follows a strict regime when it comes to exercise, diet, and sleep and claims that the biological age of his bones and his heart is far younger than his chronological age of 46. He says he is in the top 1 percent when it comes to ideal muscle fat and when it comes to his maximum oxygen consumption during physical exercise with a VO_2 Max in the top 1.5 percent of 18-year-olds. Since Johnson is preoccupied with increasing his longevity and shortening his biological age to the point that it takes precedence over anything else in his life, one wonders if this extreme form of biological biohacking is worth the effort. After all, he has decided not to have a relationship or live with anyone because his lifestyle makes it impractical.[20]

A Healthy Old Age Is the Goal

A more manageable goal for most people would be to enjoy a healthy old age, in other words, to live beyond average life expectancy and to enjoy a health span that extends to the end of their lives. We will discuss the latest research on ways of increasing one's lifespan as well as health span through a variety of ways, including developing healthy habits and a healthy lifestyle. In the next chapter, we'll examine the latest research on animals and on human subjects to boost longevity.

CHAPTER 2

The Race to Discover How to Increase Longevity

Why and how do we age? Does the body just simply wear out? Do we age because of genetic patterns, or is it anomalies and breakdowns of normal processes that bring about our demise?[1,2] While most people associate aging with physical changes such as loss of muscle mass and strength, changes in hair and skin, and a less robust immune system, researchers focus on underlying changes at the cellular level that manifest themselves in those physical changes. In this chapter, we'll examine a number of scientific breakthroughs related to understanding the aging process and increasing longevity.

Obviously before we can turn back aging, we need to understand the changes that take place in your body as you age as well as what medical science can do to reverse those changes. Much of the research on this topic has been done on mice and even on worms.

What can a nematode worm tell us about our own mortality? First of all, worms' very short lifespans (nine days or so) and their limited numbers of genes (8,000) make them ideal subjects when it comes to studying longevity because it is possible to understand long-term changes in longevity over several generations. Scientists discovered that changing a single gene on a worm could increase its lifespan from mere days to months, a 10-fold increase. Molecular geneticist Thomas E. Johnson discovered that he could double a worm's nine-day lifespan by mutating a gene he labeled *age-1*.[3] More recently, biologists Siegfried Hekimi and Bernard Lakowski discovered specific genes on a worm that seem to control the aging process directly. By manipulating these genes, which the researchers described as a biological clock controlling lifespan and metabolism, the researchers were able to slow down individual cells' metabolism so they divided more slowly. The worms lived 50 percent longer than normal.[4]

While genetics certainly plays a role in human longevity, the good news for most people is that some scientists now estimate that inheriting genes from long-lived parents only has a 35 percent impact on a person's possible longevity.[5] If that number still seems high and discouraging or if you have short-lived parents, longevity expert David Sinclair believes genetics only accounts for around 20 percent of a person's longevity.[6]

Epigenetic Alterations

Scientists have discovered that our genes as well as those in other species, including mice, are programmed to turn a cell's operations on and off. This cell programming is comparable to the software that governs how computers operate. We describe a body's "software" as its epigenome and the reprogramming of it as epigenetics. Shinya Yamanaka discovered how adding four proteins, called the Yamanaka factors, could reprogram cells.[7,8] In Chapter 5, we will explain how these Yamanaka factors can be used to reprogram cells to function as stem cells that unfortunately are in short supply as we age and are necessary to repair or replace aging cells.

Researchers have built upon this breakthrough to look for the biologic "magic bullet," the reprogramming that could reverse aging. They studied mice whose aged retinal ganglion cells lacked the capability to support vision and were able to restore vision by reprogramming these cells to their youthful state.[9]

Research published in 2010 revealed that the rapidly aging disease progeria is caused by a change in one gene, a protein required to hold a cell's nucleus together. The flawed gene makes a protein called progerin that makes cells unstable and leads to rapid aging. The disease is rarely passed down from generation to generation.[10] More recently, Juan Carlos Belmonte has experimented with aged mice that have been modified so that they suffer from progeria. His results indicate he has been able to reverse aging in these mice by reprogramming their cells. Belmonte believes that cells age because of changes to their epigenetic markers, the chemicals that wrap around a cell's DNA and apparently function as on and off switches for genes. Hence, he believes that if these changes can be reprogrammed, the cells would revert to their younger state.[11]

The Impact of DNA Changes as People Age

We can liken our DNA and the genes that carry out its orders as our software designed to work with our body or hardware. Just as computer software can become corrupted and malfunction, the same is true for our DNA. Corruption sometimes is the result of a spontaneous mutation. While we have built-in repair mechanisms to protect our genes, they can become overwhelmed. Schumacher has spelled out some of the environmental conditions can have a harmful impact on our DNA as we age, including UV light, x-rays, chemical compounds in our water and food, and so on.

The damage to our DNA can result in mutations as well as damage to DNA's ability to communicate and send instructions to cells. This reduced ability to communicate can result in cell death and "...functional loss of organs, cancer, atrophy, and inflammation."[12] Yousef Zadeh and his colleagues looked at DNA damage and its impact on aging and concluded that the conditions associated with aging described in their seminal article "The Hallmarks of Aging" could be linked directly to DNA damage.[13]

Damaged DNA can result in disruption of cells' ability to regulate proteins present within them as well as outside them. These proteins then begin to clump together since the cell's ability to eliminate these proteins has been compromised. In fact, researchers have noted excessive clumping of proteins in patients with Alzheimer's disease while long-lived people tend to have far fewer clumped proteins present.[14] Damaged DNA also can have an impact on cell replication. DNA molecules have protective caps at their ends known as telomeres that are long strands of repeating DNA bases. Each time a cell divides, the length of the telomeres shortens as some of those DNA telomere bases are removed. When the telomeres caps become too short, cells can no longer divide. Furthermore, they no longer can protect cells from disease and aging. Researchers experimented with mice that had been engineered so that all their cells contained DNA with hyper-long telomere caps. The results showed that these mice with longer telomeres had less DNA damage with aging. The mice were lean with "low cholesterol and LDL levels and also had improved glucose and insulin tolerance." They also had fewer incidences of cancer and lived longer than mice without longer telomeres.[15]

Does the research that indicates that a genetically engineered mouse with longer telomeres enjoys a greater lifespan and health span apply to humans as well? A Danish team of researchers examined 274 pairs of Danish same-sex twins aged 73 to 94 and found that the twin with longer telomeres lived longer than his brother with shorter telomeres. They concluded that a shorter telomere length is an excellent way of forecasting mortality and that the greater the differences in telomere parameters between the twins, the higher the telomere–mortality association.[16]

While DNA mutation can stop cells from dividing and replicating, so can other types of damage. Normally, the body's immune system can dispose of nonfunctioning cells before they become a problem. Unfortunately, the immune system reaches a point where it no longer can clean up and dispose of these "senescent" cells, sometimes known as "zombie cells." These cells are not totally dead, but they are not fully alive either in the sense that they are performing their normal functions. In fact, the accumulation of these cells is one biological marker associated with aging.[17] These senescent cells try to signal that they need to be disposed of, but the damaged cell is unable to respond. So, these zombie cells resort to sending out molecules that result in the body's immune system responding and causing more and more inflammation, another condition associated with aging. These senescent cells accumulate and create what researcher von Kobbe calls a "pro-inflammatory and pro-tumorigenic environment that eventually can lead to cancer, insulin resistance, osteoarthritis, atherosclerosis, and brain pathologies...."[18] Interestingly enough, a team of Newcastle University researchers discovered that while senescent cells usually only comprise a small percentage of total cells, in aged mice these zombie cells represented 36 percent of all cells.[19]

Dealing with senescent cells is complicated. While they do not cause cancer directly, they do create an inflammatory environment that can cause any nearby cancer tumor to grow. Researchers are focusing on senolytic drugs designed specifically to kill these cells. The U.S. National Institutes of Health is investing $125 million in SenNet, a research tool that is designed to identify and map senescent cells in humans and mice.[20]

As of August 2022, there were 20 clinical trials either scheduled or performed to test senolytic therapies. April 2023 saw the publication of the results of the first clinical trial to use senolytic therapy to modulate the progression of Alzheimer's disease. While the early results were described as "promising," the researchers indicated that additional studies were required.[21]

There are several challenges when it comes to the effective use of senolytic drugs.[22] Perhaps it is possible to reverse the damage done to DNA reflected in shorter telomeres and senescent cells. Researchers have done a trial using human subjects where they performed hyperbaric oxygen therapy on them. The result was that these patients' telomere length increased while the number of senescent cells decreased[23] (for more about telomeres, see Chapters 5, 11, 12, and 17).

Damage to Mitochondria and Their DNA

Mitochondria are tiny, organized structures or organelles that exist in every cell. They are critical to life because they are responsible for energy production to power cells by using aerobic respiration to generate a chemical that provides chemical energy for the cells. They also decide which cells are to be destroyed and release an enzyme to perform that task. Other tasks include the storage of calcium and the ability to generate heat when we are cold.[24]

The problem is that mitochondrial DNA has less protection than other DNA and is thus far more likely to become damaged. Because damaged mitochondria cannot generate energy, their negative impact is greatest on those parts of the body that require the most energy such as heart muscle cells and nerve cells. One popular theory is that free radicals (unstable molecules with an unpaired electron) in the form of reactive oxygen species (ROS) is produced by mitochondria as a byproduct of producing energy. These ROS particles contribute to aging by "damaging DNA, fats, and proteins."[24] Another possible explanation is that an accumulation of mutations of mitochondrial DNA can lead to premature aging. In fact, there is experimental evidence with mice to support this idea.[25]

Stem Cell Depletion and Revival

Yet another marker associated with aging is the depletion of a body's stem cells. As discussed in Chapter 5, in addition to embryonic stem cells found at birth, various organs have a number of stem cells specifically designed for them. These cells function as a repair crew to replace cells that are damaged. There are only so many of these cells, and they increasingly suffer from an inability to receive the signals sent to them as people age. The good news is that researchers have discovered a way to revive and rejuvenate these cells so they can perform their functions. A UCLA research team discovered that addition of a key antioxidant that prevents cell damage actually results in rejuvenating old muscle stem cells so that they become capable once again for repairing damaged muscle tissue.[26]

Using Epigenetic Markers to Estimate Lifespan

We have discussed a number of the markers of aging described as the "Hallmarks of Aging." Researchers have determined that it is possible to forecast people's lifespan by evaluating a number of the epigenetic markers in their bodies and concluded that their new algorithm they call DNAm PhenoAge that uses whole blood is far more accurate in forecasting lifespan as well as health span. They found that people with an epigenetic age higher than their chronological age suffered from greater inflammation, decreased efficiency of cell's ability to activate their transcriptional machinery, and decreased ability to respond to DNA damage. This single epigenetic biomarker of aging can capture the risks and outcomes across "multiple tissues and cells."[27]

Searching for the Magic Elixir That Reverses Aging

We've seen the various ways that aging manifests itself in the body, but so far there hasn't been a breakthrough, a magic potion that reverses aging. Still, recent research on mice suggests a tantalizing possibility. Researchers tied the circulatory systems together of a young mouse and an old mouse using a technique known as parabiosis. The infusion of blood from younger mice rejuvenated older mice that then lived 6 to 9 percent longer. Also significant, these older mice's biological markers improved and resembled those of much younger mice. Scientists still are not sure of why a younger mouse's blood would rejuvenate the older mouse. For such a process to work with humans, the two people tied together would have to be identical twins[28] (see Chapter 7 for more details about these experiments).

While some biohackers such as Bryan Johnson have experimented with blood plasma from younger people, in his case his son, there is no evidence that such a technique works on humans even though there are clinics that are offering blood from younger people for sale for thousands of dollars. Perhaps the secret to increase longevity lies in stimulating our own immune systems.

The Gut Biome as a Marker of Longevity

If the secret to longevity doesn't lie in transfusing the blood of those far younger, maybe it lies in something far more mundane, our gut biome. Researchers have studied over 9,000 people to establish the relationship between their gut biome and their epigenetic markers associated with aging. They found that people who keep their original gut biome composition of bacteria age far faster than those, particularly over 80 years of age, who develop a unique gut biome by leveraging microbially produced amino acid derivatives circulating in their blood age far slower. Those people retaining their original gut biome were found to have a higher mortality rate when the researchers followed up over a four-year period.[29]

Conclusions

To understand how humans can achieve longevity along with a significant increase in their health spans, it is necessary to look at the human body as a complex system much like a supercomputer with both hardware (the physical body) and software (the underlying communications that take place at the cellular level). Just as computer software can become corrupted in a number of ways, the human epigenome equivalent can also become corrupted in a number of ways, including gene mutation, telomere shortening, cellular death, and senescence.

Research over the past two decades has looked at a number of possible ways to rejuvenate old cells and restore them to youthful vigor. Scientists have successfully reprogrammed cells to become stem cells capable of repairing cellular damage. They also have discovered that there is something magical about youthful blood, at least in the case of mice, that can be used to rejuvenate cells of older mice. Unfortunately, that approach does not seem to be workable when treating older people.

As we see more centenarians and supercentenarians, scientists are actively studying the differences found in their bodies compared to people who age faster. Already we can see that this healthier, older, and slower-aging population has a significantly different gut biome when compared to the gut biome of people aging faster. This group of healthier longer-lived people show far less inflammation, far less protein clumping, and fewer senescent cells, but there is, as yet, no definitive answers to what lessons can be learned at the cellular level from this population and applied directly to the general population. What we do know now is that different organs age at different rates as people age. By applying a newly developed algorithm, it is possible to assess how well people are aging and even forecast their longevity.

CHAPTER 3

The Microbiome—Partners in Our Health and Longevity

The microbiome (or biome for short) is the collection of all microbes, such as bacteria, fungi, viruses, and their genes, that naturally live on and inside bodies. We cannot avoid them as these microbes are everywhere—on our skin, in our nose, in our eyes, and in our gut. As it turns out, that is mostly a good thing. These microbes contribute in big ways to human health and wellness. That is not to say that sometimes we become infected by some bad microbes (germs) that overwhelm the good microbes in the microbiome to cause diseases.

To give you a sense of the magnitude of the human microbiome, here are a few statistics: The average weight of microorganisms living in and on a 220-pound person is about 4.4 pounds. Truly shocking, the ratio of different microorganisms to different human cells in the body is 10 to 1. The number of different microbial species inhabiting the human body is about 10,000.[1] This is not something to be concerned about because it is a symbiotic relationship. Since the microbiome is a key interface between the body and the external environment, these microbes can affect our health in many ways. Some members of our microbiome affect not just our bodies but also respond to external environmental substances in ways that can make them more toxic, while others act to make environmental substances less harmful. They protect us against germs and nonliving pathogens (e.g., chemicals and toxins), help our immune system develop, and enable us to digest food to produce energy.

In this book, we discuss the many ways and strategies that can be used to increase longevity. Recent research also shows that in addition to eating vegetables, exercising, and getting enough sleep, we, as individuals, can improve our longevity and reduce life-shortening diseases by better management of our microbiome.

The Microbiome Affects Your Health

A person's core microbiome is formed in the first years of life, but its composition will change over time in response to different factors, including diet, medications, and environmental exposures. The gut's microbiome response to different environmental exposures can also disrupt a person's health in ways that can increase the likelihood of developing conditions such as diabetes, obesity, cardiovascular diseases, neurological diseases, allergies, inflammatory bowel disease, and others.[2,3]

The Gastrointestinal Tract or Gut and the Microbiome

The gastrointestinal tract (GIT or gut) microbiome is not a passive bystander in your health. It may not be obvious, but it is a major player in your health and longevity. The key functions of the gut are to digest your food, to secrete the various substances that your body needs to help you digest and absorb your food, and to help maintain other normal functions. Less well appreciated is the fact that the gut is also "home" to a huge variety of microorganisms, bacteria, viruses, protozoa, and fungi. This extremely complex and diverse community of microorganisms is collectively known as the gut microbiome.

To our great benefit, the gut bacteria are able to produce a variety of vitamins and synthesize all essential and nonessential amino acids as well as perform other important metabolic functions. The microbiome can metabolize many things that escape regular human digestion to recover energy and absorbable nutrients for our use as well as an extra supply of energy and nutrients to support their own growth within the gut. As will be explained in more detail below, the gut microbiome does not just help digest food, it also plays a very important role in your health.

The Gut Stimulates a Healthy Immune System

The gut, along with the skin's microbiome, is involved in stimulating the development of the host's immune system.[4] As a result, the immune system takes out organisms it doesn't "know" (e.g., pathogens or cancer cells) and is tolerant to the organisms that make up the normal gut microbiome. This goes on without you knowing it is going on. You only get sick when the immune system fails to destroy a pathogen or a cancer cell before it develops a tumor.[5] Any disruption to the gut microbiome may be associated with the immune system not being able to respond quickly enough to catch a disease or pathogen before it does too much damage.[6]

If the pathogens circulate throughout the body, serious diseases may develop or be exacerbated, such as obesity, type-2 diabetes, cardiovascular diseases, and many more. Research has shown that gut microbes can cross not only the gut walls but once absorbed can cause or exacerbate neurological diseases such as Parkinson's disease, Alzheimer's disease, and multiple sclerosis. A change in biome composition to contain pathogens can be linked to many disorders and illnesses, including cancer.[7]

The Gut's Biome and Liver Health

Researchers link the gut microbiome to liver health. Pathogens in the gut microbiome have been linked in the progression of nonalcoholic fatty liver disease to advanced fibrosis and cirrhosis. Researchers now analyze stool samples to detect microbial changes that can accurately diagnose liver fibrosis and cirrhosis. These findings demonstrate that a core set of gut microbiome species might serve as a noninvasive diagnostic test for cirrhosis.[8] Researchers have found a correlation between human oral and gut fungal microbiota and patients with metabolic conditions associated with fatty liver disease. This means it might be possible to treat this disease by replacing the "wrong" or "offending" microbiome member organisms in the gut with the microbiome organisms found in healthy patients.[9]

Effects of Microbiome on Therapeutic Drugs

The GI microbiome metabolizes eaten food or anything that comes its way. This means it metabolizes food additives and swallowed drugs too. When new drugs are being developed for oral delivery, pharmaceutical companies have to test them to see if they are inactivated in the stomach or by the intestinal microbiome to determine how much of the dose gets actually absorbed. Many potentially wonderful drugs can't be taken by mouth or are not absorbed through the intestinal tissue. That is why some drugs have to be injected or infused.

Gut Microbiome Can Enhance Cancer Therapy

Researchers have modified human microbiota composition to boost the patient's response to existing anticancer therapies, minimize correspond-ing adverse effects, and reduce drug resistance in immunotherapy and chemotherapy. Such treatment can reduce consequences from cancer surgery and radiation therapy. Clinical research results revealed that a pro-biotic treatment can significantly relieve inflammation, enhance immu-nity, and promote recovery in patients with gastric cancer after removal of the cancerous gut tissue, so it may serve as joint treatment for gastric can-cer in the future. More importantly, available human clinical study data seem to indicate that modifying the composition of the gut microbiota can improve the performance of anticancer drugs.[10-15]

Direct Tumor-Suppressive Effects

We now know that microbiome secretions are extremely diverse too. Some bacterial secretions can initiate and promote cancer while other bacterial secretions are known to inhibit cancer's occurrence and progres-sion through two mechanisms: direct killing effects on tumor cells and positive stimulation of the immune system. Additionally, some bacteria secrete toxins that exhibit a unique targeting property against cancer cells and may be potent enough to serve as anticancer agents.[16]

Chemotherapy Effectiveness Is Closely Linked to the Gut's Microbial Composition

Researchers have found a strong relationship between certain gut micro-organisms and the effectiveness of anticancer treatments. To be clear, the microbiome alone is not a cure for cancer, but, with the proper organ-isms present, it can provide a better outcome in ways that a drug alone cannot.[16] Chemotherapy is widely used for treating cancer. Many, but not all patients, respond well to these powerful drugs. One reason that cancer patients respond differently to the identical chemotherapy drugs may be the differences in the composition of their gut microbiota.[17,18]

Gut Microbiome and Aging

The gut microbiome is emerging as a key factor in the aging process. Over the past two decades, microbiome research focused on establishing a causal relationship between individuals' microbiome and their aging.[19,20] Studies have found gut microbiome pattern differences in older adults who are lean and physically active compared to their less-fit peers. Other research connected early frailty to reduced gut microbial diversity. In healthy people, the kinds of microbes that dominate the gut in early adulthood make up a smaller and smaller proportion of the microbiome over the ensuing decades, while the percentage of other, less prevalent species rises. This is a sign of healthy aging. But in people who are less healthy, the study found, the opposite occurs: The composition of their microbiomes remains relatively static, and they tend to die earlier. This can be explained, in part, by the metabolic activity of the gut microbiome and their secretions of positive and negative metabolites. One other relevant study was done in mice. In mice studies, microbiota transplantation from a young to an old mouse act as a reset button for aging by increasing the old mouse's lifespan and changing its metabolism.[21] This again suggests that the composition of microbiome is important for healthy aging.

Researchers have shown that the gut microbiomes of centenarians (≤104 years of age) and supercentenarians (104+ years) are depleted in core abundant organisms while complemented by an increase in the prevalence of rare organisms.[22] Other studies on individuals in the age range of 20 to 117 years showed that centenarians displayed youth-associated features in their gut microbiome. Several studies have reached the conclusion that the human gut microbiome is relatively stable up until old age. In old age, there is a gradual compositional shift that is driven by dietary changes, lifestyle, and health status. These microbiome changes are positively correlated with longevity. These studies and those at Duke University suggest that the gut microbiota communities do not merely coexist with the host but, in fact, play a functional role in shaping a response to the aging process.

Conclusion

Predicting longevity based on the microbiome is a subject of active research. A recently published study developed a human gut microbiome aging clock based on a gut meta-genomics data-trained deep learning model (i.e., AI-based and Big Data analysis). The model revealed that indicators of age can be derived from microbiome data. In the near future, we will be able to identify and predict longevity risk factors from the gut composition.[23]

CHAPTER 4

Keeping Our Brain Healthy as We Age

There are so many TV advertisements in which older businesspeople say they are taking various supplements because they fear they no longer feel "sharp" enough to keep up with younger colleagues. In this chapter, we'll examine how to keep our brains healthy as we age as well as how the brains of super-agers differ from that of the general population.

As people grow older, changes occur in all parts of the body, including the brain. Most of us will continue to have strong memories as we age because our ability to remember will not decline rapidly or substantively. In old age, we will also retain the skills and knowledge learned throughout our lives. Unfortunately, the parts of the brain important for learning and other complex mental activities also shrink in volume due to the loss of some brain cells as we age. Accordingly, almost 40 percent of us will experience some form of memory loss after we turn 65 years old. But even if we experience some memory loss, chances are unlikely that we have dementia. For the most part, our memory loss is mild enough that we can still live our day-to-day lives without interruption or reduction in the quality of life. Symptoms of this benign memory loss include not remembering information as well as we once did, not being able to recall things as quickly, occasionally misplacing things, forgetting to pay a bill or a password for a website, or the name of a former classmate. These are not signs you have dementia.[1]

It is unclear to medical professionals where the line is between normal age-associated memory loss and mild disease-related memory loss. This normal aging of the brain is distinguishable from disease-related decline in brain function. The normal age-related forgetfulness can simply be due to the fact that a person has not thought about a particular fact or situation for a very long time and, therefore, has trouble recalling it. There are things that can be done to minimize this aging process and keep the brain memory recall healthy and, indirectly through this, increase longevity. However, if you have concerns that your memory loss is not normal age-related forgetfulness, you should consult a doctor.

Part of the task of keeping the brain healthy is making sure the brain gets what it needs to stay healthy. The brain needs glucose (its main source of energy), oxygen, vitamins, minerals, and other essential chemicals such as proteins, fats, and amino acids for it to run properly. There are many chemicals and proteins in the body that would not be good for optimal brain function. The blood–brain barrier (BBB) operates to keep harmful chemicals out of the brain while letting in the useful and necessary nutrients.[2]

How Does the Brain Manage Your Health and Longevity?

Simply put, the brain is the body's nerve center, and it is much like a computer system. It does this through big nerve bundles, such as the vagus nerve, that carry information from the brain to the other tissues in the body and from them back to the brain. This is one of the brain's communication highways. It is responsible for the regulation of internal organ functions, such as digestion, heart rate, respiratory rate, vasomotor activity (hot flashes, flushing, night sweats, etc.), certain reflex actions— such as coughing, sneezing, swallowing, and vomiting—and many other functions because branches of this nerve highway go to every corner of the entire body.[3] It also regulates the body's cycles, rhythms, and hormone release. If something goes wrong in the brain or communication is broken between the brain and the organs in other parts of the body, some diseases occur. Two examples of this are inflammatory diseases such as rheumatoid arthritis and elevated blood pressure. Scientists are finally making progress in understanding how these communications work. Setpoint Medical is using vagus nerve stimulation to suppress the immune system to reduce inflammation in patients with rheumatoid arthritis.[4] Other benefits from stimulating the vagus nerve are: reducing inflammation, reducing symptoms of chronic depression, treating epilepsy, and boosting the immune system.[5] These examples show the importance of the brain in managing the health of the person, their quality of life, and, indirectly, their longevity.

There are things you can do to keep the brain healthy. The CDC suggests the following seven things you can do to help maintain brain health and reduce the impact of age-dependent memory loss. These are[6]:

1. Stay socially engaged and stay involved in community and other activities.
2. Be physically active.
3. Get enough sleep.
4. Maintain a healthy weight and eat healthy.
5. Maintain a healthy blood pressure level.
6. Manage blood sugar.
7. Quit smoking.

None of these things should be a surprise to you.

Brain "Mental Exercises" Improves Brain Health

Like any other organ in the body, it is very important to "exercise" the brain through mental exercises and not just physical exercises. Mental exercises involve active thinking in a way that forces the brain to figure out things. This "hard" thinking results in the brain making new connections between brain cells (neurons). Examples of this kind of brain exercise would include learning new skills or a language, staying involved in activities such as with your community school or place of worship, and spending time socially with friends and family. These activities require the brain to "think" and to be active in ways that passive tasks, for example, watching TV, do not.[7] "While passively watching TV gives you some visual stimulation, there is no back-and-forth brain engagement," explains Douglas Scharre, MD, the director of The Ohio State Wexner Medical Center Division of Cognitive Neurology: "That's probably less a benefit to your brain than activities that you're actively involved in." In general, education also affects the prevalence of dementia. Poon and colleagues' study results showed that among older adults as the level of education goes up, dementia prevalence goes down.[8]

Research has shown that there are many ways you can hone your mental sharpness and help your brain stay healthy, no matter what age you are. Doing certain brain exercises helps boost your memory, concentration, and focus, which has the additional benefit of making your daily tasks quicker and easier to do while keeping your aging brain sharp. Examples of evidence-based exercises that offer the best brain-boosting benefits include doing a jigsaw puzzle, playing cards, building your vocabulary, or learning a new language. Other brain stimulating activities that use all your senses, such as baking cookies, learning or teaching a new subject to someone else, playing music, and so on, are also beneficial. These kinds of mental activities benefit you no matter what age you are. By incorporating brain exercises into your everyday life, you'll challenge your mind, sharpen your cognitive skills, and possibly learn something new and enriching along the way.[9,10]

One interesting new area of research is the role of music on memory and concentration. Research reveals that listening to music can improve memory recall, especially for information that is emotionally important or has a personal meaning to the person.[11] According to a publication from Johns Hopkins, music provides a total brain workout and activates nearly all brain regions. It can reduce anxiety, blood pressure, and pain as well as improve sleep quality, mood, mental alertness, and memory.[12] According to a Swiss study, playing music stops brain shrinkage and boosts memory.[13] Musical intervention has therapeutic benefits for people with dementia or Alzheimer's disease because it evokes emotions and memories. When this happens, presumably, the music-stimulated brain will develop more connections between brain cells and this improves memory.[14]

Just remember that memory is complicated and a combination of a lot of things. Consider a trip to the grocery store: Remembering what you intended to buy without having a list to look at requires an ability to recall things. Remembering the layout of the store and where to find things requires more of a visual/spatial memory. These examples are different kinds of memory that use different regions of the brain and require different kinds of brain processing.[15]

Physical Exercise Has a Positive Effect on the Brain

Physical exercise improves your muscles, heart health, blood flow, and oxygenation as well as improving brain function for many reasons. Whether you are over 65 and concerned about age-related memory loss or are simply looking to implement measures to improve cognition, research overwhelmingly shows that physical exercise is one of the most important daily habits to include to prevent cognitive decline.[16]

Marat Reyzelman, MD, a specialist in Neurology and Clinical Neurophysiology at Wellsar Health System, emphasizes why we must look at exercise as an essential element in maintaining a healthy brain:

"Studies have shown that in adults who exercise regularly, there was a significantly reduced rate of brain tissue atrophy (shrinkage) as well as reduced signs of vascular tissue injury and silent stroke based on MRI imaging. There was also increased thickening of various parts of the brain cortex—areas vital for memory and thinking functions. In essence, exercise caused patients to maintain or even gain cells in important brain areas, whereas lack of exercise caused an increase in the rate of age-related brain cell loss."[17]

Reyzelman also noted that exercise is not just for the young because there is a link between brain health and heart health.[18]

Research overwhelmingly supports the importance of exercising. As stated earlier, it improves the brain by improving the health of our cardiovascular system, which leads to better brain vasculature (blood vessels), oxygen, and nutrients going to the brain.[19] For example, Ganz et al. found in the centenarian brains within their sample, 50 percent had no signs of atrophy or brain size shrinkage.[20]

Dr. Ebony Glover, director of the Affective Neuroscience Laboratory and associate professor of neuroscience at Kennesaw State University, explains that physical exercise can lead to improvements in cognition not only by protecting the brain, but also through a process called neurogenesis, where new neurons (brain cells) are formed in the brain and neuroplasticity is increased. Neuroplasticity describes the flexibility of brain cells to form and reorganize connection between brain cells. This capability is super important for normal brain function as well as for learning, memory, and overcoming minor injuries. It is also the reason that stroke patients regain some function over time. "Physical activity appears to lead to neurogenesis, neuroprotection and cognitive improvements, primarily through the production of chemicals called neurotrophins." He also explains that "The brain is one of the heaviest oxygen consumers in the body. A higher supply of oxygen to the brain has been shown to positively affect cognitive processes, such as learning and memory."[21] Improving cardiovascular health improves the oxygen supply to the brain.

Many studies have suggested that the parts of the brain that control thinking and memory are larger in volume in people who exercise than in people who don't. "Even more exciting is the finding that engaging in a program of regular exercise of moderate intensity over six months or a year is associated with an increase in the volume in certain brain regions." Exercise can also boost memory and thinking indirectly by improving mood and sleep and by reducing stress and anxiety.[22] For an older person, the kind of exercise that would be beneficial is walking/jogging, biking, swimming, lifting weights, and moderate-intensity cardiovascular exercise. The thing to remember is that this kind of exercise needs to be done regularly and multiple times a week. The good news is that the benefit is for your entire body and not just for your brain.

"Rewiring" the Body's Nervous System to Improve Communications Within the Body and Increase Longevity

Neuroplasticity is the ability of the nervous system to change its activity and connections to other brain neurons following external stimuli or following injuries such as stroke or traumatic brain injury. Basically, healthy brain cells use neuroplasticity to rewire themselves to regain function following damage or to make newly wired connections following a stimulus such as learning a new language. Neuroplasticity helps the brain resist aging by adapting to negative brain events, to repair or work around irreversibly damaged areas (when possible), and to make new connections to enhance function following proper stimulation. All of these delay age-dependent memory loss and sustain health span and longevity.[23]

To be clear, neuroplasticity can also be negative, for example, when the brain changes to succumb to chronic joint pain, phantom limb pain, or addiction. As we have described above, a variety of cognitive training techniques can enhance neural and cognitive function and even brain mass. This does not mean that there is no brain deterioration that occurs with age, but the training stimulates neural activity, and this slows the decline. This neural activity then stimulates the brain cells to make new connections and rewire themselves in response to the stimulation or the need to overcome a damaged part of the brain. Dr. Park and colleagues at the Center for Vital Longevity at the University of Texas at Dallas studied neuroplasticity following cognitive training. Their research suggests that challenging leisure activities that stimulate core cognitive processes, such as working memory and reasoning, may prove to be more effective than say computer-based training due to the ability of older adults to sustain interesting leisure activities indefinitely.[24] In summary, together with aerobic physical exercise and mental exercise, neuroplasticity is required for strong brain function and delaying brain aging.[25]

Sleep Is Important for Brain Health

Sleep is an essential part of everyone's daily routine, and you spend about one-third of your life doing it. It is essential for good brain health and affects nearly every tissue and system in the body. In fact, your brain stays remarkably active while you sleep. Upon falling asleep, thousands of neurons in the brain switch from waking to sleeping states. Recent findings suggest that sleep enables the brain to conduct housekeeping activities that remove toxins and clean brain fluids that build up while you are awake.[26]

There are four stages of sleep. Stage 1 is the transition from wakefulness to sleep and your muscles relax, your heartbeat slows, and your brain waves begin to slow. In Stage 2, you go deeper into sleep, your body temperature drops, and your brain waves continue to slow. Stage 3 sleep is non–rapid eye movement (non-REM) sleep, and this is the sleep required to feel refreshed in the morning. It is not just that your muscles are very relaxed, but it is difficult to awaken you from this sleep. In this stage, the brain waves become even slower. Stages 1 to 3 are all non-REM sleep.

Stage 4 is REM sleep. This is when you dream for an average of two hours/ night, your brain waves become active, and your heart rate and blood pressure increase. Your brain is not sleeping most of the time you are asleep. It is busy consolidating memories, sorting, filing, and storing information, "cleaning up" and removing biological waste that accumulate from the day's activities. Lack of sleep prevents these brain maintenance activities from getting done, and serious negative consequences will eventually result, if you don't catch up. Thus, sleep is important for memory. During your sleep and REM sleep, the brain uses that time to convert some short-term memory and consolidate new memories to long-term memory.[27]

You can dream during any phase of sleep. The exact reason for dreaming is unknown, but it is most vivid during REM sleep. It is clear, however, that it is involved in processing emotions and is a part of the sorting and filing of memories that the brain needs to do. Stress and anxiety are associated with frightening dreams, and these dreams are also part of how the brain processes information.[28]

College students often stay up late studying and "cramming" for a test. The research on this subject does not support the long-term benefits of this practice. Students who stay up late cramming may have a short-term benefit, but, without catching up on sleep, those benefits may diminish as the brain will not be able to process and store that information correctly. Also, by being so sleepy during the exam, their memory may not function optimally, and the recall of recently learned information may also be less than optimal. Furthermore, lack of sleep has a negative effect on many of the body's systems and can lead to getting sick. Your body produces less infection-fighting antibodies when sleep-deprived.[29]

Your sleep patterns change as you age. Older people tend not to sleep as deeply and wake up often during the night. In some cases, physical and mental health conditions may interfere with sleep, such as going to the bathroom frequently during the night, being anxious, or experiencing joint pain. This more frequent awakening may make older adults think they get less sleep, but studies suggest the total amount of sleep remains about the same as when they were younger—6.5 to 7 hours a night.[30] This number varies significantly between individuals of the same age. There is no specific amount an individual needs except that their body will "tell" them when they are sleep-deprived.[31]

Finally, among the lifestyle habits of centenarians is longer average sleep. It should be noted that the brain clears β-amyloid, the protein associated with the development of Alzheimer's disease, during sleep. Researchers have shown longer sleep duration is associated with less β-amyloid accumulation in the brain.[32] More than half of centenarians in one study reported sleeping eight hours or more per night at age 70 years and older.[33]

Centenarians Have a Neuronal Reserve That Delays Cognitive Decline

Studies of centenarians show that most do not show cognitive decline until their 90s and some don't show any.[34] For these centenarians, there is a resistance to dementia due, in part, to the presence of a cognitive-neuronal reserve that is still available. These studies suggest that a young brain has a reserve of neurons, and, as the brain ages, this reserve is "used up." The loss of brain tissue and brain reserves shows up as cognitive dysfunction at some point. The goal then is to focus on things that promote brain health while we are young and middle-aged before this brain reserve is used up. To reemphasize again, biological aging is not tied to chronological aging and the CDC's (Centers for Disease Control and Prevention) recommendations can help slow biological aging.[35]

Dementia Reduces Longevity

Dementia is not a given for older people, but it does shorten their lifespan. It is very difficult to know how long someone with dementia will live because the disease progression is so unpredictable. With dementia, a person's body may continue to be physically healthy. For Alzheimer's disease, longevity after diagnosis is about 8 to 10 years depending on the age at diagnosis. For vascular dementia, it is about five years with an increased risk of stroke or heart attack. For Lewy body dementia (LBD), it is about six years with increased risk of falls and infections.[36] However, dementia causes the gradual loss of thinking, remembering, and reasoning abilities, which means that people with dementia at the end of life may no longer be able to make choices about their healthcare or communicate their symptoms and/or therapy wishes.[37]

In a Danish study of people who turned 100 years old, 51 percent showed the prevalence of mild to severe dementia while 37 percent had no signs of dementia. Of the demented centenarians, 12 percent had diseases such as B_{12} or folate deficiencies, hypothyroidism, and Parkinson's disease, and 50 percent had cerebrovascular or cardiovascular diseases known to be risk factors in developing dementia.[38] Beker and colleagues studied centenarians and found that after reaching age 100 years, cognitive performance remains relatively stable during ensuing years. They concluded that these centenarians might be resilient or resistant against different risk factors of cognitive decline.[39]

Are Brain Supplements Useful?

Some diseases are caused by vitamin deficiencies. If you have a deficiency of a vitamin or mineral or another important nutrient, then supplements will be helpful. There is no doubt that the brain supplement market is huge. It was reported in a Harvard report that 25 percent of adults over 50 years of age take supplements designed to improve brain health with the promise that it will improve memory and sharper focus without any proof that they work.[40] In 2021, the brain supplement market was estimated to be $8.23 billion, and it is expected to grow at 8 percent/year to reach $17.4 billion by 2028.[41] If you are not vitamin-deficient and are eating a healthy diet such as the Mediterranean diet, one rich in vegetables and healthy oils, it is unlikely supplements will provide a further boost. Experts agree a healthy diet and lifestyle are the most important components of supporting brain health.[42] Healthy diets provide all the nutrients, vitamins, and minerals needed to support optimal and normal brain health. There is no scientifically verified evidence that these kinds of supplements support the improvement of brain tissue, brain vascularization, or enhance brain function over normal. It is for these reasons the Global Council on Brain Health recommends that most people do not take dietary supplements to improve brain health but, instead, focus on regular exercise, a healthy diet, and intellectual stimulation to improve brain function and health.[43] For more details about supplements see Chapter 7.

Natural Products Versus Supplements

There was the natural products industry before the supplement business became popular. A natural product is something obtained from living things such as a plant or animal. The basis for this started in ancient times when man began to search for cures to human diseases. The healer or, in more modern times, the medicine man, would have someone eat an herb or chew on some tree bark and so on that they believed had some medicinal activity. So many supplements have this hint of medical benefit as a basis for their claims. This will be discussed in greater detail in Chapter 7.

Mental Illnesses Reduce Longevity

Throughout this book, we have discussed longevity and brain health in different ways. The statistics are clear that people with serious mental illness currently die 10 to 20 years earlier than the overall population.[44] Serious mental illnesses such as schizophrenia or bipolar disorder have a substantially reduced life expectancy compared with the general population. Much of this reduction is attributable to a two to three times greater risk of cardiovascular disease and death. The prevalence of cardiovascular disease is up to 3.6 times greater in people with serious mental illness.[45] Often early death in people with serious mental illness is also driven by high rates of physical health conditions such as obesity and type-2 diabetes that may be secondary to drug therapy treatment.[46]

People with serious mental illness have a much higher prevalence of smoking compared with the general population. Although smoking prevalence in the general population has reduced over the past few decades, smoking prevalence among people with serious mental illness has remained largely unchanged with over 60 percent of people with schizophrenia reporting current cigarette use.[47] There is no way around the fact that mental illness either directly or indirectly leads to shortened health span and lifespan. Any therapy that reduces or prevents mental illnesses is expected to have benefits in brain health.

Conclusion

Research additionally shows that one can improve brain health and slow aging by maintaining their health through mental and physical exercises, proper sleep, and dealing with medical issues such as high blood pressure, diabetes, or mental health problems promptly and proactively. Research supports the view that we are born with excess brain capacity and, over a lifetime, we use up that extra capacity through just normal life or disease. Many centenarians show that they still have some extra brain capacity that helps them live longer and delay or slow the development of dementia. Through the study of animals that live longer, scientists and doctors have a better of understanding now about why some live longer. Some of the differences are biological and genetic that we, at the present, cannot change. For now, all we can do is to follow the pathway of maintaining brain health throughout our life and, especially as we get older, to slow the brain aging process. The benefits of this behavior to longevity are clear.

CHAPTER 5

Stem Cells to the Rescue?

Stem cells are the body's wonderful "jacks of all trades" that can be used to repair damaged tissue and organs. Scientists have been able to revitalize aging mice with a healthy dose of these magic workers. While mice have been the first beneficiary of stem cell therapy, we're now starting to understand their impact on humans. Embryonic stem cells are the most versatile of the various types of stem cells. They can be taken from embryos created by in vitro fertilization when the embryo is no longer needed. These embryos come from eggs fertilized in fertilization clinics but never implanted in women's uteruses and donated with the women's consent.[1] These cells are pluripotent, meaning they can generate all the body's cells with the exception of an umbilical cord or placenta.

Some people now are utilizing companies that will freeze a baby's umbilical cord, a rich source of embryonic stem cells. The idea is that these cells later can be thawed and used to repair that same individual in the future. Scientists can divide embryonic stem cells in a petri dish and create an entire army of new cells of whatever type of cells that are needed.

The politicization of the abortion issue resulted in the National Institute of Health publishing guidelines in 2009 for the use of embryonic stem cells to ensure that no lives are lost in the harvesting of embryonic stem cells. Besides the limitation on the source or lines of stem cells that can be used (i.e., from nonviable embryos or nonembryonic tissues), there also are requirements for donor approval of any stem cells used.

Adult stem cells, also called somatic cells since they are present at birth, are located in various parts of the body, including the bone marrow and fat. They are found in limited numbers and under normal conditions can only divide and produce the types of cells where they reside. Bone marrow adult stem cells, as an example, only produce blood cells. Professional athletes have begun embracing stem cell therapy. Scientists can harvest stem cells, grow them in controlled conditions, and then inject them into the damaged area that needs repair. Bone marrow transplants remain the most common examples of stem cell therapy. One issue, of course, is the reaction of a patient's immune system to the presence of cells taken from someone else. The result is that such transplants require a significant number of drugs to silence the body's normal immune system response.

Some people have begun going to clinics that will extract and then save their stem cells in case they need them later in life to repair age-related conditions like heart disease or arthritis.[2] Forever Labs charged $7,000 for the process, which it says is the price for longevity.

Humans are not gifted with a large number of adult stem cells, and they decrease in number as they age. That's why researchers will remove some of these cells and then grow them in culture to build an adequate supply for experimentation. As people age, their adult stem cells age as well and, sadly, lose their potential for self-renewal and tissue regeneration.[3]

Mesenchymal stem cells (MSCs) are adult stem cells gathered from bone marrow, adipose tissue (fat), and peripheral blood cells, but bone marrow is the major source. They are used to treat a number of different conditions, including degenerating joints and damage to bones and cartilage. They also are used for aesthetic purposes. Because body stem cells grow old over time unlike embryonic stem cells that enjoy immortality, scientists prefer to draw body stem cells from younger patients. Luckily, MSCs are relatively easy to find and harvest, and they grow rapidly in culture.[4]

A five-year study of using MSCs taken from a patient's fat cells showed improvement in musculoskeletal issues, such as hip, knee, and ankle osteoarthritis. The results showed major improvement by Year 3 and included reduction in swelling and cartilage improvement as well as reduction in pain.[5] These treatments utilize a patient's own MSCs, thus avoiding the issue of its immune system rejecting these cells.

MSCs and Increasing Longevity

Scientists recently injected select proteins known as Yamanaka factors into elderly mice's muscular stem cells and rejuvenated them so that they performed like brand-new MSCs. When the experimentation moved to human patients, these researchers found that the process when applied to isolated cells from the cartilage of people with and without osteoarthritis resulted in reducing the secretion of inflammatory molecules and improved the cells' ability to divide. Imagine sometime in the future being able to treat arthritis without the need for drugs.[6]

Similarly, UCLA scientists recently found that when they restored glutathione, a key antioxidant that prevents cell damage, they were able to rejuvenate old muscle stem cells in mice. While treating mice is still a distance from treating humans, it is a significant understanding and a breakthrough on the road to keeping stem cell functionality young so that they can maintain tissue regeneration across a patient's lifetime.[7]

Stem Cells Under Attack

Adult stem cells age like the rest of the body, and that results in them losing their effectiveness, a condition known as stem cell exhaustion. That condition can be a blow to the person's immune system because there is reduced production of bacteria-killing and virus-killing white blood cells. It's actually a "war" going on in our bodies between the immune cells and factors and infectious organisms, and we don't always win. Senescent cells are those that no longer can divide and create new cells. For a variety of reasons, senescent cells that don't just die become a problem for adult stem cells. These zombie-type senescent cells secrete chemicals that increase inflammation and suppress the immune system. If life is not tough enough for stem cells, they also can be damaged or even mutated to the point that they become cancer cells induced by senescent cell factors.[8]

An iPSC Breakthrough

In 2006, Shinya Yamanaka discovered a way to reprogram adult stem cells to create new cells not limited to where the original body stem cells were found. These cells are called "induced pluripotent stem cells" or iPSCs. In other words, he was able to take an adult blood stem cell, as an example, and create new cells for the heart. This complex process required determining what kinds of signaling a body stem cell received to turn it into a specific type of cell and then manipulating several genes in order to customize cells for different parts of the body. It's no surprise that Yamanaka received the Nobel Prize for his efforts.[9]

It's important to note that the primary use of these iPSCs at this time is in research because there are several limitations to actually injecting them into a patient, including the development of tumors. Still, this process holds the potential for therapeutic benefits once the current limitations are resolved. In fact, there have been clinical trials to use iPSCs to treat adult macular degeneration since the eye does not seem to mount the same level of anti-immune response as other parts of the body.

Overcoming the Limitations of iPSCs

Scientists recently discovered the reason for the body's often negative response to iPSCs. The answer lies in a patient's DNA. An epigenome refers to a person's genetic makeup and the way selected genes turn on and off and transmit molecules to cells with directions regarding their behavior. Apparently, iPSCs still retain a memory of sorts of the type of cells they used to be. That memory causes these cells now playing an organ-specific role to act inefficiently or even in a hostile manner when infused into a patient's body.

These researchers figured out exactly how the reprogramming process works and utilized a technique called transient-naive treatment (TNT) to "erase" any lingering memories iPSCs still retain of their former roles. The result of these experiments is that these iPSCs become much more functionally and molecularly similar to embryonic stem cells than the ones artificially produced.[10]

How Stem Cells Could Increase Longevity

While some lower animals can replace their lost limbs in days, humans cannot. For one thing, we lack the enormous number of stem cells found in those animals. Stem cells can repair damaged organs but not, as yet, rejuvenate an entire person. Researchers are trying to uncover the complex balance in the human body maintained by anti-aging genes. Klotho is a gene that scientists found could suppress aging in mice. The problem is that, if overexpressed, it caused just the opposite reaction, including the senescence and depletion of stem cells. Another way stem cells could help increase human longevity has to do with telomeres, the DNA endcaps, discussed earlier, that help protect human chromosomes from being damaged.[11]

When cells divide, these telomeres shorten and can result in inflammation and cells becoming senescent. Stem cells can activate telomerase, an enzyme that can regulate the length of telomeres. If scientists could control this process, they could reduce many of the diseases associated with aging. At this point, we do not really understand how stem cells communicate with the cells they are attempting to repair. Telomerase, however, can have negative effects such as tumors if too much is present, by enabling "bad cells" to live longer. So, learning how to regulate the amount of this enzyme stem cells produce is critical. Researchers also are trying to understand a variety of juggling acts that stem cells perform. They not only try to balance the amount of telomere shortening, but they also can activate genes that can suppress tumors.[12]

Stem Cell Therapy Tourism

The FDA has approved a very limited number of stem cell therapies. Of course, there are a number of stem cell therapies in clinical trials. One way to get access to a life-saving procedure would be to explore ClinicalTrials. gov. This website can be searched by type of disease and even by location of the trial. There is a long arduous road toward getting government approval of a new therapy, and some people have been taking shortcuts.

A new phenomenon called "stem cell therapy tourism" has evolved. Clinics around the world have begun advertising for patients while promising miraculous cures. They are often found in exotic locations such as the Cayman Islands and Antigua and promise the added benefits of resort living while recovering from the procedures.

These procedures are very expensive and are unregulated. One problem is that it is easy to read about anecdotal "proof" that such therapies work. While a friend or relative might report that they found immediate relief from whatever condition they suffered from following stem cell therapy, that is not a rigorous data-driven proof that the procedure worked.

CHAPTER 6

CRISPR and Gene Editing Tools

Jennifer Doudna and Emmanuelle Charpentier received the 2020 Nobel Prize in Chemistry for discovering the *CRISPR/Cas9* genetic scissors, a tool for editing DNA. As pointed out in Chapter 2, DNA errors are responsible for a variety of human afflictions such as sickle cell disease as well as for programming cell errors that disrupt cells' normal behavior and accelerate aging. In other words, DNA errors impact both human health span and lifespan.

CRISPR stands for Clustered Regularly Interspaced Short Palindromic Repeats. These repeats were found in bacteria with DNA sequences between the repeats that matched viral sequences. It is believed that it serves as a tool for a bacteria's immune system. Bacteria and viruses have waged a war on humans for eons. Doudna and Charpentier discovered that bacteria transcribe these key viral DNA characters to RNA when a virus infects them. The RNA instructs a protein to cut out a targeted, particular area of the viral DNA sequence. Doudna and Charpentier used an enzyme called Cas9 (CRISPR-associated Protein 9) that is guided to the target DNA sequence by a small RNA molecule called a guide RNA (gRNA). The scientists designed the gRNA to recognize and bind to the specific DNA sequence location that the Cas9 enzyme is designed to cut. CRISPR cuts the double DNA strands at that point. Scientists have now discovered enzymes in addition to Cas9 that can offer even more precision. Cpf1, for example, leaves a "sticky" end to one DNA strand to facilitate addition of a new sequence to give the DNA new properties. This approach makes it easier to perform more precise gene edits.[1]

While scientists have mapped the entire human genome, the problem of using CRISPR to mitigate diseases is that there appears to be side effects when multiple characters of the DNA code are cut. The Chinese scientist who broke the law and edited the genomes of twin girls to make them resistant to HIV may have shortened their lives. Researchers reported that people "with two disabled copies of the *CCR5* gene—the version that protects against HIV infection—are 21 percent more likely to die before the age of 76 than people with at least one working copy of the gene."[2]

Cutting multiple characters of the DNA code is not an issue when it comes to treating sickle cell disease that is caused by a single-letter mutation in the genetic code. In late 2023, the U.S. Food and Drug Administration (FDA) approved a therapy for that disease that utilizes CRISPR. Unfortunately, at this time the treatment is projected to cost over $2 million. Jennifer Doudna believes the price will drop as market forces drive the cost down.[3]

Treating Huntington's Disease with CRISPR

Huntington's disease generally doesn't strike until people are in the age range between 35 and 55 years, but then death usually follows anywhere within 10 to 25 years.[4] This inherited disease causes nerve cells in parts of the brain to break down and die. Its effect is noticeable because it attacks those areas of the brain responsible for voluntary movement as well as other brain areas. It impacts people's ability to move, their ability to think and understand, and even their mental health. Researchers have tackled Huntington's disease using CRISPR as a tool. They discovered that an error within the Huntington (*HTT*) gene creates a mutant protein that destroys neurons. As a proof of concept, these researchers used CRISPR to permanently disable the Huntington gene's mutant function. The result was a 50 percent increase in the lifespan of the mice treated.[5]

The Use of Base Editing

One of the problems with using CRISPR is the side effects caused by this tool's cutting of both strands of DNA. Base editing is a new approach that makes precise changes to individual letters of the DNA code and serves as a less invasive approach than CRISPR. Harvard researcher David Liu developed base editing to swap out a single letter on one DNA strand. This technique is usually described as a "cousin" to CRISPR. Hutchinson–Gilford progeria syndrome is a condition where a single-letter change in the gene is responsible for generating the protein lamin A. Lamin A supports the membrane that forms the cell's nucleus. This mutation results in a damaged nuclear membrane, and the disease progeria, which also causes premature aging. Liu used this base editing approach to treat progeria. He has successfully treated mice with this induced condition, and these mice lived 500 days longer than untreated mice. The next stage would be to treat children since up to now there has been no cure for this terrible disease that usually causes death by the age of 14. Base editing is now used to treat brain disorders as well as eye and ear diseases in mice.[6,7]

CRISPR Cancer Treatment in Humans

One of the most promising uses of CRISPR, when it comes to cancer research, has to do with reprogramming a cancer patient's own T-cells to make them more effective in fighting cancer. Researchers noted that cancer cells often are able to fool a patient's T-cells associated with their immune systems and, thus, avoid detection. A Phase 1 study of 16 cancer patients consisted of researchers removing some of those patients' T-cells and then customized programming of those cells to make them able to detect the specific proteins the cancer cells contained and then attack them.[8,9]

CRISPR Could Ease the Shortage of Organs for Transplant

Surgeons at the University of Pennsylvania have successfully attached a genetically altered pig liver to a brain-dead person and found that the organ functioned normally for 72 hours. The experiment represents a step toward using pig organs to help deal with the more than 10,000 U.S. patients waiting to receive a liver transplant. eGenesis of Cambridge, Massachusetts, used gene editing and CRISPR to make 69 genetic edits to these pigs to prevent the human patients' immune systems from instantly rejecting these organs. The company has transplanted these organs into monkeys who were able to live for more than two years. Imagine the increase in health span if the technology is improved and applied to other transplant organs in short supply![10]

CRISPR's Long-Term Impact on Aging

Researchers have identified the *KAT7* gene as a driver of cell senescence. They used CRISPR-based gene editing to inactivate KAT7 and, thus, rejuvenate human cells. While this research is still in its infancy, the researchers labeled their results as promising.[11] More recently, researchers have focused on the impact of CRISPR-Cas9 in age-related disorders. These include neurodegenerative disorders, inflammatory diseases, and cancers that affect a growing population of people over 60. The hope is that this therapy can correct for gene mutations and then target cancer cells by making them more sensitive to chemotherapeutics while keeping them from proliferating.[12]

CRISPR and Gene Editing Could Impact Both Health Span and Lifespan

While the uses of CRISPR and gene editing are in their infancy, it is clear that prices for these procedures eventually will decline as Jennifer Doudna pointed out in her discussion of a CRISPR treatment of sickle cell disease mentioned earlier in this chapter. What is encouraging is that there already are small-scale human trials being conducted using these new tools, and they are showing some positive effects. One major issue is that researchers still must grapple with the impact of cutting DNA strands on off-target genes that might not have a clear functional relationship to the targeted genes. Still, the fact that these tools are beginning to show progress with the production of animal organs suitable for human transplant as well as determining which genes are responsible for cell death is encouraging.

CHAPTER 7

The Drug Industry's Efforts to Boost Longevity

Although we are not close to a pill or drug to extent lifespan, there is clear scientific evidence from research in mice that it should be possible. As mentioned in Chapter 2, some experiments in the 1970s connected the circulatory system of a genetically identical young mouse with that of an old mouse. The blood of the young mouse circulated into the older mouse. By doing this, the older mouse's lifespan was increased.[1] This process, called parabiosis, demonstrated that there are substances in a young mouse's blood that will help the older mouse live longer. Conboy and others reported in 2005 that by briefly connecting the circulatory system of young and aged mice, old mice exhibited youthful features in the brain, muscle, and liver, and increased cognitive function.[2] In 2023, researchers showed that if you conduct parabiosis for 12 weeks, the mouse lives about 10 percent longer than the genetically comparable mice that did not have the procedure. Even more interesting was the markers of age in blood and liver tissue showed changes opposite to aging and similar to the results of limiting calories. The benefits of parabiosis lasted for months after the procedure.[3] Clearly, this research shows that the blood of young animals contains natural substances and cells that can slow down aging and perhaps reverse it. It is not a procedure that can be done in humans except for genetically identical people (for example: identical twins). Identical human twins, however, are the same age and therefore there will not be a benefit for their sharing their blood. The experiments in mice, described above, demonstrate that there is something in the blood from a younger animal that slows and maybe even reverses some aspects of aging in older animals. Zhang and other scientists are now trying to pin down what it is in the blood of younger mice that seem to reverse aging in the older mice. Some have speculated that stem cells are key to reversing aging. This was covered in more detail in Chapter 5.

Supplements and Natural Products

Part of the drug industry's efforts to improve health and longevity are dietary supplements. What is in these supplements, and are they really useful? Many contain a variety of vitamins, omega 3 fatty acids (found in fish oil), vitamin E, and various B vitamin mixtures among other things. It is important to understand that supplements are only useful for restoring normal levels of important vitamins, minerals, hormones, and so on, if they are abnormally low. In this way, they restore your health as long as you don't overdose.[4] It is also important to note that herbal supplements are exempt from Food and Drug Administration (FDA) regulation and have not been subjected to testing in an FDA-approved clinical trial—so buyer beware. For this reason, supplements claiming medical benefits should be viewed with caution.

Still, there is a class of drugs called "nootropics" or smart drugs that may improve memory, thinking sharpness, and learning. These smart drugs work best for individuals who are mildly cognitively impaired. They work by increasing the supply of glucose and oxygen to the brain, have anti-hypoxic effects, protect brain tissue from neurotoxicity and, in some cases, inflammation. The most common of these is caffeine, a stimulant that also increases levels of several neurotransmitters such as acetylcholine, which helps with short-term memory and learning. There are other drugs in this category such as Deanol, Nicergoline, Piracetam, and Naftidrofuryl.[5] Their biological effects result from providing temporary stimulation of blood flow, neurotransmitter release, improved local nutrients, and related biological activities but do not permanently improve brain function. In addition, some nootropics also have undesirable side effects.[6]

Natural Products Versus Supplements

Natural products are chemicals and substances that are made by a living organism such as a plant or animal and found in nature. Long before drugs were manufactured in factories, people used plants and animal materials for medicine. The benefits of natural products as medicine have been recognized for thousands of years. From medicine men to modern times, potions, extracted juices, and all kinds of elixirs derived from natural products have demonstrated their medicinal value. In modern times, scientists have been conducting controlled testing of natural products extracted from a plant or animal for biological activity against infectious organisms, heart disease, cancer, and many other kinds of diseases. Natural products have provided many useful drugs. It is estimated that 50 percent of drugs approved by the FDA were isolated or derived from plants.[7] What makes plants and animals great sources of potential drugs is that often they have unusual chemical structures that evolved to protect themselves from disease and/or predators. Many of these same materials have utility in treating human diseases. For example, some of these unusual molecules also reduce blood pressure and inflammation or have benefit in treating cancer and other human diseases. Examples of early natural products that became a drug are morphine (analgesic, Merck in 1826) and aspirin (analgesic, Salix 1899). Other early drugs are cocaine, codeine, digitoxin (cardiotonic), quinine, and pilocarpine and paclitaxel (for cancer).

Often, the natural product activity is very weak in its natural state because the medicinal material in the natural product is in too low a concentration to be very useful. It may also be that the natural structure is not fully optimized for treating the disease. Chemists then isolated or extracted the active substance from the natural source to provide the concentrated active material. There is an entire pharmaceutical industry built around harvesting natural plants and animals from the land and sea in the hunt for new drug candidates. It is estimated that between 35,000 and 70,000 plant species have been screened for medicinal activity in the search for new medicines.[8] Some supplements that claim to have medical benefits from herbs, extracts, or mixtures of natural substances may have some weak benefit. Almost certainly the active pharmaceutical drug derived from that same natural product will be a more potent formulation and have the added benefit that it has been extensively studied to be certain that its benefits and safety issues are clearly understood. To improve the overall drug profile, scientists and doctors are chemically modifying these unusual chemical structures to improve potency and reduce side effects. Indirectly, they promote longevity by curing a disease or improving your quality of life.

To really increase longevity, a substance/drug would have to interfere with the natural aging process (senescence) or reverse it another way. The ones that look most promising are based on addressing some metabolic or disease-related problem that is associated with premature aging and especially by decreasing inflammatory diseases. Examples of interesting natural products found so far include quercetin, rapamycin, resveratrol, spermidine, curcumin, and sulforaphane. Their administration increases longevity and stress resistance in model organisms such as yeasts, nematodes, flies, and mice. From this group, rapamycin, resveratrol, and curcumin are currently in additional testing at the National Institute on Aging to assess their potential for eventual human longevity testing.[9]

Antioxidants Reduce Oxidative Stress

Oxidative damage is another process that appears to be one of the main factors in aging. The damage results from undesirable oxygen side-reactions during normal cellular metabolism resulting in cellular damage, cellular senescence, and premature cell death. Antioxidants can prevent these processes and extend healthy longevity due to lowering the body's level of oxidative stress.[10] The bulk of the studies suggests that dietary/natural products increase health span—rather than lifespan—by minimizing the period of frailty at the end of life.[11] There are many studies that support the view that "Mediterranean or a blue zone" style high-veggie and low-red-meat diets are good for longevity. In summary, natural products have produced many drugs that have improved health and indirectly lifespan, but research is continuing to definitively prove that any dietary regimen or natural product increases longevity directly.[12]

A New Generation of Drugs

One of the most exciting areas of pharmaceutical research is the progress being made in treating formerly incurable diseases such as sickle cell anemia, obesity-related diseases, and Alzheimer's disease among many others. These new generation therapies are not your traditional kinds of drugs in pills that you take once or twice a day. They are based on a very technical understanding of the biology underlying the diseases. These biological drugs are frequently very unstable in part because their biological molecules are derived from proteins, DNA, and RNA and have fleeting lifetimes in the blood or tissues. However, they have an outsized effect on the body because they are frequently the "sparkplug" that activates an entire sequence of events that give them an outsized positive effect. Despite their less-than-ideal physical properties, their remarkable activities on chronic diseases are clear.

The leading edge of this new generation of therapies are just now hitting the marketplace. Ozempic (a GLP-1 receptor antagonist) is an excellent example of this class of biological drugs. It is the trade name of one of four currently approved drugs in this category. This drug was developed for its effect on reducing glucose levels in the blood of diabetics. It also helps the patient to significantly reduce their weight while taking the drug. Ozempic patients would be expected to live longer if they keep their diabetes under control and if they can keep their weight within a healthy range long-term. Their impact on longevity still remains to be seen. Nevertheless, it is already clear from careful clinical studies they are improving the health of patients.

Improved Longevity Due to Curing Diseases

Aging, in part, is clearly a result of the cumulative damage caused to the body by various diseases. As much as 15 percent of centenarians have no clinically demonstrable disease at age 100. About 43 percent are "delayers" who did not exhibit an age-related disease at age 80 and about 42 percent who are "survivors" had clinically demonstrable disease before the age of 80. For supercentenarians (age 110+ years), health span indeed approximates lifespan, and the data show that the older they are the healthier they have been.[13] This suggests that as medicine cures more diseases, there will be less damage to the body, lower inflammation, and so on. This will improve not just the current quality of life or health span, but presumably longevity will improve in parallel with better health. The longevity benefits should accrue to individuals with the specific cured disease such as sickle cell disease rather than the entire population.

Pharma Companies Working on Anti-aging Drugs

The pharmaceutical industry has identified several drugs and natural products that may increase longevity, including the following: antidiabetic drugs—metformin and acarbose; anti-inflammatory and antioxidant—resveratrol; immunosuppressant—rapamycin; antioxidant—quercetin; supporter of basic cell functions and protein synthesis—spermidine; antioxidant—curcumin; and antioxidant—sulforaphane.[14] Recent clinical trials are registered in ClinicalTrials.gov and ClinicaltTrialsRegister.eu.[15] Each of these longevity candidates interacts with the body differently, but the general theme is they all have some anti-inflammatory and anti-oxidant activity.[16] Reversatrol found in red wine and various berries has been shown to increase the lifespan of fruit flies and a short-lived verte-brate animal (fish).[17] Another promising drug is rapamycin, which has anti-viral and anti-fungal activities. It also inhibits cell proliferation. Rapamycin and the drugs mentioned above have been shown in animal studies to slow aging, extend lifespan, and reduce age-related diseases. They are now being studied further to verify the indirect observations of extended lifespan.[18]

Because humans have quite varied diets and lifestyles, it is very diffi-cult to assess the benefits of a therapy on longevity or even health span in people. So, for now, scientists and doctors are continuing to gain evidence from animals to understand the biological processes that promote reduced blood and cellular markers of aging and their longevity impact in short-lived species.

New Tools for Longevity Researchers—Artificial Intelligence

With the development of artificial intelligence (AI), a new frontier has been opened in longevity research. The variables that influence longevity can be mind-numbing and require big computer systems and databases to be useful. This is perfect for a machine learning system such as AI that can handle so many facts and information quickly and then look for patterns that promote longevity. Dr. Kristen Fortney (Stanford University) used bioinformatics to study the genetics of supercentenarians—people who live to the age of 110 and beyond. Now, she is at the forefront of biotech efforts to turn longevity science knowledge into medicine. As CEO of the new startup company, BioAge, she is hoping to use AI to develop unique treatments to extend health span and lifespan. Specifically, BioAge is using AI to analyze the distinctive molecular features of people who live the healthiest, longest lives, and then use that knowledge to develop therapies that could help everyone age more successfully. AI is producing a comprehensive molecular picture of aging as well as common features in centenarians and the sometimes-subtle patterns that are unique. From this analysis, BioAge expects to discover many different but generally applicable aging mechanisms, rather than being limited to a handful of targets chosen in advance.[19]

New Directions in Drug Development

As cells age, they eventually become senescent and play their role in aging and the generation of age-related diseases. Senescent cells described in Chapter 2 are still alive but are not dividing or contributing as much to the health of their respective tissues as younger, non-senescent cells. Their presence is not really helpful to the organism and are associated with increases of a wide variety of neurodegenerative diseases, including cancer. The prevalent hypothesis of scientists and doctors today is that slowing down the senescence process will result in increases in longevity. Recent research makes it clear that just the presence of senescent cells has a negative effect on the body.[20]

It may not be possible with today's methods to prevent cells from becoming senescent, but it may be possible to develop drugs that target senescent cells and kill them. The class of drugs that specifically target and kill senescent cells are called senolytics. A number of senolytic drugs have been identified recently.[21,22] It is still early days for the longevity testing of these senolytic drug candidates. As with any new chronic therapeutic approach, the safety over a lifetime needs to be evaluated too. In the case of senolytics that have the property of causing cells to die, it is important to evaluate their long-term safety because they may also impair the general repair capacity of the organism and consequently lead to faster post-treatment development of new senescent cells. More research needs to be done on the impact of senolytics on people.[23] (Senolytics are also discussed in Chapter 11.)

Summary

The drug supplement and the natural products industry has been focused mainly on curing diseases that have cut an individual's lifespan short. This will increase the average lifespan by improving the health and quality of life for specific individuals. To date, no drug or material has been shown in humans to increase their longevity or age. This may be changing now. Research in animals have identified a number of potential candidate materials that are working their way toward human studies. The verifying process to demonstrate that these materials actually increase longevity could take decades. The use of new tools such as AI and Big Data analysis could provide the insights needed to shorten this process and help identify drugs and materials that would genuinely increase average lifespan. To be clear, there are no scientific data that show human lifespan has a required limit of 100 to 120 years of age.

CHAPTER 8

New Medical Tests for Early Detection of Diseases

In the near past, if patients were not feeling well, they would go to a doctor and tell the doctor their symptoms, and the doctor would choose the appropriate therapy. Until recent decades, there were only a few very informative diagnostic tests besides blood pressure, temperature, and the like. Today, there are literally thousands of diagnostic tests for nearly every imaginable disease or condition. Some are invasive and require obtaining a tissue sample, but others are minimally invasive such as taking a blood sample, and, now, finally, there are noninvasive diagnostic tests using spectroscopic devices or identifying disease markers in saliva, urine, or other body fluid. In this chapter, we will review the state of the art for diagnostic testing as well the status of diagnostic markers for biological age and longevity.

Current Standard Screening Tests Used During Routine Physicals

Common results from blood tests include: Complete blood count (CBC), which measures and counts the various cells in your blood; the basic metabolic panel, which measures chemicals, minerals, and electrolytes; blood enzymes and proteins (e.g., creatine kinase and troponin for heart damage); blood tests for heart disease (cholesterol and triglycerides); and blood coagulation panel (shows if clotting is normal).[1] The common urine tests include checking for infections, kidney disease, and diabetes, as well as for appearance (infections), concentration (dehydration), and contents (proteins are a sign of possible kidney disease).[2] In aggregate, these tests tell the doctor that you are generally in good health, if all of these test results are in the normal range. Should something be out of the normal range in these initial, general diagnostic tests, there are then secondary tests that are more specific for diseases of a specific tissue or organ to help narrow down the specific issue.

Prospective Detection of Diseases Before Symptoms

Many noninfectious diseases such as cancer involve some changes in cells and tissues before becoming a full-blown disease. If a test were available to check the tissue for these pre-cancerous changes before it became a "full-blown" tumor, then it would be possible to interrupt its progression into cancer. This is quite possible with today's understanding of human biology and diseases, and it will become much better in the near future. For example, in colonoscopies, doctors remove polyps. Although most are harmless, some may progress into cancer. Their removal prevents their potential development into a GI cancer later on.[3] It is believed that some foods can promote the development of polyps. These include fatty foods, such as fried foods; red meat, such as beef and pork; and processed meats, such as bacon, sausage, hot dogs, and lunch meats.[4] Polyps develop in many other tissues in addition to the GI track. It is important to be checked out if you have symptoms that are not normal. In another example, most uterine polyps are benign, but up to 13 percent of endometrial polyps can lead to uterine cancer. The point here is that polyp removal is a way to prevent cancer before it develops. Most cells exhibit pre-disease changes, but, for internal organs, doctors prefer to examine markers in blood or other fluids rather than taking an "invasive" tissue biopsy for examination.

Depending on the tissue, many things may promote the development of pre-disease changes, but a common thread is usually inflammation.[5] It is not just a marker for the development of polyps but is a causative agent for many other diseases such as rheumatoid arthritis, diabetes, inflammatory bowel disease, asthma, and many more. Inflammation has well-recognized markers in blood. Again, as noted above, an easy way to check for these pre-cancerous changes are in bodily fluids, but even newer tests are becoming available. Biotechnology has developed to the point now where individual cells can be analyzed or the DNA or RNA can be extracted and analyzed. Developing specific tests for disease markers found in these biological materials are an area of very active research. One of the hottest new areas of minimally invasive diagnostic research is called "liquid biopsies."

Liquid Biopsies and Other Modern Tests for Disease Markers

A liquid biopsy is a blood test that detects signs of cancerous tumors. The test detects individual tumor cells floating in blood and cell-free cancer DNA in blood. This works because as a tumor grows some tumor cells can break off from the tumor and circulate in your bloodstream. If these cells are not killed, they may stick to a new location and form a metastasis. The liquid biopsy is a very sensitive test that can identify these few cancer cells in blood. Sometimes even before the tumor is large enough to be detected by standard methods such as x-rays, tissue biopsies, or the development of symptoms, a liquid biopsy can detect the cancer cells or their DNA/RNA. The FDA has already approved some liquid biopsy cancer tests, and many companies are working hard to expand the portfolio of such tests.[6] In Chapter 11, liquid biopsies are discussed in more detail.

Looking for cancers one-by-one for each tissue type is a very slow and expensive process. The Galleri test[7] looks for 50+ types of cancers with a single blood test. The concept behind this test is that many cancers have similar markers. So, they are bundling those cancers together into one diagnostic based on the common or similar marker. If the test has a positive hit, then they will conduct additional testing to narrow down the list to determine which kind of cancer it is and where it is.[8] In some cases, the DNA isolated from blood in the Galleri test or DNA/RNA isolated from other sources is unique enough to have a high probability of coming from a specific kind of cancer. Such a positive test should be followed up by the patient with a medical professional to confirm the potential diagnosis. (https://www.mdvip.com/about-mdvip/blog /what-are-multi-cancer-early-detection-blood-tests)

Current medical practice is not to use these newer tests on a routine basis and not to test younger patients unless they present symptoms. This means that often the test then is only confirmatory and not used to catch cancer early. Liquid biopsies are currently focused on detecting abnormalities by looking in blood for things that are not normally found in a healthy person's blood. If tests like the Galleri were routinely performed during routine checkups, it could catch many cancers very early and improve the outcomes. The main issue for reducing adoption now is that the test is expensive. Over time, the technology will improve, and the costs will decrease. The hope is in the future they will become part of the standard battery of diagnostic tests during routine physicals. An additional reason for this optimism is the increasing use of AI in the analysis of diagnostic samples.

DNA and RNA Testing in Blood, Saliva, and Other Body Fluids

DNA and RNA are found in all body fluids, in addition to blood, and the testing now is relatively ubiquitous and inexpensive. Among the earliest changes in a pre-cancerous cell are those found in the DNA, RNA, and the cell's shape. A recent study using cell-free DNA in blood combined with machine learning was able to detect cancer "signals" across multiple cancer types and predict the origin of the cancer signal with high accuracy. The results from this study demonstrate that this test could complement existing screening diagnostics and increase the number of cancers detected through population screening.[9] As with the Galleri test, this test would be a useful screening tool not just for cancers but also for all DNA-based diagnostic markers. This potentially would be useful for longevity markers that are DNA-based, such as for senescence (when cells stop growing and dividing), telomere shortening (leads to cell senescence and cell death; see Chapter 2 for more details), and so on. In another example, Foundation Medicine has an FDA-approved test that will analyze over 300 genes in blood. The company believes it is the most comprehensive FDA-approved liquid biopsy test on the market.[10]

Noninvasive Diagnostic Approaches

For this section, we define minimally invasive as the taking of a blood, or another internal fluid sample for a diagnostic test. A noninvasive diagnostic would not require any body tissues (biopsy) or internal fluids (such as blood, cerebrospinal fluid, or lymph) to obtain useful information. Modern medicine has developed many instruments for looking inside your body from the outside and seeing what is going on. X-rays, CT, MRI, ultrasound, PET, and other instruments are very useful tools for looking at big issues within your body, such as a cancer lump, aneurism, or lung damage. They are also expensive and can only do a few patients a day. Consequently, they are reserved for diagnosis or confirmation of serious medical issues. They are not for routine health management or following a disease progression over time. As we described earlier, this is why developing a panel of diagnostic tests for routine exams with a blood or urine sample or other body fluids is such an important advance.

Equally important, but so far less advanced, is an even newer area of research—diagnostic tests that can be done through the skin or the eye. As mentioned earlier, the health apps are a category of personalized medicine that measure through your skin—heart rate, oxygen saturation, and so on. They do more than just give a person an insight of how they are doing in relation to the app parameters. It also alerts the individual and sometimes the doctor of a medical issue that needs immediate attention. It can also enable the patient to track their health trends over time without going to the doctor each time they want an update on blood sugar or pressure. Chapter 10 covers wearable devices that provide information through the skin.

For chronic diseases, if the eye were the window into what was going on in brain tissue, it would enable doctors to follow the progression of brain and perhaps other diseases over time just as easily as they follow your eyesight or macular degeneration over time. It needs to be pointed out that repeated sampling of eye fluids (tears, conjunctiva, aqueous humor, and vitreous humor) for biomarkers has already enabled objective measurement of disease process or biological responses to a drug treatment.[11] This is fine, but a powerful new understanding of how the tissue in the back of the eye can signal disease is a new field. As you can imagine, this is becoming a powerful way for doctors to track diseases with clinical symptoms such as Alzheimer's disease where β-amyloid plaques are visible in the back of the eye. If these technologies could be applied early and combined with routine eye exams, they might identify some chronic diseases before clinical symptoms develop. This would enable doctors to prescribe therapies earlier in the development of the diseases in order to slow/prevent progression. It could also be used in the development of new therapies, or manage their routine use once approved. Then the doctor could follow the disease progression longitudinally as well as the drug's benefits over time.

Artificial Intelligence Impact on Diagnostics

Artificial intelligence (AI) is already being applied to help identify tissue abnormalities, bone fractures, and tumors in clinical laboratory testing. It leverages large datasets to improve accuracy, reduce costs, and save time while minimizing human errors and assists clinicians with decision making.[12] Hologic is a company that has an AI application for diagnostics. It has just gotten FDA approval for its cytology test that uses AI to analyze the images from many tissue samples and then select those that show a potential anomaly. This saves the pathologist time and energy by selecting and examining only the tissue samples (on microscope slides) that need further evaluation. A pathologist looks at hundreds and perhaps thousands of tissue slides a day. The use of AI will reduce the cost and speed up the diagnosis of biopsies. In another example, a Mayo Clinic spinout company called EKO has developed an AI stethoscope that can diagnose in 15 seconds three kinds of heart problems that have no obvious symptoms. The Mayo Clinic is using AI with the Apple watch to detect a weak heart pumping action.[13]

AI in longevity research is just now starting to ramp up, but it is clear that it will have impact in this area as well as throughout the health care arena. Mario and colleagues have recently published a scientific review discussing the markers of aging and how AI research may accelerate our understanding of aging and longevity.[14] In summary, AI is already having a consequential impact on diagnostics and physician decision making and will have an important impact on longevity and aging research in the future.

Longevity Markers

Entrepreneurs have immediately taken advantage of this new area of medical research to create apps that you can download onto your phone or computer to help you optimize the areas that you can do yourself without a doctor's intervention. Many of these apps are fitness trackers, and others suggest weight loss, dietary, and other behavior changing recommendations that are correlated with longevity research in certain blue zone areas. They come with ways to log into the app and track your compliance against the recommendations and provide motivational games and suggestions. You will find a lot of these on the Apple App store[15,16] or Google Play among many others.[17] A different set of non–medically approved apps and FDA-approved medical devices track specific medical conditions. These are also beneficial for longevity because they test for specific diseases under the assumption that these diseases are leading causes of death and, therefore, are the ones to watch. To be honest, so far these are more correlated with improved health span than longevity.

Just as the blood and tissue markers can indicate the person's health or disease, similar but different markers may be applied to assessing longevity. This field of study is young, and the best markers are not decided yet by the scientists and doctors who study this subject. Murata and his colleagues studied the health records of centenarians and non-centenarians (people who did not live to 100 years old) over 35 years to learn about what biomarkers were most predictive of longevity. They studied 1,224 participants (84.6 percent females) who lived to 100 years and found that higher levels of cholesterol and iron and lower levels of glucose, creatinine (kidney function), uric acid (kidney and thyroid function), and five other blood chemicals covered in routine blood tests over the decades were associated with living to 100 years. In fact, even at 65 years and onwards people who were destined to become centenarians showed these favorable biomarker levels and differences with non-centenarians.[18] Overall, the scientific community is still undecided about what the best cholesterol level is correlated with longevity.

A Japanese study found that inflammation biomarkers (such as IL-6, TNFα and CRP) were important predictors of exceptional longevity.[19] Clearly, if you are not physically fit and have heart disease or a chronic inflammatory condition, you may not live as long as someone who doesn't. In some ways, these investigators too are confusing health span with longevity, and no doubt they are useful to know and should be addressed with the appropriate medical solutions to lengthen health span. However, longevity also relates to the normal aging of cells, and different and convenient inexpensive tests should be developed to track aging of key body organs and tissues.

Aging constitutes progressive physiological changes in an organism. These changes alter the normal biological functions and eventually lead to cellular senescence. López-Otín and colleagues have proposed markers suitable for assessing biological aging. They proposed 12 markers of aging that include gene instability, senescence, chronic inflammation, mitochondrial dysfunction, and others. All 12 of these markers are interrelated and relate to cellular response to stress, genetic mutations or changes, and maintenance of homeostasis.[20] This and the López-Otín 2013 paper[21] were the basis for researchers focusing on more relevant aspects of biological aging and less on health span.[22]

There are also new data from genetic analysis that some genes are turned off/down or are more active in centenarians. These include the *STK17A* gene that is critical in repairing DNA damage, the *COA1* gene that is involved in energy production, and the *BLVRA* gene that is involved in the elimination of dangerous reactive oxygen species. If this research is confirmed, then there can be additional markers of aging.[23]

Summary

While longevity research is still in its early stages, clear progress has been made in not just understanding the value of conducting routine diagnostic tests for common illnesses but to use this information to address these diseases early to minimize their negative effects on the body. Medical care is clearly making progress on new therapeutics for diseases more common in older people, such as Alzheimer's disease, as well as lifestyle issues, such as obesity and type 2 diabetes. Clear progress has also been made in educating scientists and medical professionals to the difference between lifespan-focused diagnostics and longevity diagnostics. As a consequence, research specifically focused on longevity markers is increasing rapidly. Researchers are currently validating a number of possible clearly relevant longevity markers in the hopes of developing convenient and inexpensive tests for them.

CHAPTER 9

3D Printing Could Lead to Longer Healthier Lives

3D printing, better known as additive manufacturing, was first developed in the 1980s. Rather than create an object by filling in a mold or carving/assembling it from a block of material, this approach builds a 3D object by "printing" successive layers of material based on "orders" received from a computer-assisted drawing program. It is only in the past two decades has this technology been applied to creating biological outputs by using "bioink," a soupy mixture of stem cells as well as other cells and additional biological materials such as collagen. For creating 3D objects, it is necessary to first create a "scaffold" to support the bioink being "printed."

The process begins with generating the cells necessary to create the product that the 3D printer will print. That generally means harvesting and cultivating organ-specific stem cells. These cells are then mixed with ingredients such as gelatin or alginate to make a printable bioink. This "ink" is then "printed" by syringes that squirt the cell mixture into the layers and locations that fill in the scaffold with the stem cells and other cells imbedded in the approximate locations necessary to grow into the desired tissue.

The real value of 3D printing is that it will help people live longer and live healthier lives. In other words, it will increase both the health span and the lifespan of people. Why? Much like a car that needs increasing maintenance as it ages, people's organs wear out over time or are damaged during life. Imagine being able to replace a person's heart or lungs. That person would otherwise suffer a clear degradation of quality of life as those organs began failing versus a much longer and pain-free life with 3D-printed replacement organs. It is also well within technological possibility to use the person's own stem and other cells in the printed tissue/organ to reduce the potential for rejection. The same, of course, is true for

3D-printed prosthetics. While some products like 3D-printed hearts and lungs are still in the future, we'll provide a timeline as to when they are likely to be available as well as what 3D products are currently available.

One very practical use of medical 3D printers is to "print" organs based on scans of the patient's body. The practical application is to help surgeons preplan their actual surgery with an exact replacement shape of the tissue/organ being removed. This is particularly true if there are tumors or other unusual conditions that make the surgery anything but routine. It is already being done with prosthetics.

Prosthetics

Worldwide, there are more than 57.7 million people living with the loss of a limb. For many of these patients, the cost of a new limb is far more than they can pay. Additionally, there are children who will need several replacement prosthetic limbs as they grow.[1]

3D printers offer a number of advantages when it comes to producing prosthetics. Unlimited Tomorrow promises to drop the price of limbs from $80,000 to $8,000 with its TrueLimb product. Customers scan their residual limb at home and then send those images to the company. It then prints the customized limb and mails back the battery-powered prosthetic that includes a number of sensors to interpret topographic movements. In other words, the artificial limb responds accordingly when the patient wants to lift his arm to drink out of a cup.[2] The beauty of 3D-printed prosthetics is that they are customized for each patient, and they are not limited to limbs. In 2014, Dutch surgeons designed a customized 3D-printed implant made of plastic to replace the entire top of a woman's skull.[3]

Dentistry is a field where 3D printing is rapidly progressing. One company is now 3D printing clear aligners for its patients. The process begins with patients taking impressions of their teeth with an at-home impression kit. As an alternative, they can also go to a center to have an intraoral scan. A dentist analyzes the impressions and/or scans and creates a plan for treatment. The plan is used to 3D print the clear aligners that are then sent to the patients.[4]

3D printing dental applications can be even more extensive. An 83-year-old woman in the Netherlands received a 3D-printed jaw reconstruction composed of titanium powder with a bioceramic coating and a dental bridge added to the reconstructed jawbone so that the patient could have new teeth implants.[5]

Replacing Tissue for Burn Victims

There are over 2.4 million burn victims every year. Sometimes doctors will treat the burn area with an allograft, a skin graft taken from the back skin of a cadaver. The idea is to use this material to help heal the burn, but it is not a permanent solution because activation of a burn victim's T-cells causes the body to reject this material. The current long-term solution is for doctors to take skin from the victim's body where there are no burns and graft that skin onto the burn areas.[6] In the future, it will be possible to take the patient's own skin tissue to regrow the necessary cells and then 3D print them onto the patient's burn areas. This 3D-printed tissue would not be rejected.

In a major breakthrough, Rensselaer Polytechnic Institute in New York 3D-printed skin patches with blood vessels. That 2019 demonstration was a key step toward printing skin with blood vessels. The next necessary step is to be able to integrate these blood vessels at the microscopic level with the blood vessels and nerves already in the patient's own skin.[7]

Think of the complexity, though, because researchers have to be able to create all the twists and turns and bends and branches of a vascular system. Korean researchers are well on the way to achieving this goal. They created implantable 3D-printed blood vessels and then implanted them into a rat.[8]

What about treating burn victims in hospitals and not just in laboratory settings? Researchers at Wake Forest's Institute for Regenerative Medicine are working to develop a mobile skin bioprinting system that enables doctors to roll the printer to a patient's bedside, scan and measure the wound area, and then print skin, layer by layer, directly onto the wound's surface.[9]

From Blindness to Sight

Researchers are using 3D printers to develop eye tissue as well as biodegradable contact lenses and drug delivery to the eye.[10] In a proof-of-concept experiment, researchers 3D-printed a cornea in only 10 minutes. They created a unique bioink mixing healthy corneal stem cells with other ingredients. They scanned the patient's eye and then 3D-printed the cornea customized to fit the patient's unique eye, including its size and shape. Obviously, this is only the first step in a long process, but it could mean rescuing countless people from blindness. Researchers are also working on the 3D printing of retinal tissue.[11]

Breast Grafts and Implants

One approach to breast reconstruction is to 3D-print a clear resin that can be molded to the patient's body.[12] CollPlant has been developing 3D-bioprinted breast tissue. Researchers have designed these grafts to gradually degrade and be replaced by the patient's own tissue. It's designed to be a much safer process than current breast augmentation procedures that include silicone implants or fat transfer operations.[13] What is fascinating about this process is that CollPlant has replaced the animal or cadaver-sourced collagen in its bioink with the patient's own fat cells, a mixture that provides the physical scaffolding for the tissue, and rhCollagen.[14]

Replacing Entire Organs

Almost 106,000 Americans are currently on waiting lists for organ donations, and 17 people die each day while on those waiting lists.[15] Let's review the current state-of-the-art research focused on achieving this "holy grail" of medical 3D printing—the creation of working, full-sized organs that can replace diseased organs. Think of the major diseases so many Americans suffer from, and the possibilities offered by this potential lifesaver: diabetes (print a new pancreas), heart disease (print new replacement valves or an entirely new replacement heart), bladder cancer (print a new replacement bladder), and ovarian cancer (print new ovaries). We're probably a couple of decades or less away from this scientific area becoming practical, but it is already being studied in our best medical institutions.

A Replacement Pancreas

Polish researchers working for the Foundation of Research and Science Development bioprinted a functional prototype of a pancreas that included stable blood flow into pigs during a two-week period of observation.[16] The lead scientist on this project was quoted as saying that the "goal of the project is to create a functional pancreas. One that can be transplanted without major problems."[17]

Future Replacement Kidneys

Companies such as San Diego–based Organovo have spent years trying to develop a 3D-printed kidney. Researchers have not overcome all the obstacles needed to be overcome to produce a fully functional kidney with all the blood vessels, urine ducts and nerves functioning. Transplanting kidneys into children is a particularly difficult task. Researchers provided surgeons with 3D-printed kidneys that they could use for preoperative review and surgical simulation. The result was that three children with end-stage renal failure received kidney transplants and were progressing successfully at the time of their 16-month postoperative checkups.[18]

There are at least two major drivers pushing for the development of a fully functional 3D-printed kidney. One is the lack of sufficient numbers of kidneys available for transplant, and the second driver is the enormous potential cost savings. When a patient's kidney fails, keeping a patient on dialysis is estimated to cost around $270,000, and the cost of a kidney transplant is around $442,000 according to research published by the American Society of Nephrology in 2020.[19]

Replacement Livers

Oganovo has been able to 3D-print liver patches in mice and began human trials in 2020. Since then, it has sold its human liver research operations to Samsara Sciences.[20] Printing patches can act as a stop-gap measure until a patient can receive a liver transplant.[21]

Replacement Lungs

Lungs offer a real challenge to medical researchers seeking to 3D-print them because of their size and complexity. United Therapeutics Corporation recently (2023) 3D-printed a human lung scaffold that included 4,000 kilometers of capillaries and 200 million alveoli capable of oxygen exchange in animal models. Their goal is to be cleared for human trials within five years.[22]

Replacing the Heart

Research continues toward the goal of 3D-printing a heart. Researchers have created a heart cell made from stem cells, but it does not beat as strongly as a fully functional heart. Stanford researchers have 3D-printed a mini-heart that took four hours to produce. When connected to a pump that drives oxygen and nutrients through it, this tissue does develop on its own and increases in both maturity and function.[23]

Researchers also have printed a mini heart that beats on its own. One useful function it will perform is to test how new medications affect heart tissue without having to resort to human testing. Researchers also have 3D-printed a heart valve that possesses the same anatomical architecture as a human heart value. The next stage is to test it on sheep.[24] Researchers have also 3D-printed a fully vascularized mini human heart composed of human cells taken from a patient along with carrier cells.[25] Finally, researchers have produced 3D-printed hearts that match those of patients along with the valve that needs to be implanted. Surgeons then can practice placing the replacement valve in the patient's "heart" before the actual operation.[26]

A Timeline

This technology holds tremendous potential, but there are still technical limitations that need to be overcome. One of the many current limitations is the inability of current medical 3D printers to print the mixture of different types of cells required in most organs; an organ composed of a single type of cell will not function. There might be a breakthrough on the horizon. Researchers at Stevens Institute of Technology are developing a new type of 3D printing process that uses microfluidics. This means they will be able to produce much more precise manipulation of liquids through tiny channels to produce output at the cellular level to make more complex tissues. In addition, this process would permit the printing of multiple different types of bioink that could form a single organic structure.[27]

Researchers have already made impressive achievements when it comes to printing tissue as well as proof-of-concept organs. The real breakthrough will be the 3D-printing of organs with the same functionality as a patient's original organs, including complete vascular and nervous systems. Most experts peg this next stage as being somewhere between one and two decades into the future. Clearly, some organs will be easier to print than others. In many ways, the timeline for 3D-printed organs is tied to concurrent developments in stem cell research since using a patient's own cells eliminates the concern over the body rejecting the 3D-printed organ and the use of anti-rejection drugs for drugs.[28]

3D Printing for Longevity

While some futurists envision a time when people will improve the quality of their lives by voluntarily adding various 3D prosthetics such as 3D-printed legs designed to enhance outdoor sports, there are far more practical advantages to 3D printing when it comes to increasing longevity. Today skin grafts from 3D printed material can be the difference today between life and death. While "printing" the vascular system within an organ is still an obstacle, the timeline most experts believe is short before that problem will be overcome. Diabetes is a major killer, so imagine being able to replace a defective pancreas and providing someone with a much longer and much healthier life. The same can be said for people whose lungs are so limited that they are unable to live a normal life. A new set of lungs would provide a much longer and a much more enjoyable life. This goal is still years away, but it is easier to imagine a nearer-term solution where fully functional 3D-printed tissue is added to a compromised organ/tissue to improve its functionality. This alone would be a huge benefit to the patient with a poorly functioning organ.

CHAPTER 10

Wearable Devices to Stay Healthy as We Age

The traditional the process of getting health care is rapidly changing. This is a topic worth exploring because over 150 million wearable devices were sold in the third quarter of 2023 and about 492 million were sold in 2022.[1] The acceptance and adoption of these new technologies is progressing rapidly globally. In this chapter, we will provide more detail about wearable devices that will help us stay healthy as we age and allow us to actively engage in our own health care management.

We are focusing in this chapter on wearable medical devices that are worn by individuals. Wearables are "seamlessly embedded portable computers…worn on the body."[2] Wearables are not limited to medical devices used by health care specialists to follow a patient's health status longitudinally. They also can be non–medically approved devices with the objective of helping the user to stay more aware of their own activities' impact on their health and to promote healthy habits and behaviors. This second kind of device are called "activity trackers."

Activity trackers are not medical devices. To be so designated, they would require FDA approval before they could make that claim. Some manufacturers do not have an interest in offering a true medical device because they want to avoid the kinds of claims that require the extra expense of proving their medical benefits to the FDA. The benefits of wearable "non-FDA-validated" devices have stimulated a whole new industry to spring up and provide real-time monitoring and diagnosis information for the health-conscious users. In earlier chapters, we have briefly mentioned the development of devices and instruments among the new developments in medical technology. In the following sections, we will expand with some examples of the wearable device segment and briefly review some other technologies that are impacting the medically and non–medically approved wearable space.

Fitness Trackers

Fitness trackers are basically electronic devices that measure and collect information about an individual's movements and physical responses. Early activity trackers were basically pedometers that used accelerometers and altimeters to estimate the speed and distance traveled. From this, even calories burned could be calculated. Among the earliest trackers were wearable heart rate monitors. Today, with the development of the smartphone, loaded with specially designed apps and the phone's prodigious calculation capabilities, far more sophisticated sensors can be integrated into the activity tracker app. These modern devices can monitor not just exercise-related activities but also mood, sleep, water intake, medicine usage, potential illnesses, and an ever-increasing number of other things. Consumer Reports has recently reviewed this category of products.[3] They can be worn on wrists (bracelets, watches), fingers, armbands, attached to skin nearly everywhere appropriate for the measurements. Some are designed for athletic training, others for children, and still others for adults and individuals with special needs. There are even trackers in earphones that can measure blood pressure, electrocardiograms, heart rates, and body temperature directly from ear capillaries.

Still, these wearables should not be categorized as medical devices. If something looks abnormal in the output from such a tracking device or app, then the user should contact a health care professional to address the potential issue. Most trackers are also not designed for privacy. The information being collected may leave a digital footprint, for example, on your smartphone. If this is a concern, then the user needs to investigate the privacy protections for the selected device in advance of adoption. This issue will be covered in more detail in a later section.

Trackers constitute an area with a huge number of similar products. For this reason, we can only mention a selected few that help us make the point for how they benefit health span and longevity. The real benefit from using tracking devices is the increased awareness they provide of the benefits from physical activity and proper eating habits. As stated throughout this book, these habits provide clear benefits for health span and longevity.[4]

Medical Uses of Wearables

There is a parallel proliferation of FDA–medically cleared wearable devices beyond those stationary devices used in medical facilities to track, monitor, and diagnose health conditions in a presenting patient. Wearable devices are prescribed by health care professionals for chronic conditions where remote, continuous monitoring is important for the patient and their doctors. Some examples follow.

Glucose Monitoring and Insulin Delivery Pumps

For diabetics, monitoring their sugar levels (in particular, glucose) is important for maintaining a healthy metabolism. For decades, diabetics have been monitoring their blood sugar levels by pricking their fingers and then putting a drop of blood into a sugar meter. This gives a sugar level at one specific time. It doesn't provide the blood sugar levels after a meal or during sleep and so on, unless the procedure is repeated multiple times a day. A better solution would be continuous sugar monitoring so the diabetic can know exactly when the sugar levels are out of a healthy range. Such a wearable is now available as a 24-hour-a-day wearable patch providing real-time sugar levels. Two companies that offer such a device are Dexcom and Abbot's Freestyle Division. Their products and those from other companies measure the sugar levels and send the information to a monitor or a smartphone. The so alerted patient can take appropriate action if the reading is too high or low.[5] These wearable sugar monitors have reduced the number of low-blood-glucose emergencies, fewer finger sticks, and a better health state, in general, for diabetics.

The development of wearable insulin pumps by Medtronic/MiniMed, Insulet, and others has been proven to help maintain a healthy sugar level within the optimal target range. Still the diabetic needs to know how much insulin beyond their basal levels the pump needs to deliver and when. The optimum would be to develop an "artificial pancreas" to close the loop between automatically measuring sugar levels and automatically delivering the correct amount of insulin. In the last few years, such smart devices have been brought to the market. They take the information from a continuous glucose monitor, and then a smart device (e.g., smartphone) takes that information and relays it to a wearable continuously delivering insulin pump that then delivers the required insulin to maintain optimal sugar levels. Furthermore, these closed loop devices can be monitored by health care professionals to be sure they are working properly and to recommend changes to the patient if less-than-optimal readings are observed. This closed-loop system helps the diabetic avoid hypoglycemia and hyperglycemia to improve their quality of life and, indirectly, their longevity.[6]

Cardiovascular and Heart Monitors

For people with heart conditions, monitoring heart activity provides an important early warning of potentially life-threatening events. As with many diseases, catching the problem early and addressing them immediately can help mitigate the worst outcomes. According to the American Heart Association, the number of people dying of a heart attack each year has dropped from 1 in 2 in the 1950s to 1 in 8.5 now because of improved diagnosis and treatment options. Also, stroke, the third leading cause of death in the United States in the 1930s, is now the fifth because of aggressive health and intervention programs to reduce the risks associated with strokes.[7] The development of continuous cardiac monitoring devices addresses this problem of not having a recording device detect the cardiac event real-time. Some of the earlier heart monitors were designed to be activated when the patient feels symptoms. The disadvantage of this kind of monitor is that it will not monitor subthreshold heart rhythm events if the patient does not notice them. These subthreshold events are common in heart patients. It is essential for the doctor to be aware of them so that actions can be taken early and possibly mitigate the issue before the problem becomes clinically observed.

For people with a variety of heart issues, these devices can record active and resting heart rate, heart rate variability, walking asymmetry and steadiness, atrial fibrillation, cardio fitness, and even an electrocardiogram (ECG). Heart monitors are inexpensive and convenient to use. Clinical-quality heart monitors, however, depend on electrodes attached to your chest and a device that records and processes the ECG collected from the electrical impulses. There are several types of devices that have different diagnostic capabilities and different communication and reporting capabilities. A Loop Memory Monitor will save an ECG if the patient feels symptoms and pushes a record button. Then the patient can review it and report/share the results with a health care professional.

Newer monitor designs will also start on their own if they detect abnormal heart rhythms. A Symptom Event Heart Monitor records symptoms when the patient turns on the device. Patch recorders have no wired leads from the electrodes to the monitor but can wirelessly communicate with the monitor. This system can continuously monitor ECG activity for up to 14 days when the patches/batteries need to be replaced. Modern devices will simultaneously send their data to a health care professional in real-time to enable the doctor look at the data and respond quickly if the computer program detects an event needing attention.[8] Sometimes, people with heart conditions will report anxiety associated with a heart event. For patients who record their ECG continuously, the doctor can analyze the order of events to determine if the anxiety event precedes or follows the heart issue.[9]

Heart Rate Is a Window to Your Heart's Health

For older people, your heart rate will vary due to a variety of conditions. Regular exercise, medications, stress, and various medical conditions, all play a part in your heart's condition and beating rate. Your resting heart rate is taken when you are calm, relaxed, sitting, and not sick. Too low a heart rate (below 60 beats per minute) can result in lightheadedness and even fainting. A low heart rate is called bradycardia and can be dangerous. A high resting heart rate can also be a signal that something is wrong such as abnormal hormone levels or anemia. In the case of low or high heart rates, you need to see a health care professional to diagnose the cause(s). For adults and older adults, the heart rate range should be between 60 and 100 beats per minute. On average, for a 70-year-old, the target heart rate of 75 to 128 beats per minute during exercise is okay. There are many reasons for a high resting heart rate (called tachycardia) that include high blood pressure, obesity, low physical fitness, stress, pain, fever, and a variety of medical conditions and illnesses. It is important to recognize that the lower your heart rate is the less work the heart needs to do to meet your body's needs. For an otherwise healthy person, the best way to lower your heart rate is to increase your physical exercise. Physical exercise strengthens your heart muscle so it is stronger and will require fewer beats to pump the required amount of blood.[10] This is one of the benefits for an older adult to exercise and take walks to improve heart health and indirectly longevity.

Blood Oxygen (Pulse Oximeter Diagnostic Devices)

Blood oxygen measurement (pulse oximetry) is already very common in a variety of wearable devices. The pulse oximeter is a rapid, through-the-skin measurement of the oxygen saturation level of red blood cells in a body. Oxygen saturation levels between 95 and 100 percent are considered normal for adults and children. A consistent level below 95 percent is considered abnormal. People over 70 years of age may have oxygen level average closer to 95 percent. If you're using an oximeter at home and your oxygen saturation level is 92 percent or lower, on average, then a health care professional should examine you to see if there is a medical issue. The brain, a major user of oxygen, is damaged when oxygen levels drop below 80 to 85 percent. Some symptoms of low oxygen saturation (hypoxia) are headache, shortness of breath, rapid heart rate, confusion, and bluish color in skin, fingernails, and lips. The bluish discoloration of the skin or mucous membranes occurs when oxygen levels fall below 67 percent. If it's at 88 percent or lower, the recommendation is to get to the nearest emergency room as soon as possible to address any medical issue needing attention.[11] Even short periods of low oxygen can damage specific cells in the brain. Low oxygen levels are a well-known cause of brain damage in premature babies.[12] Low oxygen saturation over time, for example, in people with sleep apnea, can cause progressive damage to the brain or heart. Certain areas of the brain are more sensitive to low oxygen saturation than others. Low oxygen also means that the blood has higher-than-optimum levels of carbon dioxide. This can also be a problem as carbon dioxide changes the blood pH[13] (see Chapter 15 for more details about sleep apnea).

The importance of the oxygen saturation level has prompted wearable device makers to include blood oxygen measurements with their medical and nonmedical devices. This is especially important if the user has respiratory issues from disease, smoking, or lung damage. Pulse oximeter systems also have been incorporated into wearable rings, watches, and other medical and nonmedical tracking devices.

Weight Loss and Obesity

In the United States, nearly 1 in 3 adults are overweight, 2 in 5 are obese, and 1 in 11 are severely obese.[14] It is estimated that 40 percent of older adults are obese. Weight loss programs for adults aged 65+ consist of restricted caloric intake and programs of aerobic and resistance exercises. Weight loss in conjunction with exercise leads to significant improvements in cardiometabolic status, reduces intramuscular fat deposition, and leads to increased muscle mass, strength, and physical function, all which can reduce long-term mortality.[15] Obesity is well known to be a risk factor for many different medical conditions, all leading to increased morbidity and mortality. Various interacting factors influence the prevalence of obesity, including people's upbringing, lifestyle, environment, and genetics. Popular strategies for losing weight focus mainly on reducing calorie intake and increasing "energy expenditure." These have had limited success as obese persons often lose motivation over time and regain any weight lost. A new strategy is needed to maintain motivation and modified behavior if these programs are to be more successful.

It is impossible to watch TV or any media including streaming services on the Internet that does not have many ads touting weigh loss drugs or products. The health consequences of obesity are really negative, and, for health span and longevity, ignoring them is at your "peril." The advent of inexpensive, wearable fitness trackers and related wearables is impacting this field too. A Harvard study that pooled data from 31 different fitness studies involving over 2,200 people showed that people who wore commercially available fitness trackers like Fitbit or Jawbone for an average of 12 weeks lost an average of 6 pounds and 2 Body Mass Index (BMI) points. They concluded that using these devices was a constant reminder and motivator to the individual to pursue healthy exercise and eating goals.[16] Research into the effectiveness of interventions programmed on wearable fitness devices suggests that these programs with reminders, tracking, and "nagging" do help the wearer lose weight.[17] However, long-term weight loss (>1 year) is often unsuccessful because, to remain successful, the person has to change the lifestyle that resulted in becoming obese. In many cases, focus lapses as the novelty of the approach wears off over time. In summary, wearable devices give the wearer information about their exercise, food intake, and other activities to keep the wearer motivated. The more modern and complex devices provide additional health information as they combine other diagnostic measurements to the output of the information presented to the wearer. The data show these devices motivate and help the wearer to be more alert to their weight and eating and other behaviors conducive to weight loss. These wearables work as long as the wearer continues to sustain their changed lifestyle, or they will not maintain the weight loss. Simply said, staying motivated will result in improved health span and increased lifespan.

Hearing Aids, Hearing Implants, and More

A key contributor to longevity is keeping the brain stimulated and engaged. In other chapters, we have discussed the importance of social engagement and doing activities that involve physical exercise and mentally taxing activities. Even in old age, these activities are really important in helping to keep not just your brain "thinking" but also optimizing your physical health. One underappreciated area is the impact of hearing and hearing-related diseases on people's health span and longevity. Severe hearing loss is associated with increased risk of mortality, cognitive decline, and poor physical health.[18] The risk could be reduced by consistent hearing aid use.[19] It is now believed that a loss of the ability to communicate with others among older people leads to social isolation, loneliness, and frustration. The result is a gradual dulling of the brain's mental acuity, and, consequently, it will negatively impact the brain's management of important physiological functions and health span. Unless the patient is deaf, the use of hearing aids of various kinds reverses this impact of hearing loss.

One really new idea is to combine an existing headphone product with a hearing aid. Apple announced recently it has been given FDA clearance to include a clinical-grade hearing aid feature in its AirPods Pro 2 product in an over-the-counter headphone product.[20] Its cost is the same as for the regular product, which may bring the technology down to a more affordable price point. If it works well as a hearing aid and is not just a sound amplifier, then it could be a game changer.[21] As far back as 2019, Apple's Tom Cook has said that he expects Apple's greatest contribution to mankind will be in health products.[22] At the same time, Apple also announced that it would be adding sleep apnea–tracking capabilities to its newest Apple watch making it another FDA-cleared wearable medical device.

For people who are profoundly deaf through damage to the inner ear sound receptors, a cochlear implant is an option. There were over 8,500 cochlear implantations in 2019. This device has an inner ear implanted electrode array and sound processor outside the body communicating with the electronic array inside the ear. For many, the cochlear implant enables them to "learn" to hear again and enables them to enjoy many of the advantages available to hearing people. One especially gratifying area is that many children who are born deaf and get a cochlea implant very young grow up being able to hear "as if they could always hear." One recent study says about 78 percent of deaf children have cochlear implants.[23]

One other wearable product in the hard-of-hearing area are products that are simple sound amplifiers. These products capture ambient sound and simply amplify all the frequencies about the same amount. This is not a hearing aid–type product in the usual sense as they don't adjust the sound volume tuned to the person's reduced hearing frequencies as a hearing aid would. If not careful, the person could damage their hearing in areas where they do not have hearing loss while making the frequencies with hearing loss louder. They could be worn in an area where the sound of a product such as a TV is not loud enough, and the wearer can amplify the sound without bothering others in the area.[24]

Sleep Trackers

Getting enough sleep is an important component of good health. We will discuss sleep in more detail in Chapter 13, but sleep trackers are wearable devices we will cover in this chapter. Sleep disorders and insomnia can be caused by many things. It can simply be caused by a change in your circadian rhythm resulting from travel, excessive daytime napping, being in an unfamiliar place, changes in lifestyle, and bedtime changes. It can also be associated with mental stress, depression, some medicines, and stimulants in food and drink. The advent of modern electronics has stimulated a wealth of wearable over-the-counter products that track sleep to help the user to understand their sleep patterns and then enable them to address solutions that will improve their sleep.

Sleep tracking wearable devices use a variety of endpoints. These endpoints include an accelerometer that measures arm movements and heart rate and blood oxygen. The idea is that because, for example, the heart slows as you move into Stage 2 (deep sleep) of our four-stage sleep cycles, the tracker knows you have entered a different stage of sleep. During REM sleep, the body has reduced limb movements too so the tracker can estimate that stage you are in too.[25] These data go into an algorithm to estimate the amount of time you sleep and the quality of your sleep.[26] One common sleep tracking system is the Apple Watch paired with Apple phone that can measure these common diagnostics of sleep.[27] Another one is the Oura Ring (Oura Health Oy), which has received clearance from the FDA and has a CE mark from the European Union. The Oura Ring uses three small sensors in the interior of the ring equipped with infrared light to track the wearer's heart rate, blood oxygen level, breathing regularity, heart rate variability, temperature, and movement activity. The results are calculated and presented to the wearer to understand the quality of their sleep.[28]

For the data to be even more useful, the information generated by the wearables will need to be integrated with health systems and potentially inform therapy planning. This will enable doctors, health care professionals, and insurance coverage companies to track any serious issues longitudinally.[29] In this way, the wearable data can be incorporated into a broader health care program to improve health span and longevity.

In summary, the development of wearable medical devices and fitness trackers is changing how a patient's medical status is followed and diagnosed. It is one of the important health-related developments derived from the electronics revolution. These wearables in all forms are also raising the patient's awareness of their health status enabling them to be proactive in its management. This clearly directly translates to improved health span and longevity.

CHAPTER 11

Cancer and Its Challenge to Longevity

To live a long healthy life there are two main health-related components: The avoidance of disease and the reduction of non-disease-related biological aging. As people live longer, diseases relating to increasing age such as memory loss, essential tremor, muscle atrophy, increased frailty and so forth become more prominent, the medical profession is increasingly focusing on new areas of aging medicine to mitigate these issues. This topic of biological aging is discussed in another chapter (Chapter 2). The focus of this chapter will be on cancer.

Benefits of Early Detection of Cancer

Cancer is one of the most important human diseases to prevent. A number of cancers are preventable according to the Siteman Cancer Center because they can be caught through early screening before they become a significant problem. Addressing these cancers with appropriate screening and doing your best to follow your doctor's the recommended actions to reduce your preventable rate of cancer can go a long way in reducing your incidence of cancer.[1] Siteman lists the 12 preventable cancers as: bladder, breast, cervical, colon, kidney, lung, ovarian, pancreatic, aggressive prostate, skin/melanoma, stomach and uterine. They also recommend the eight actions we have been discussing throughout this book about how to increase longevity. These actions also apply to preventing/reducing the incidence of cancer. They include: not smoking, maintaining a healthy weight, exercising regularly, following a healthy diet, drinking alcohol in moderation, protecting yourself from the sun, managing infections promptly and screening regularly for these preventable cancers. Cancer cells are different in a variety of ways from normal cells. They have many unique characteristics which include: looking different under the microscope, not repairing themselves or dying (immortal), not specializing for the tissue they are in, not sticking together (thus they can spread to new areas of the body), and dividing and growing without the usual restraints (thus forming a tumor at each remote location). Taken together these are the characteristics that make cancer so dangerous.[2]

Methods for Early Detection of Cancer

A number of tests are already in common use for early detection of cancer including: mammography for the breast, HPV and PAP tests for cervical cancer, PSA for prostate, colonoscopy, sigmoidoscopy and stool-based tests for colorectal cancer, skin exams of moles and CT and x-Ray for lung and other cancers throughout the body.[3] People need to take these tests at regular intervals to catch potential issues early. Newer tests are now coming onto the market that use DNA, RNA and tumor cells and tumor cell markers in blood. One example of this is the minimally invasive technique called liquid biopsy. As mentioned earlier in Chapter 8, liquid biopsy detects cancer in a blood sample because cancer cells break off from a tumor and circulate in the blood (circulating tumor cells) while looking for a place to land and start a metastatic site. Cancer cells also shed DNA and other proteins into blood. In some cases, liquid biopsy has been shown to detect minimal residual disease (from a former cancer patient) or new metastatic disease as much as two years earlier than by imaging with for example CT or x-ray. Imaging methods are of limited value until the tumor is large and established. Liquid biopsy does not rely on the size of the tumor for detection. Early cancers are more likely to be curable and thus early detection allows for therapy before the cancer gets "established." This technique has recently been extended to other physiological fluids such as saliva, urine and even cerebrospinal fluid.[4] What is especially exciting about these liquid biopsy-type analyses is that they can detect many kinds of cancers for which there had not been a specific test developed previously. Once alerted to the presence of the cancer by this test, the physician can use other techniques to identify its location and provide therapy.[5] It is reasonable to expect that before too long a liquid biopsy or saliva test will be incorporated into a patient's routine annual physical exam as a way to catch cancer early.

Different Causes of Cancer and Implications for Longevity

Cancers have been found in every tissue in the body except, perhaps, the heart. Unfortunately, there is no single cause of cancer even though a single carcinogen could cause cancer in different kinds of tissues and organs. The five-year survival rate for childhood cancer is 80 percent, but for older adults it is only 68 percent. Stanford Medicine lists several general categories of cancer: Lifestyle, family history (read genetics), exposures to cancer causing viruses, environmental exposures (read pesticides and industrial waste) and some kinds of chemotherapies and radiation.[6] Examining all the potential causes of cancer is too detailed a topic for this book. In general, there are many causes we don't have control over and some we can avoid reducing our chances for getting cancer. Causes we don't have control over include family genetics, spontaneous mutations and inherited disease. Causes we have some control of include lifestyle factors such as smoking, high-fat diets, working with toxic chemicals, and exposure to cancer causing viruses. Normally, our body repairs minor damage to cells and, if it cannot, the cell can be programmed to self-destruct (apoptosis) and be replaced with a healthy cell. The message here is that over time minor cellular damage builds up through normal life activities. In most cases, the cell just becomes senescent. This buildup can also cause some cells to develop abnormal "behaviors" leading the cell to die, or barring this outcome, they go "rogue" and become pre-cancerous or cancerous.[7] As individuals we should focus on the things we can do to minimize exposure to potential causes of cancer. Unfortunately, cancer is partially a consequence of life. For this reason, following regular medical health checkups, following up on anything suspicious is essential. As discussed throughout this book, early diagnosis of cancer and early treatment improves health span and indirectly longevity.

Cancer Cells Keep Growing and Are Immortal

Normally cells are stimulated to grow and to specialize by proteins called growth factors that instruct the cell when to grow, divide and its specialization type. Under regular situations the production of growth factors only occurs when they are needed. Normal cells have a number of checks and balances that prevent the cell from over growing. For example, if the location has enough of a specialized cell type in say a muscle tissue, normal cells will stop growing and dividing. Normal cells in a mature tissue will stop growing and only divide when needed to replace a dying cell or following a stimulus that promotes tissue growth such as when a muscle is exercised. One way the cells controls growth is through the production of the enzyme tyrosine kinase which acts as an on/off switch for cell growth. Normal cells will block this enzyme that promotes cell growth and division when growth is not needed. However, cancer cells produce inhibitors of tyrosine kinase which is one of the ways it can continue to grow even when contact inhibition should tell it to stop. Cancer cells also need nutrition to grow. To get this nutrition, it over produces angiogenic factors that stimulates blood vessel growth into the tumor. Once the tumor has a source of nutrition, growth goes into overdrive. Doctors are now using and developing inhibitors of these growth promoters and mechanisms as a way to treat or at the least slow its growth.[8]

The other aspect of cancer cells is that they don't die nearly as often as normal cells do or go into senescence. This is due, in part, to the fact that they produce telomerase, an enzyme that prevents telomere shortening. As discussed in Chapter 2, telomere shortening is responsible for cells becoming senescent and cells with short telomeres stop growing and dividing. Cancer cells are immortal because the enzyme telomerase keeps their telomeres long, so they will not become senescent. This is part of why cancer cells are so dangerous. (For more about telomeres see Chapters 2, 5, 12, and 17.)

Normal Cells Are Not Immortal

One of the reasons people are not immortal is that most of our cells are not immortal. Mortal cells, unfortunately, become senescent. This means that slowly, over time, the cells in our various organs become senescent or die leading to increasingly dysfunctional tissues. Because senescent cells stop dividing, they stop replacing tissues and organs with new "young" cells. The result contributes to the tissue's aging process. Eventually, these senescent cells die without producing a replacement and the various tissues are degraded—"aging."

To learn more about the importance of telomeres and longevity, geneticist Richard Cawthon and colleagues at the University of Utah studied two groups of people divided by the length of their telomeres. It found the people with longer telomeres live an average of five years longer than those with shorter telomeres.[9] They also found that among people older than 60, those with shorter telomeres were three times more likely to die from heart disease and eight times more likely to die from an infectious disease. There also is some evidence linking shortened telomeres to Alzheimer disease, hardening of the arteries, high blood pressure, and type-2 diabetes. These and other studies support the view that your telomere length is important for longevity.

Telomeres alone, however, do not dictate lifespan. Cawthon and colleagues noted that the risk of death doubles every eight years. Their study estimated that the differences in telomere length only accounted for 4 percent while the risk of death from chronological age was 6 percent. When combined with gender and chronological age, their scientific aging model only accounted for 37 percent. So, what else contributes to aging independent of telomere length? An important factor that contributes to aging is oxidative stress, which damages our DNA and contributes to inflammation. Together, these two factors—oxidative stress and inflammation—reduces our ability to fight infection and our ability to counteract damaging substances such as alcohol and cigarettes. Cawthon suggests that if oxidative stress became routinely repairable, then humans might live much longer. Another important aging factor is glycation (sugars reacting with biological molecules in your body and negatively modifying these tissues). Through the process of glycation, glucose modifies your DNA, proteins, and lipids leaving them less able to their jobs. Glycation gets worse with age.[9] These additional factors contribute to our aging, and understanding this process will provide scientists and doctors with biological pathways to study for increasing health span and longevity.

Reducing the Incidence of Cancer

Cancer is a disease that usually comes from "damaged" normal cells, cells damaged by oncoviruses, external chemicals, or radiation. Sometimes, it comes from a mutated/damaged DNA or an improper division of a normal cell. For this reason, there is no easy way to prevent all cancers.

We cannot know in advance when these events will occur. There are things we can do, however, to reduce the incidence of cancer. These include[1,10]:

1. Avoid cancer-causing chemicals or foods associated with higher incidence of cancer. Smoking, drugs, and liquor are clearly associated with causing the mutations that cause cancer. Some of the chemicals used to preserve meat have been shown to cause cancer in separate screening studies. Eating foods that have too high a level of pesticides or heavy metals may also provide avoidable health issues.

2. Do regular cancer pre-screening to look for pre-cancerous changes in tissues as part of your regular checkups. Identifying pre-cancer changes in cells before they progress to cancer has an obvious benefit. With this information the patient can take proactive measures to prevent these changes from becoming "full blown" cancer. An example of this is that during a colonoscopy the GI doctor removes intestinal polyps that can become cancerous.

3. Do the activities discussed throughout this chapter and book to keep your body healthy. Living a clean life together with exercise, proper food, sleep, and so on is associated with longer lives. This is because the entire body is healthier and, therefore, has less internal inflammatory and other diseases. This is especially true for things that reduce inflammation and so on, so the body can fight off any abnormal cells to prevent them from "escaping" to form cancer.

4. Early identification of invasive (metastatic) cancer, such as through a liquid biopsy, is a way to reduce cancer spread before it becomes established in multiple locations. Outcomes are better the earlier you find and treat the cancer, or any other disease for that matter.

As stated throughout this book, the main points are that living lives in a way that avoids risky exposures and staying healthier biases the results for avoiding cancer in the first place.

Improving Cancer Outcome and Longevity

The country's cancer death rate has declined by 33 percent since 1991. The American Cancer Society believes that this is the result of improved treatments but, most importantly, reduction in smoking.[11] This report also noted that the overall cancer survival rate for five years was 49 percent in 1970 and now is 68 percent. The survival rates for cancers between 1975 and now have significantly improved. Some examples include[11]:

Lung cancer from 12 to 23 percent
Female breast cancer from 75 to 91 percent
Colorectal cancer from 50 to 65 percent
Kidney cancer from 50 to 77 percent
Leukemia from 34 to 66 percent

The article points to improved screening to find it at an earlier stage but also to immunotherapy and to a very interesting variety of creative new drugs such as checkpoint inhibitors and targeted therapies.

In normal situations, a healthy cell presents "checkpoints" on its surface so that the immune system will not mistakenly destroy it. However, cancer cells take advantage of this to avoid being killed by the immune system.[12] Many cancers are removed by the body's immune system and/or have their programmed cell death process activated and never develop to a point where they are detected. The cancers that do develop are the ones that are able to avoid being detected. One way cancer cells become "invisible" to the immune system is by presenting proteins (called checkpoint proteins) on their surfaces that mask them from detection by the immune system surveilling "checkpoints." Recognizing this avoidance system, scientists are developing new kinds of therapies called "checkpoint inhibitors" to change the interaction of these proteins with the immune cells so they will be targeted for killing.[13] It is a promising approach that will synergize therapies targeting specific cancers and hopefully reduce the damage to normal cells around the cancer.

Another very modern kind of cancer therapy is called CAR-T-Cell therapy. This fancy name describes a way of taking your own immune T-cells and reprogramming them to recognize a specific kind of cancer cell. These reprogrammed cells then are injected back into the patient and attack the cancer wherever the cell finds them.[14]

Finally, after surgeries to remove a tumor, there can be some cancer cells left behind. These residual cancer cells need to be removed, or they will grow back to form a new tumor, and the benefit of the surgery may only be temporary. Doctors are now using new targeted chemotherapy agents to mop up any residual cancer cells missed following surgery that removes the main tumors.[15]

These new medicines and medical approaches are improving outcomes and have fewer side effects than traditional cytotoxic drugs that may kill good cells as well as cancer cells. They do this by basically hijacking the ways cancer cells operate and then using it against them. For the patient, this means a better and longer, more enjoyable lifespan. It also means improved longevity for the patient and the population as a whole.

Curing Cancer Alone Will Not Prevent Diseases of Old Age

Earlier in this chapter, we discussed and focused on cancer as a major cause of death. However, curing cancer alone will not prevent the many other diseases of old age. As a reminder, the major age-related diseases include hearing loss, cataracts, arthritis, diabetes, osteoporosis, stroke, chronic kidney disease, chronic obstructive pulmonary disease (COPD), dementia, Alzheimer's disease, and Parkinson's disease, just to name a few.[16] As modern medicine develops effective therapies the society's average longevity will increase. On an individual's level, the quality of life may not be better as the ravages of age progressively take hold. As an illustration, on average people who only live to 50 will see fewer diseases of old age such as Alzheimer's disease or hypothyroidism. Other diseases develop over a lifetime and sometimes are accelerated by "misbehavior" such as smoking or drinking. On the biological level, aging results from the accumulation of a wide variety of molecular and cellular damage over time. As diseases are conquered people will live longer, and the diseases of old age will become more prominent. A lot of how people age has a genetic component. As we described in earlier sections, inflammation, oxidative stress, and glycation also play a role in the degradation of our body and health and cause the unevenness of aging between individuals. These changes are just consequences of life and are not from a regular disease.

Scientists and doctors are actively looking at genes, cells, hormones, eating patterns, and other clues for how to prevent or slow aging. What is clear now is that exercising, certain diets, and maintaining a healthy body weight (i.e., eating fewer calories) have a big payoff in health span and longevity. Exercising for endurance (aerobic), muscle strengthening, balance training, and flexibility are more beneficial than just walking. Beyond the benefits of a proper diet, amply discussed throughout this book, the benefit of a low-calorie diet is also clear. Why this is the case even if followed for a lifetime is not understood. Some speculate that a low-calorie diet may slow metabolism.[17] Fontana and Hu reviewed studies that considered optimal body weight, health, and longevity and concluded the lowest mortality is associated with a BMI (body mass index) of < 25 kg/m^2.[18] Body fat is an endocrine organ too, and, when there is too much of it, then body fat promotes metabolic diseases such as type-2 diabetes.

Scientists and doctors do not have a handle on how to stop aging on a whole-body level. What is clear now is that your different tissues and organs age at different rates. Just as individuals age at different rates so do your organs. Scientists now can track aging of specific organs by looking at various biomarkers of the different organs. A recent study by Dr. Wyss-Coray at Stanford conducted genetic activity to understand aging across nearly 5,000 proteins and in the blood from over 5,600 people. His team showed that almost 20 percent of people have accelerated aging in a single organ while less than 2 percent have accelerated aging in more than one organ.[19] They also found a correlation between certain diseases and accelerated aging of particular organs. For example, people with hypertension and diabetes had "older" kidneys than their age-matched peers. This opens the prospect that in the future one may improve health span and indirectly longevity by addressing an aged kidney, for example.

Senescence is what is believed to ultimately impact longevity in the absence of disease and in people who follow all the guidelines for a healthy life. The biology of senescence of cell division arrest has been shown in cell culture to occur in the absence of the protein p16 expression and when the protein p53 is inactivated.[20] To be clear, this is very early research, and it is not a clinical solution for senescence. There is a class of drugs in development called senolytics that remove senescent cells from the body. This may be showing promise in clinical studies as they seem to be restoring damaged tissue to prior levels of function.[21] This is encouraging, but researchers still haven't demonstrated the long-term longevity benefits of such therapies beyond removing senescent cell.[22]

The Skin, Cancer, and Longevity

The skin is your body's largest organ comprising about 15 percent of your total weight.[23] Simply put, your skin protects your body's insides from the very many outside world dangers and is both a barrier and a sensory organ. As a result, it has an outsized effect on your health and lifespans. The skin is a remarkably complex organ that varies in thickness in various parts of the body. It maintains its health by constantly shedding (turning over) the outer layer of cells that may be damaged or senescent and thus revealing lower-level cells that "move up" to replace them. The turnover time for young skin cells is 28 days but increases to 84 days by age 80.[24]

As we age, the skin composition changes too. The aged skin thins significantly, due to the loss of many of the kinds of cells in the various layers of the young skin. Among the consequences from this thinning is a reduction of important immune and other protective cells in the skin and on the surface.[25] One example is the loss of melanocytes (a pigment cell) resulting in the graying of your hair and loss of skin color.[26] The loss of elastic fibers contributes to the wrinkling of the skin.

An important and often overlooked component of the skin's health is the contributions from the microbiome. As described in Chapter 3, the microbiome is the collection of all microbes that miraculously survive on the outside of our bodies despite the discouragements from soap, sunblock, lotions, and antibiotics we smear on our skin. To be clear the skin microbiome is different in various places on the body and reflects your age, health status, and exposure to outside environmental conditions and, of course, germs. One important function of the skin's microbiome is not just to protect from dangerous germs but also to educate your skin's resident immune cells to prepare the defense networks against potentially invading pathogens.[27] As we age, the changes in the skin's microbiome may contribute to the reduced health of the skin and its immune system.

The skin's visibility makes it easy to see the developing chronological aging changes when compared to normal young skin. These superficial changes include wrinkling, sagging, dryness, pigment and blemish development into neoplasms (cancer), nail integrity (brittleness), and hair color and volume changes. The medically related changes include decreased mechanical strength, altered immunity, skin cell senescence, vascular changes, and decreased skin protective functions. In the following sections, we will review how some of these changes impact your health and longevity.

Skin Cancers

Skin cancer, the most common form of cancer, most often develops in areas exposed to sunlight but not always. One type of skin cancer, basal cell carcinoma, a cancer of the cells that produce new skin, is believed to be caused by the UV light from the sun damaging the cells' DNA. A second form, squamous cell carcinoma, is a growth in the cells in the middle layer of the skin, is usually not fatal if treated promptly and before it spreads. A third form, melanoma (the pigment cells in skin), is believed to be caused by UV from the sun or other forms of ultraviolet light such as from tanning lamps. Melanoma cells are found mainly on the exposed skin and are irregularly shaped dark black or irregularly colored "mole-like" spots. If found early and removed or treated promptly, it is usually successful. In many of these and related skin cancers, it is believed that UV radiation damages the cells' internal machinery and their DNA. Avoiding UV light and the use of sunscreens will reduce the incidence of skin cancer. Having regular checkups with dermatologists to identify early any suspicious skin areas is also important to enable early removal of growths before they become a problem.[28]

Therapy options vary with the kind of cancer and the stage of the cancer. However, since the cancer is on the surface, topical chemotherapy may well offer a convenient option. Minimally invasive options include freezing, light therapy, or lasers. Minor surgical options include biopsy, and, for deeper-level cancers where the cancer may already be spreading within the skin, the Mohs procedure is effective. Mohs is used for many skin cancers, including for basal cell carcinoma and squamous cell carcinoma. One benefit with the Mohs procedure is that it has a high cure rate and leaves a small scar.[29] The outcomes for skin cancer therapies are high as long as the cancer has not spread beyond the initial skin site. Health span and lifespan are clearly dependent on active identification and management of skin cancer and other skin diseases.

Artificial Intelligence (AI), Cancer, and Skin Health

The easy visibility of the skin to medical personnel for data collection is enabling the rapid progress in application of AI for screening and diagnosis of skin cancer and other skin diseases. This is also made possible by the availability of large datasets and image data that the AI systems can analyze together with patient demographics and past medical history. This has been especially helpful for melanoma and non-melanoma skin cancers.[30] The development of smartphone usage and medical apps allows patients to screen themselves first and then send the self-assessed tele-dermatology data to medical professionals for confirmation and management recommendations. Moreover, powerful benefits from AI usage are significantly illustrated in many medical publications. For example, AI increased the abilities of 23 nonmedical professionals to correctly determine a diagnosis of malignancy from 47.6 to 87.5 percent without compromising specificity.[31] AI is not perfect, yet, but it is getting better as researchers diversify its training with curated information. When given 26 skin conditions that make up 80 percent of common cases, AI had 93 percent accuracy and 83 percent specificity.[32] AI is rapidly approaching the level of dermatologist's performance for diagnosis of various forms of skin cancer and other skin diseases.[33]

Skin Diseases and Longevity

Skin diseases affect people's quality of life, self-esteem, social relationships and mental health and are often visible to others. The common skin diseases include acne (blocked pores), atopic dermatitis (itchy, dry skin), cold sores (small fluid-filled blisters that appear on or around the lips), hives (inflammation-related itchy red lesions; often related to the herpes simplex virus), vitiligo (patches of skin that lose pigment), and psoriasis (scaly skin). The symptoms of these diseases include burning, itching, and skin discoloration caused by inflammation and swelling. The prevalence of these diseases differs around the world and even across socioeconomic groups, but it is clear that most of the deaths from skin diseases occur in people over 80 years of age. A global study of skin and subcutaneous diseases showed that fungal infections accounted for 34 percent and bacterial infections accounted for 23 percent of new infections and together they accounted for 95 percent of the deaths from such infections. Fungal skin diseases are the major contributors to incidence worldwide.[34] On the positive side, the skin microbiome contributes to wound healing, the immune response, and works with the body to promote the restoration of the skin's barrier in acute and chronic infections/wounds.

Maintaining "Younger" Skin with Microbiome Management

As one ages, the diversity in the aged skin microbiome increases. This is also true for postmenopausal women. Research on younger skin compared to older skin shows a decrease in some of the dominant bacteria and increases in less desirable bacteria. This suggests that one might develop an indicator of skin "age" by evaluating the skin microbiome and the associated skin secretions and biomarkers. It also suggests that dietary supplements (prebiotics, probiotics, and post-biotics) and cosmetics containing healthy skin microbiota may be beneficial and, as noted below, help maintain skin hydration. One researcher, Li et al, suggested the potential for developing a new medical field of skin therapy that focuses on manipulating the skin microbiome composition and using microbiome transplantation to produce healthier skin with all the associated benefits.[35] Another important factor in skin health and appearance in the aged is hydration. "...The balance of the skin microbiome's good and bad bacteria can change trans-epidermal water loss," said Dr. Shilpi Khetarpal, a dermatologist at the Cleveland Clinic. "Think of a grape turning into a raisin. With our skin, it works the same way. The microbiome can influence the hydration." He also noted that the skin microbiome can directly influence how we age. Dr. Qian Zheng, Head of Advanced Research, North America, at L'Oréal, noted that this opens up the potential for new products to monitor and adjust the skin microbiome that helps maintain health and reduce skin aging.[36] Clearly a well-hydrated skin will be healthier, look fuller, and have less pronounced wrinkles.

Skin and Longevity Research

It is important to distinguish the differences between anti-aging treatments that focus on the visible signs of skin aging and skin longevity that focuses on the root cause of aging at the cellular/molecular levels. Having a youthful skin (youthful skin's biological age) encompasses smart dietary habits, lifestyle choices and supplementation with skin management, and therapies that slow down the biological aging. Perhaps the most important action is minimizing DNA damage (e.g., UV light damage) and promoting repair mechanisms that involve managing inflammation from injury and disease, low-grade inflammation, and oxidation (read: reactive oxygen species and free radicals).[37] Topical management of these aging processes has been a boon to the cosmetics industry as they include ingredients that address the causes of cell damage to improve skin longevity and anti-aging in their products. Some of these products also have ingredients that promote hydration and maintain elasticity of collagens and elastin. Other products include pro-biotics and post-biotics that help to restore and/or maintain microbial balance as the skin secretions change and alter the microbiome environment of the skin. Lopez-Otin has identified 12 hallmarks of aging, and addressing these with effective skincare is essential for slowing the aging process and promoting long-term skin health.[38] This research highlights the complexity of trying to improve skin longevity, and overall human longevity, in general, through skin health.[39] These researchers recognize the importance of skin health and longevity by not just addressing the potential of skin diseases, inflammation, and cancers but also to the general benefits of a robust skin immune system and its payoff to health and longevity.

Blind trials have shown that even basic skin treatment reduces levels of systemic cytokines in the blood. A longer-term study in older people found that similar care reduced moisture loss, inflammation, and cognitive decline. Specific treatment for skin conditions impacts psoriasis, atopic dermatitis, and a range of other issues. While the skin is the area being treated, treatment is likely to have an effect on body-wide conditions and longevity.[40] In this way, caring for our skin will reduce body-wide deterioration. We know that severe skin damage, from burns, or disease, eliminates the barriers' important impermeability and impacts overall health. Skin that thins with age, or disease, or through lack of appropriate treatment, can allow particles through even under normal conditions, thus increasing skin disease and possibly contributing to other serious systemic illnesses.

Growing evidence suggests that damage to the skin can have knock-on effects for the rest of the body, driving distal inflammation, muscle and bone loss, and possibly even cognitive decline. The more your skin deteriorates, the more the "rest of you" ages prematurely. In this emerging view, your skin doesn't just reflect signs of aging—it contributes to it. There is even tentative evidence that taking better care of our skin could slow the harmful effects of aging and improve our overall health.[41] "Our skin is one of the first parts of the body to show signs of aging. It becomes wrinkly, especially in active places like the corners of our eyes, and age spots can appear. Such changes may seem—quite literally—skin-deep, but we shouldn't underestimate the skin's importance to the rest of the body," said Wendy Bollag at Augusta Univ. in Georgia.[42]

Drugs That Promote Skin Longevity

The data summarized above suggest that promoting skin health has a benefit to not just skin longevity but longevity in general. The review of skin health and approaches to improving skin health in the above sections focus mainly on topical administration of various substances that cover or penetrate slightly the skin. For example, rapamycin cream or ointment has been patented to prevent and treat skin aging.[43,44] Suppression of cellular senescence by rapamycin was demonstrated in numerous in vivo studies.[45]

When considering longevity, there are drugs taken systemically that also show benefits to skin health. For example, as described elsewhere, there is increasing evidence that rapamycin functions as an anti-aging drug through its inhibition of the factor mTOR to impact senescence of cells not just topically on skin but also systemically.[46] Metformin is another drug that is showing promise as an anti-aging drug.[47] Although it is early days for this research, there is some evidence that GLP-1 receptor agonists may positively influence cellular pathways associated with longevity.[48] Still other research on lower species like fruit flies in

Prof. John Tower's lab show that the anticancer drug, mifepristone, may have some anti-aging benefits.[49]

In summary, the skin is not a passive barrier between the outside world and your insides. It is an active participant in your health. Skin cancer is an area where early detection and treatment has long-term benefits to your health and longevity. Skin health is important to reduce local and systemic inflammation and to activate and train the immune system to respond to potentially dangerous things. The benefits of a healthy skin are not just in reduced aging for appearance but also by promoting healthy skin cellular compositions that leads to a more robust longevity to the entire body.

CHAPTER 12

You Are What You Eat

It is likely that most readers grew up tired of hearing their mothers urge them to eat their fruits and vegetables. Despite that, their mothers for the most part were correct. We'll examine the latest research on the relationship between food, diets, and supplements and an increased health span and lifespan. We'll also touch on the difficulty of finding unbiased information on the topic and the need to rely on reputable medical research rather than on social media or even the country's Agriculture Department's dietary recommendations because of the influence of food industry lobbyists on their recommendations.

"Trust Me," Says the Government

Since 1916, the U.S. government has been recommending the types of food and the portions required for a healthy diet. What is fascinating is that science has often played a limited role compared to the lobbying efforts of the food and dairy industries. Not only that, but the composition of the plate itself has changed markedly over the years. In 1916, for example, the USDA published its very first food guide for young children and divided food into five groups: milk and meat, cereals, vegetables and fruits, fats and fatty foods, and sugars and sugary foods.[1] The USDA revised its recommendations during the 1930s to reflect people's limited funds and again in the 1940s. The recommendations in 1943 now consisted of seven basic food groups: (1) green and yellow vegetables; (2) oranges, tomatoes, grapefruits; (3) potatoes and other fruits and vegetables; (4) milk and dairy products; (5) meat, poultry, fish, eggs, and beans; (6) bread, flour, and cereals; and (7) butter and fortified margarine. Someone posted an additional recommendation to "eat any other foods you want."[2]

By the 1950s, the recommendations listed just four food groups: milk, meat, fruits and vegetables, and grain products. There was certainly lobbying going on by the various food manufacturers, and that increased during the 1970s and 1980s with the creation of the food pyramid. The latest iteration called My Plate not only focuses on portions to prevent obesity but also adds a fifth food group—namely, oils.

Over the years, the success of lobbyists in nullifying the work of nutritionists is shocking. The 1992 version, for example, gave dairy its own section because of lobbying by the dairy industry. According to Luise Light, a nutritionist who worked for the USDA during this period, she was shocked to find that the pyramid was "sold to the highest bidder." Food giants managed to codify 6 to 11 servings of bread, cereal, rice, and pasta per day. She was quoted as saying, "…the Ag. Secretary's office altered wording to emphasize processed foods over fresh and whole foods, to downplay lean meats and low-fat dairy choices because the meat and milk lobbies believed it'd hurt sales of full-fat products."[3]

By 2011, the pyramid was now labeled My Plate and consisted of portions for each of the food groups to combat obesity, something the earlier pyramids probably had a major role in facilitating. Food manufacturers concerned with profits and not health or longevity seem to have found a "sweet spot" for attracting consumers with their highly processed foods.

The Influence of Big Tobacco and Highly Processed Foods

Big tobacco has had a significant impact on consumers' health by promoting highly processed foods. For a couple of decades (1980s–2000), Philip Morris and R.J. Reynolds acquired the major food companies Kraft, General Foods, and Nabisco. That meant they produced some of Americans' favorite comfort foods, including Kraft's Macaroni & Cheese and Oreo cookies. An article in the medical journal *Addiction* pointed out that these tobacco companies found the sweet spot (the combination of sweet and salty flavors) that made their customers addicts to these products to the point that they contributed to the growing obesity of the American public.[4,5]

Avoid Causing Inflammation When You Plan Your Meals

So much of longevity research has focused on the impact of inflammation. Researchers have discovered that a major difference between centenarians and the rest of the population is that the centenarians have low levels of inflammation.[6] In fact, researchers have zeroed in on the fact that aging is associated with "inflammation," the high level of inflammatory markers, and activation of immune cells associated with aging. It is encouraging that at least a few diseases caused by inflammation can be helped by changing one's diet. So, eating right can improve a person's health span as well as their lifespan. The researchers concluded that "In summary, we propose that inflammation may be viewed both as a clinical biomarker of the failure of resilience mechanisms and as a causal factor in the rising burden of disease and disabilities with aging."[7]

What makes chronic inflammation so harmful to a person's extended health and lifespans is that it accelerates the number of senescent immune cells. Remember those are moribund cells that reduce the effectiveness of the immune system. The result is a weakened immune system and the inability to clean out these dead/moribund cells and pro-inflammatory factors released by these senescent immune cells. It's a repeating cycle that ultimately damages key organs, including the liver, bone marrow, and lungs. In addition, researchers have found links between chronic inflammation and Alzheimer's disease, cancer, type-2 diabetes, heart disease, and arthritis as well as overall brain health.[8,9]

Modify Your Diet to Prevent Inflammation

It is possible to modify your diet to fight inflammation. Experts agree that for most people, in addition to exercising—and avoiding highly processed foods, high-fat dairy, fried foods, and red or processed meats—fruits and vegetables provide the best medicine for that condition. Leafy green vegetables such as spinach and kale as well as broccoli, chard, and arugula are ideal inflammation fighters because they are high in antioxidants. Adding whole grain foods, fatty fish such as salmon, olive oil, and nuts to an anti-inflammatory diet is ideal. Furthermore, eating legumes, rich in minerals such as magnesium, are also associated with lowering inflammation. Fruits such as strawberries, cherries, blueberries, tomatoes, and oranges should also be part of an inflammation-fighting diet. The citrus is important because it is rich in Vitamin C which protects cells against oxidation, a condition that leads to inflammation.[10]

Sugar Is Public Enemy Number 1

Researchers have identified sugar along with highly processed foods as causes of chronic inflammation.[11] Sugar also has been shown to accelerate biological aging by affecting the "wear and tear" on a body at the cellular level.[12]

Coffee

Coffee is a major source of polyphenols. Research has shown that coffee drinkers can drink as much as three to five cups a day (around 400 mg of caffeine) and enjoy reduced risks for type-2 diabetes, some cancers, and heart disease and overall lower risk of mortality. In other words, drink coffee and increase one's health and lifespans.

British researchers did an in-depth review of more than 200 previous studies on the subject of coffee's relationship to health and concluded that moderate coffee drinkers had less cardiovascular disease, and premature death from all causes, including heart attacks and stroke, than non-coffee drinkers. A study of 1,700 older coffee drinkers indicated that coffee is associated with lower levels of inflammation. In addition, other studies have shown an inverse relationship between coffee and cancer as well as other chronic diseases.[13,14]

A Plant-Based Diet Increases Longevity

It is well-known that humans need a certain amount of protein in order to build strong muscles and bones. The amount of protein required varies by age. There has been quite a lot of research on the negative effects of eating red meat even though it is packed with protein. A plant-based diet is one where the protein comes from such protein-rich sources as legumes, nuts, and whole grains. A study involving participants from 20 different countries found a link between meat consumption and type-2 diabetes. One solution is to transition to a plant-based diet. In fact, a research study found increased longevity—coupled with a lower risk of all mortality causes, including cardiovascular disease mortality—for people adopting a plant-based diet.[15–18]

Perhaps the most convincing study to show the benefits of a plant-based diet is one conducted with 22 pairs of identical twins where one twin ate a vegan diet while the other twin ate a meat diet. Over the eight weeks of the study the vegan eaters' low-density lipoprotein (bad cholesterol) dropped on average by 15.2 mg over eight weeks while the omnivore dieters' bad cholesterol dropped by 2.4 mg. In addition, the vegan eaters dropped 4.2 more pounds than the omnivores and their insulin which regulates blood sugar dropped by approximately 20 percent.[19,20]

Intermittent Fasting and Longevity

Intermittent fasting has become more popular. First of all, there are several different ways of following this regime. One approach (16/8) is fasting for 16 hours and confining meals to eight hours a day, say 9 a.m. to 5 p.m. Another approach (14/10) is fasting for 14 hours a day while having an eating window of 10 hours. Yet another way to follow an intermittent fasting regime is known as the 5/2 plan. This means capping calories at 500 for two days a week (one 300 calorie meal and one 200 calorie meal) while eating a healthy normal diet the other five days. Finally, a fourth variation is fasting twice a week for 24 hours each while eating a normal healthy diet the other five days.[21]

Harvard researchers discovered that intermittent fasting provided some positive results. Evidence is accumulating that eating in a 6-hour period and fasting for 18 hours can trigger a metabolic switch from glucose-based to ketone-based energy. As long as people don't snack between meals, people's insulin levels go down and then the body uses fat and stored sugar as energy. The goal is to get sugar levels down far enough to exit type-2 diabetes and insulin resistance. The researchers concluded that fasting improves people's metabolism, lowers blood sugar levels, and lessens inflammation while improving overall health and lowering cancer risk. One theory the researchers advanced is that fasting is evolutionarily embedded within us in the sense that primitive man went through periods of famine in between successful hunts.[22,23]

Are there benefits for obese men who practice intermittent fasting? University of Alabama researchers conducted research using a form of intermittent fasting known as "early time-restricted feeding." This is a scheme where the group was broken into two groups—one who consumed all meals during an early eight-hour period of the day (7 a.m. to 3 p.m.) and a second group that consumed all meals over 12 hours between 7 a.m. and 7 p.m. Neither group lost weight, but the group consuming food over eight hours (7 a.m. to 3 p.m.) had dramatically lower insulin levels and significantly improved insulin sensitivity and blood pressure.[24]

Unfortunately, some recent research suggests that one negative side effect of intermittent fasting could be an increase in the risk of heart disease-associated death. The study analyzed data on the dietary habits of 20,000 adults across the United States who were followed from 2003 to 2018. They found that people who adhered to the eight-hour eating plan had a 91 percent higher risk of dying from heart disease compared to people who followed a more traditional dietary pattern of eating their food across 12 to 16 hours each day. People who already had existing cardiovascular disease who followed the intermittent fasting regime had a 66 percent higher risk of dying from heart disease or a stroke. To make matters even worse, people who already had cancer were more likely to die of that disease if they followed an intermittent fasting routine. So, perhaps the best advice is one your mother probably gave you and that is eat everything in moderation.[25]

Learning from the Blue Zones

In Chapter 1, we discussed the "blue zones," areas of the world where people live far longer. Their diets are 95 percent plant-based, and they eat whole foods such as rice, corn, soy, fruits and vegetables, or prepared food like tofu or manna bread. What they avoid are processed foods. They eat fish each day and a small portion of meat once a week, but no processed meats. While residents eat a very small portion of dairy, they eat beans every day and snack on nuts. They limit their bread to sourdough, which doesn't raise their sugar levels and severely limit their sugar by eating foods that are sweetened by fruit or honey. They drink coffee and tea and avoid sugary drinks.[26] The key to the success of the blue zone residents' diet was the vegetables they ate. Squash is rich in vitamins A, B, and C and also magnesium and potassium. The residents benefited from the antioxidants in the black beans they ate as well as protein and fiber. The tortillas they ate were high in complex carbohydrates that helped maintain the residents' energy while the corn they ate provided fiber that helped satiate their appetites.[27]

The Mediterranean Diet

The Mediterranean diet is a plant-based diet that includes healthy fats like olive oil as well as whole grains, vegetables, fruit, beans, lentils, nuts, and seeds. Wine in moderate amounts is also part of this diet. While dairy, poultry, and fish are part of the diet, it does not include red, fatty, or processed meat.[28] Researchers followed 850 French citizens over the age of 65 for over a decade and discovered that those who followed a Mediterranean diet were less likely to experience cognitive decline as they aged. Participants were split fairly evenly between women and men, and all were dementia-free at the start of the study. They monitored a panel of biomarkers (like healthy omega-3 fatty acids EPA and DHA, found in foods consumed on the diet) every few years and performed five neuropsychological evaluations on each participant during the course of the study. Those who closely followed the plant-based diet, rich in healthy fats—as evidenced by results of blood tests, and not participant-completed food diaries or questionnaires—were less likely to experience cognitive decline as they aged. This group also lowered their body weight, blood sugar, blood pressure, and cholesterol, as well as increased their life expectancy.[29]

The Atlantic Diet

The Atlantic diet is a variation of the Mediterranean diet because both focus on eating fresh fruit, vegetables, fish, olive oil, and moderate amounts of wine. The Atlantic diet, found traditionally in northwest Spain and Portugal, includes 3 to 4 servings a week of fish and lean meat. One key difference is that it also includes more brassicas (turnip greens and turnips, cabbage, cauliflower, and kale). Another difference is that the Atlantic diet includes starches such as bread, potatoes, and chestnuts while the Mediterranean diet includes more pasta. While both diets are healthy, the Atlantic diet's test subjects enjoyed superior results when it came to their level of body fat and their lipid profiles.[30,31]

Fasting-Mimicking Diet

The fasting-mimicking diet (FMD) is a low-calorie, low-protein, and high-fat plant-based diet that includes fasting five days a month. It has shown improvement for obese patients in key biomarkers, including glucose, ketone bodies, and insulin-like growth factors, similar to results obtained by fasting and drinking water. Researchers did a head-to-head comparison between the fasting-mimicking diet and the Mediterranean diet for four months. Both groups lowered risk factors such as weight, fat percentage, and total cholesterol. The FMD group did not experience a loss in lean body mass while those test subjects on the Mediterranean diet did.[32,33]

An Anti-aging Diet

Researchers have discovered that if they reduced rodents' calories anywhere from 20 to 50 percent while ensuring adequate intake of vitamins and minerals, these animals lived longer, healthier lives with less disease than normally fed rodents. While intermittent fasting with breaks between feeding lasting a day or two also produced robust results, the researchers believe that it was the limiting of calories rather than the fasting itself that produced such good results.[34]

Dietary Supplements and Spices

Spices can be another inflammation fighter, though most people don't typically consume large volumes of them. Curcumin, a compound found in turmeric, has been linked to reduced inflammation in animals. Curcumin has been shown to be effective in treating chronic conditions like rheumatoid arthritis, inflammatory bowel disease, Alzheimer's, and common malignancies like colon, stomach, lung, breast, and skin cancers.[35]

Garlic

Research has shown that garlic supplements can also have a positive impact on reducing inflammatory markers. Garlic has a broad range of biological effects with promising anticarcinogenic, antioxidant, and immunomodulatory effects. These characteristics in garlic arise from the presence of sulfur and a variety of chemical compounds that can reduce inflammatory markers.[36]

Turmeric

As stated above, curcumin, a compound found in turmeric, has been linked to reduced inflammation in animals. In addition, it has been shown to be effective in treating chronic conditions like rheumatoid arthritis as well as various cancers.[35]

Omega 3

Omega-3 is an essential nutrient for health. People who eat fish a couple of times a week probably are receiving sufficient amounts of it, but not everyone has that many fish meals in their diet. Other sources of Omega-3 include walnuts and flax seed oil. Our bodies cannot produce this key fatty acid, so we need to supplement it in our diet. It is associated with a reduction in inflammation as well as providing heart and brain health.[37]

Nicotinamide Mononucleotide

Nicotinamide mononucleotide (NMN) when taken orally is rapidly absorbed and converted by the body to NAD+. Several studies indicate this supplement suppresses age-related adipose tissue inflammation, improves insulin secretion, and improves mitochondrial function.[38]

Rapamycin

It almost sounds like a scene out of an Indiana Jones film. Researchers on Easter Island (also known as Rapa Nui) discovered this substance.

They brought it back and discovered it has the ability to extend the lives of older female rats by 14 percent and male rats by 9 percent. Scientists have discovered it has similar effects on other animals as well, including worms, marmosets, and fruit flies. Today, many people are taking rapamycin off-label in low doses.[39,40] So, what exactly does rapamycin do? Apparently, it suppresses the mTOR complex, a basic pathway concerned with cellular health. The result is a cascade of positive effects that include a decrease in inflammation and an increase in the removal of cellular "trash."[41]

CoQ10

As people age, their level of CoQ10 declines. Researchers believe that CoQ10, an antioxidant, could be useful in reducing mitochondrial damage associated with aging. It also might reduce the likelihood of getting age-related diseases, including cancer, heart, and kidney damage.[42,43]

Spermidine

Spermidine is a polyamine found in whole grains, mushrooms, and several soy products. Researchers say it supports autophagy, the removal of dead cells, a process critical for healthy aging. It also has the effect of simulating the beneficial effects of fasting. Finally, it offers protection against the breakdown of the caps at the end of our chromosomes known as telomeres.[44,45]

Summary

It is clear that your diet has an influence not just on your immediate health but also on your health span and longevity. The data are not clear how the intervals between your feeding influence your health or negative inflammatory processes. It is clear that the body needs an interval between meals to clear out, store, and process the food you eat. This means that your body needs some time when the blood stream is not full of the metabolic products from your meals to "clean up." Together, these data may suggest that intermittent periods of eating is better than a continuous, frequent small meals regimen although this has not been studied rigorously.

Additionally, food scientists are identifying some natural food sources that may have health and longevity advantages. These studies are suggestive, and, as clinical studies of their benefits progress, it may provide a natural food pathway to improve our health span and longevity.

CHAPTER 13

Sleep as a Key to Longevity

Getting a proper amount of sleep plays a role in supporting your heart and overall health and longevity. A recent study reported at the 2023 World Congress of Cardiology found that 8 percent of deaths from any cause could be attributed to poor sleep patterns. The study noted that getting enough hours of sleep was not sufficient. The quality and restfulness of the sleep showed a clear relationship with all causes of death and with longevity.[1] The study also supported the conclusions that people with good-quality sleep lived longer across ethnic groups. Any discussion of longevity must include the role of sleep. In this chapter, we will discuss sleep, its surprisingly important role in your health and longevity, and how it impacts nearly all aspects of your life.

During sleep, the human body cycles through several distinct stages several times a night with each one lasting for about 90 minutes. These stages are called non–rapid eye movement stages N1, N2, N3, and REM (rapid eye movement). Each stage is characterized by variations in muscle tone, brain wave patterns, and eye movements. Stage 1 (N1) is a light sleep with low-amplitude brain waves. Stage 2 (N2) is a deeper sleep, and the average person spends 45 percent of their time in this stage where their heart rate slows and body temperature drops. Stage 3 (N3) is a deep sleep characterized by lower-frequency and higher-amplitude brain waves, and one spends about 25 percent of their time in this stage. It is often difficult to awaken someone in this stage of sleep. Finally, there is Stage 4 (REM) sleep for about 25 percent of the time. REM sleep is associated with dreaming, and for many it is not as restful sleep. The eyes and diaphragmatic muscles are active while skeletal muscles do not move. Brain EEG activity is similar to someone who is awake during REM, and there is increased oxygen usage by the brain.

How much you sleep, and the quality and time spent in each stage, is altered by age, medications, circadian rhythm, and other disorders.[2]

Newborns can sleep for 16 to 18 hours; children, for 11 hours; and teenagers, 9 to 10 hours a night. In general, adults need 7 to 9 hours a night, but individuals 65 and older often need less sleep. There are also gender differences in the amount of sleep needed and the cycles during sleep. As humans, we spend a third of our lives sleeping. While we are "resting," our brain and body are not. To be clear, sleep has a huge impact on our health, mental state, and longevity.[3] Sleep is a surprisingly complex subject. As we close our eyes and drift out of awake consciousness, the brain and the body engage in a wide variety of activities necessary for good health and longevity.

Sleep Impacts Health

During sleep, the cells in your muscles, organs, and brain repair and renew themselves, release hormones, and adjust your metabolism. A sleep deficit impacts these tissues in ways that contributes to high blood pressure, heart and cardiovascular disease, diabetes, depression, and obesity, to name just a few. Sleep deprivation has also been associated with reduced immune function, reduced/weak metabolism, mood disorders (mood swings [rapid change from one state of mind to the another such as, for example, from elation to depression in a very short time], feeling negative, or anxious), and disease resistance. If you are sleep-deprived, then there are consequences as you don't get the full benefits from these important renewal activities.[4]

Additionally, sleep supports the brain's need (capacity) to change and rewire itself based on learning and experience, which is essential for cognitive health and memory consolidation. Also, it regulates the hormones responsible for appetite, thus playing a role in maintaining a healthy body weight and reducing the risk of metabolic disorders.[5]

Anyone who has not had enough sleep notices immediately an impact on their brain's function. Sleep is an important time for the brain's nerve cells to communicate with each other. Among other things, during sleep the brain is "cleaned" in a kind of housekeeping that removes toxins and unnecessary detritus (including damaged proteins) that build up during waking hours. Sleep also affects memory because this is when the brain consolidates and transitions memories from short-term to long-term storage. Some sleep can be "caught up" on weekends, but it may not be sufficient to overcome all the missed activity during the week. It is better to sleep the proper length each day.[6] All this brain activity is important.

Lack of Sleep Impacts Brain Function

Scientists have long noticed that lack of sleep has an effect on memory, but there also is a relationship with dementia. A long-term Harvard study followed 2,800 people 65 and older and found that those who slept under five hours a night were twice as likely to develop dementia compared to those who slept six to eight plus hours a night. A different study of 8,000 people found that sleeping less than six hours a night was associated with a 30 percent increase in dementia risk compared to those who slept seven plus hours.[7] It is still not clear to scientists and doctors what is going on here. One hypothesis is that during sleep our brain clears out unneeded and damaged proteins and other materials that accumulate during the busy "thinking" part of the day. For example, β-amyloid (Aβ) is a protein our brains make during the day, and when we sleep it is cleared out. Xie and colleagues have shown that clearance of Alzheimer's disease biomarkers is accelerated during sleep compared to wakefulness. They also showed the rate of buildup of Alzheimer's disease biomarkers is greater during wakefulness than during sleep.[8] Under conditions of insufficient sleep, the brain may not be able not clear it all out. It then would accumulate until brain dysfunction occurs. In other words, a buildup of these markers may result in dementia and the dementia-related diseases such as Alzheimer's disease. This is still a theory, but it is being tested currently.

The reverse is also true. Dementia is associated with poor sleep. Throughout the night a person can go through four to six sleep cycles that vary in length. People with dementia spend less time in Stages 3 and 4 of sleep and more time in the earlier stages, which worsen as dementia progresses. It is Stages 3 and 4 where the body restores itself the most. Additionally, dementia changes the person's circadian rhythm. Individuals who have Alzheimer's disease are often unable to follow a 24-hour sleep–wake cycle and, instead, sleep more during the day and less at night.[9]

To summarize, sleep is essential for good health and good brain function. During parts of the sleep cycle, the body is very busy doing all the necessary "housekeeping" required for good brain and body health.

Too Much Sleep Is Not Good Either

While how much you need to sleep changes as you age, there is an optimum sleep length specific to different age ranges in healthy people. Sleeping too much can be a clear sign of health problems. One study showed that sleeping for over 10 hours a day was associated with psychiatric diseases and higher body mass index (BMI), but not with the other chronic medical conditions related to too little sleep described above.[10] In another study that included over 30,000 people who slept over nine hours a night, there was a 23 percent increase of stroke. Those who both slept over nine hours a night and additionally napped for 90 minutes during the day had an 85 percent increased stroke risk.[11] Recapping, your body does a lot of "housekeeping" stuff during normal sleep. If you don't sleep enough, it doesn't finish its work. If you sleep too long, the body is finished with its housekeeping work and wants to get up and do all the things requiring an alert active state. If your body wants to sleep too long, it is a sign that something else is wrong. The point in these studies is that, if you go beyond a normal, optimal length of sleep for your age, it is not beneficial to your health and, if you chronically "oversleep," you increase your risk of medical issues.

Narcolepsy Is Neither Daydreaming Nor Normal Daytime Sleep

Narcolepsy is a chronic neurological disorder that affects the brain's ability to control sleep–wake cycles and causes sudden "attacks" of sleep. The cause is not well understood, but the best guess is it involves genetic factors and abnormal signaling in the brain. A narcoleptic will spontaneously sleep for seconds to several minutes at a time. In some cases, they will sleep for an hour or longer if left uninterrupted. People with narcolepsy may feel rested after waking but then feel very sleepy throughout much of the day. Many individuals with narcolepsy also experience uneven and interrupted sleep that can involve waking up frequently during the night.[12] People with narcolepsy frequently enter REM sleep rapidly and report dreaming vigorously. Stimulants, antidepressants, and other medications may be helpful in reducing the consequences of narcolepsy.[13]

Impact of Hormones and Drugs on Sleep and Longevity

For many people falling asleep quickly and staying asleep throughout the night just doesn't happen often, especially for older people. Although the total amount of sleep obtained may be sufficient, the annoyance of not getting continuous sleep, suffering insomnia, or just intermittent nighttime sleep has prompted an entire sleep aids "industry." The pharmacy isles are full of over-the-counter (OTC) products. OTC products include herbs (such as Valerian), hormones (melatonin), and, if allergies keep you awake at night, there are antihistamines (such as those containing diphenhydramine and/or doxylamine succinate). In addition, for serious sleeping issues, there are prescription drugs too. It is beyond the scope of this chapter to cover all the sleeping aids, but we will illustrate with a few examples. The point of this discussion is that getting a proper amount of sleep is important for your health and longevity.

Melatonin

The most popular OTC sleep aid is the natural hormone—Melatonin. It was found in a 2012 survey that 3 million Americans used melatonin.[14] Natural levels of melatonin in the blood are highest at night, and it plays a role in the sleep–wake cycle. Some research suggests that melatonin supplements might be helpful in treating sleep disorders, such as delayed sleep onset. It doesn't have the side effect of making you sleepy as do the antihistamines but appears to shift the timing of sleep onset. So, to get the most benefit it should be taken 20 to 120 minutes before bedtime. Melatonin may also provide some relief from insomnia and jetlag.[15] Since melatonin is a natural hormone in your body, it is considered safe to take in moderation and intermittently. For best results, you shouldn't do things that work against its action. This means avoid stimulants such as caffeine or other similar products in the evening before bedtime. It works best if you take it about two hours before bedtime and then "wind down" the day's activities as you approach bedtime. Most importantly, if it is not working for you don't continue to take it. Contraindications against taking it include being pregnant or breastfeeding, having an autoimmune disorder, a seizure disorder, or depression.[16]

Valerian

Valerian is an herb that has been used for centuries to treat insomnia and anxiety. Unfortunately, scientific studies with controls are mixed about its effectiveness.[17]

Antihistamines

Histamines are a natural substance produced in your body that helps fight off germs and a variety of other effects associated with pollen and allergic conditions. Histamine also helps to keep people awake. Antihistamines are a class of drugs that are designed to work against allergies and the effects of histamines. Antihistamines are a relatively safe OTC drug that are optimized for treating allergies as they block the side effects of histamine. They also have the side effect of making some people drowsy (sedating). Products such as Benadryl, NyQuil, Tylenol PM or Motrin PM, and other sleeping aids contain diphenhydramine as the active agent to help make you sleepy. It is helpful as it does induce a form of sleep, but it is not designed to be a sleep aid. There is research that suggests sleep quality is reduced when taking antihistamines and its effectiveness decreases over time. For adults over 65, it is not recommended to take sleeping aids without the consent of a doctor. All sleeping aids have side effects and can cause memory loss too. The main point here is that antihistamines and stronger sleeping aids do help induce sleep, but it is important not to become dependent on taking them or to take them on a regular basis.[18]

Effects of Other Commonly Used "Drugs"

Two of the most commonly consumed "drugs" are caffeine and alcohol. Studies have shown caffeine reduces how long you sleep because it is a stimulant.[19] As described in Chapter 12, there is a positive side to taking caffeine. A research study has shown that people who drink up to eight cups of coffee per day may slightly lower their risk of early death compared with nondrinkers, according to a large new study. Note this is coffee and not caffeine. The research surprisingly also showed that it doesn't matter if the coffee is caffeinated, decaffeinated, brewed, or instant.[20]

Alcohol is consumed for a large variety of purposes. One of them is that for some it has a relaxing effect. Alcohol does not promote sleep. Furthermore, excessive alcohol consumption results in poor sleep quality and insomnia.[21]

There are hormones associated with keeping you awake. Two of them are cortisol and adrenaline. Both of them make it difficult for you to relax and initiate sleep. They both keep your mind racing.

Cortisol

The stress hormone, cortisol, is produced by the hypothalamic-pituitary-adrenal (HPA) axis. When cortisol is released, it increases your heart rate, blood sugar, breathing rate, and alertness. It also stimulates your immune system to respond to illness and injury. On the negative side, it can affect your mood. It also helps coordinate your sleep cycles and is the hormone that is responsible for waking you up in the middle of the night. When the HPA axis is disrupted through chronic stress, or illness, this can result in insomnia and other sleep disturbances.[22,23] Short-term sleep loss can also lead you to crave foods that are higher in fat and sugar because your body produces extra cortisol, the stress hormone, when you're sleep-deprived.[24]

Adrenaline

Adrenaline basically gives your body a boost of energy. It also makes the heartbeat faster, causes blood pressure to increase, can leave you feeling restless, and makes it more difficult to fall asleep.[25] There is a very pronounced circadian rhythm for adrenaline excretion. Nighttime sleep reduced adrenaline excretion contributing to the circadian sleeping pattern. There is also a correlation between adrenaline secretion and self-rated fatigue.[25] Basically, high levels of adrenaline are associated with sleep disorders.

Hypnotics and Sedatives

Hypnotics, drugs that induce sleep, and sedatives are drugs that are used to relax the patient, reduce anxiety, and help with muscle relaxation, without necessarily inducing sleep. Sleeping aids have a long history. Drugs like bromides and barbiturates were among the first effective ones. More selective agents were developed later in the nineteenth century.

Hypnotics are specifically aimed at inducing sleep and are usually prescribed for individuals experiencing difficulty falling or staying asleep. A hypnotic drug produces drowsiness and facilitates the onset and maintenance of a state of sleep that resembles natural sleep in its electroencephalographic (ECG) characteristics. As scientists learned to understand the behaviors of animals, more sophisticated drugs were developed in the chemical classes: barbiturate, phenothiazine, and benzodiazepine. Drugs in these categories include Luminal (a seizure medicine with sleep promoting effects) and Seconal (short-term treatment of insomnia).

Sedation is a side effect of many drugs that are not considered active on the brain (e.g., antihistamines). Examples of sedatives are Ambien and Lunesta. In all cases, hypnotics and sedatives are powerful drugs with many side activities. They should not be used chronically or casually and only under the care of a health care professional.

In many cases, sedative and hypnotic activities are present within the same drug because they act directly on brain tissue. Finally, there are drugs that have overlapping activities—sedative-hypnotics. Common prescription drugs in this category include Xanax, Librium, and Valium. These drugs are effective in relaxing and promoting sleep, but all have the side effect of becoming habit-forming, overdosing, and abuse. For this reason, using them requires care, and they should only be used under a doctor's supervision.

Sleep and Longevity

The importance of sleep on your health is clear, but the data on using sleeping aids are not encouraging. A regular sleep pattern, characterized by regularity in timing and duration, has been associated with a lower hazard of all-cause mortality.[26] Irregular sleep–wake patterns have been associated with higher mortality risk, including dementia.[27]

A 2023 study addressing sleep and longevity further highlights the importance of both quantity and quality sleep in reducing all-cause mortality and cardiovascular mortality. The study found that young people who have more beneficial sleep habits are incrementally less likely to die early. Moreover, the data suggest that about 8 percent of deaths from any cause could be attributed to poor sleep patterns.[28]

In another study, researchers followed over 21,000 twins for more than 22 years. They asked questions about the twins' sleep habits and looked at their longevity. They found a significantly increased risk of mortality was observed both for short sleep in men (+26 percent) and in women (+21 percent), and for long sleep (+24 percent and +17 percent, respectively). The results confirm that not getting proper sleep increases mortality in both men and women. Additionally, Hublin and colleagues evaluated the use of sleeping medications and found these people had a 33 percent higher risk of mortality because the use of these drugs indicated difficulty sleeping.[29]

In a different study of 171,321 adults aged 18 years and older from the National Health Interview Survey (2013–2018) with a linkage to the National Death Index records showed that adherence to a proper sleep time improved longevity of men about five years and women about 2.5 years.[30] Still another study focused on day-to-day deviations in sleep parameters and biological aging or the speed at which your body is aging. (Note: This is different than chronological aging.) What they found is that people with inconsistent sleeping patterns had a higher biological age compared to those with a regular sleep schedule. They felt that the acceleration of biological aging reflects damage inside your body.[31] The calculation of biological age is somewhat controversial, but, as a general concept, it is relevant here. The point of this reference is that sleeping the proper amount for your age may also help slow biological aging and increase longevity.[32]

Sleeping Aids and Longevity

On average, life expectancy in individuals using sleeping pills (vs. nonusers) was shorter by 5.3 years in men and 5.7 years in women.[33] Among men, at age 50, sleeping pill users with short sleep duration had 3.9 years (< four hours/night) and 5.4 years (> eight hours/night) shorter life expectancy. For male extreme sleepers at age 30, taking sleeping pills was associated with approximately nine years reduction in life expectancy, resulting in a reduction of life expectancy by up to 12.6 years compared with sleeping pill nonusers with an average of six to eight hours of sleep. Among women, significantly shorter life expectancy was found in sleeping pill users with long sleep times (>eight hours/night), compared with the medium sleepers without taking sleeping pills at the same age.[34] Furthermore, elderly people are more sensitive to potential side effects of sedative-hypnotics, and studies have found that the risks generally outweigh any marginal benefits of hypnotics in the elderly.[35]

CHAPTER 14

Mind over Matter: Reducing Stress as a Key to Health Span and Lifespan

No discussion of increasing both health span and lifespan is complete without a discussion of stress, as an inevitable and normal part of life. Both good stress and bad stress result in your body releasing hormones that trigger common signs of stress: butterflies in the stomach, racing heart, sweaty palms, and more. Common chronic stressors include relationships, money, work, health or mental problems, and loss. It motivates you to meet your daily activities and is part of making you smarter by learning from the events in life causing stress. Good stress (or eustress) is your body's mental and physiological response to internal and external interactions. There are a number of positive attributes to stress:

- Stress is a powerful motivator.
- Stress can enhance your resilience and problem-solving skills.
- Stress can strengthen your relationships.
- Stress can promote personal growth and self-improvement.
- Stress can improve cognitive function.

Knowing that something is causing you good or bad stress isn't always a bad thing as the experience can be positive if you recognized it. Once recognized, you can learn how to make better decisions and how to deal with it in the future.[1] When stress occurs without serious threat or fear, your physiology responds with pulse increases and a hormone surge. Students studying for an exam will be stressed, but, even though there is some "fear of failing," that is eustress. Athletes are good-stressed by their coach pushing them to perform at a higher level. A rollercoaster ride or a first date can be stressful, but again this is okay eustress. Stress caused by escaping from danger or a "close call with a dangerous situation" is also good. To be sure, stress at a moderate level is acceptable. How we deal with stress determines if it is good and healthy or bad and unhealthy. Stress pushes us out of our comfort zones and forces us to confront challenges head-on. Through these experiences, we learn more about ourselves—our strengths, weaknesses, and capabilities—leading to personal development on many levels as well as self-discovery.

Even good stress can become bad if it is intense and unrelenting. Bad stress is the kind that wears you out, leaves you with anxiety and distress. The result of bad stress is also reflected throughout your body. Bad stress causes headaches, insomnia, high blood pressure, and weight gain among many other negative physiological effects.[2] Ultimately, what distinguishes good stress from bad is how you react or feel about the experience.[3] In this chapter, we will discuss stress—the good, the bad, and the ugly. Then we will discuss how it can be managed to enable improved health and lifespans.

How Stress Affects Your Body and Mind

Stress, as a biological term, relates to the effects of outside forces or stimuli and the person's internal thinking and response to these events either when they happen or after they have occurred. Your body has developed a complex set of responses to stress that work to protect the body from the threats, if any, that cause the stress. These responses are in the form of the release of biologically active proteins, hormones, and other materials that act on tissues and organs throughout the body and the brain. If the stress is positive and temporary, it can be good. The old anecdotes quoting the saying "mind over matter" for resisting disease refers to the idea that a positive attitude offers some protection against disease.[4] The medical explanation for this relates to the facts that chronic negative stress suppresses the immune system.[5] Negative stress can cause a variety of impacts on your body and, if severe and chronic, a variety of diseases. In the 1960s, it was recognized that stress affects the nervous system and causes changes in different parts of the brain. It also impacts cognition, short- and long-term memory,[6] and sometimes learning.[7] To be clear, stress sometimes improves and sharpens memory too. An example is the stress students experience studying for an exam or athletes preparing for a competition.[8] Stress also negatively affects the cardiovascular system, the gastrointestinal system, as well as other parts of the body.[9]

How Is Stress Positive?

Positive stress comes from anticipation of something exciting. Low-level stressors stimulate the production of brain chemicals called neurotrophins that strengthen the connections between neurons in the brain.[9] This may be the primary mechanism by which exercise (a physical stressor) helps boost productivity and concentration. It may also increase your immune response.[10] Stress can improve cognitive function. This kind of cognitive improvement is an important part of becoming a more capable person by learning how to cope with stressful situations in life and overcome them. Stressful events keep the brain alert, and you perform better when you are alert. Dr. Kaufer from UC Berkeley studied how short-term stress primes the brain for improved performance. Confirming other scientific reports, her study shows that those shorter moments of stress that you overcome quickly help generate new brain cells and brain cell connections that ultimately improve mental performance.[11] There are data now that show mild stress stimulates not just brain cell growth but also reorganization in several parts of the brain. This growth may be related to the release of dopamine in the brain. If the stress is significant, however, the results on brain cells are very negative. This will be discussed more in the next section.[12]

How Is Stress Negative?

Stress also has a negative side. When stress becomes chronic, we feel no longer in control of a situation, and this has negative effects on our physical health throughout the body as well as the brain. Stress is estimated to affect half of the U.S. population at one time or another with sexual abuse the most common for women and physical assault for men. Research suggests that stress also can bring on or worsen certain symptoms or diseases. WebMD reports that 75 to 90 percent of all doctor's office visits are for stress-related ailments. The lifetime prevalence of an emotional disorder is more than 50 percent and is often due to chronic, untreated stress reactions.[13] The stress–depression link was enhanced by dysregulation of several stress-sensitive biological systems, such as the immune system, microbiome, and endocrine system.[14]

The symptoms of chronic stress overload are increased heart rate, chest pain, general body aches and pains, shortness of breath, and feeling tired, anxious, and depressed. These symptoms not only affect your mind but are simultaneously physically damaging to your body. The longer the stress lasts, the worse it is for both your mind and body. You might feel fatigued, unable to concentrate, or irritable for no good reason, for example. But chronic stress causes wear and tear on your body, too. When stressed, the body releases adrenaline (increases heartbeat) and cortisol (which induces the release of sugar for increased brain activity). The overexposure to cortisol and other stress hormones disrupts almost all of your body's processes and suppresses the immune system. This can put you at increased risk for a variety of physical and mental health problems, including anxiety, depression, digestive issues, headaches, muscle tension and pain, heart disease, heart attack, high blood pressure, stroke, the reproductive system (fertility issues), sleep problems, weight gain, and memory and concentration impairment. If the stressor ends, then all things go back to normal, and all is good. However, if the stress becomes long-term then chronic exposure to cortisol and other stress hormones puts the person at higher risk for many diseases in that list.[15] Traumatic stress is associated with a range of poor health outcomes, such as heart disease, diabetes, stroke, and asthma, among others. Repeated acute stress damages the circulatory system, particularly in the coronary arteries, and this is thought to tie stress to a heart attack.[16] PTSD is a form of stress response affecting about one-third of the population at some time with about 15 percent becoming chronic stress. PTSD is twice as common in women as in men and affects 8 percent of the U.S. population at some point in their lives.[17]

Chronic stress may also cause disease that result from changes in your body or the coping mechanisms such as overeating, smoking, and other bad habits. This includes the consequences of job stress. Other forms of chronic stress, such as depression and isolation and loneliness, have also been implicated in increased cardiovascular risk.[18]

Repeated acute and chronic stress contributes to inflammation in the circulatory system, particularly in the coronary arteries. One consequence of this inflammation is plaque deposits onto the artery walls thereby narrowing them. This narrowing of the artery walls is one pathway that is thought to tie stress to a heart attack. If stress is chronic and doesn't go away quickly, the person's physiological response may result in increased cholesterol levels—also a negative outcome. When stress starts interfering with your ability to live a normal life for an extended period, in other words chronic stress, it becomes even more dangerous. The medical and scientific literature is replete with references to how stress is a factor in bringing on or worsening diseases. Traumatic stressors, the most severe kind of stress, can lead to dangers to life (suicide), to self (self-injury), an intense feeling of fear, an intense feeling of horror, along with other mentally and physically debilitating issues such as depression and helplessness.[19] To be clear, no one can completely avoid stress, but how we respond to it and how pervasive it is will have a lot to do with your health, health span, and lifespan.

Effects of Stress on the Brain

It is commonly believed that the brain stops growing by adulthood. However, this is not actually true as new nerve cells are continually being generated in the hippocampus where they are essential for learning and emotions. Nerve cells are also making new connections throughout life. It has been shown that chronic stress results in smaller brain volume.[20] An animal study showed that a single socially stressful situation can destroy newly created neurons in the hippocampus. This region has been shown for humans too and can lead to depression.[21] In animal studies, it has been shown that stress-induced changes in the hippocampal structure are associated with memory deficits. On a positive note, social enrichment or learning can enhance generation of new neurons in the brain as can treatment with antidepressants or anticonvulsants and reduce some of the brain cell loss and stress-related memory loss.[22]

One important conduit of brain information to the body and the immune system is through the vagus nerve.[23] Among its many activities, the vagus nerve is responsible for relaxing tension and counteracting the activity of the sympathetic nerves and return the body to a positive state. Simply stating, it is a positive stress response that downregulates the body's response to it.[24]

Effects of Stress on the Immune System and Consequent Disease Susceptibility

From simple observation of sick people, doctors have long known of the negative impact of stress on diseases and, therefore, indirectly, on the immune system. In 200 AC, Aelius Galenus (Galen of Pergamon) noted that women who were more positive and exposed to less stress had a lower likelihood of getting cancer.[25] Careful observations by many doctors and scientists on the impact of stress on your health over time laid the foundation for research into the basis of how stress impacts health. Your immune system is responsible for fighting off disease, and a suppressed immune system negatively impacts your health. Without exaggeration, longevity requires a strong immune system and a positive response to stress.

Stress can decrease the activity of natural killer cells that are important parts of your immune system. The suppression of these immune component cells can lead to more rapid growth of malignant cells, genetic instability, and tumor expansion. Studies have shown that the concentration of norepinephrine increases during stress and suppresses the immune function of phagocytes and lymphocytes that are also part of your immune system.[26]

In 1990, it was shown that stress mediators from the brain can pass through the blood–brain barrier (BBB) and exert their effects on the immune system.[27] Even more interesting is that the brain sends impulses through the vagus nerve to the immune system. These signals can suppress or stimulate immune function. As a result, dysregulation of the immune system can be due in part by signals from the brain. The vagus nerve signaling to the immune system is suppressed during inflammatory conditions in the body.[28] As stated earlier, the vagus nerve is supposed to downregulate stress and the physiologic state of alarm. If its operations are suppressed during severe stress, the body's response for repair, growth, and other activities will be overcome by the resulting inflammation and other negative effects.

The Gut Microbiome Influences Stress Management

In Chapter 3, we discussed the gut microbiome and its many properties and activities. It is clearly not a passive player in our health. There is clear evidence for a gut–brain axis that influences stress responses. Both preclinical and clinical studies provide evidence of the effect of our gut's modulation of stress.[29]

The gut microbiota harbors at least 100 times as many genes as the human genome.[30] The co-evolution of the human genome and the gut microbiome resulted in complex interactions between the gut, enteric nervous system, and central nervous system.[31]

When under stress, the person can have digestive issues, diarrhea, and other negative manifestations. What is not well recognized is that the gut and the microbiome within have a role in stress management too. Also not well understood is that the brain and gut are in constant communication and that changes in the gut microbiome are linked to mood, mental health, psychological symptoms, depression, emotion regulation, and cognitive function, and, as was described before, a host of all kinds of other health issues.[32] Part of the microbiome's response to stress is to change its organism composition.

New research on people who were more resilient to stress has shown that their microbiome was linked to reduced inflammation and a less leaky gut barrier compared to those who were not resilient. Research in people with a variety of psychiatric conditions have a microbiome enriched in pro-inflammatory bacteria and less of the anti-inflammatory bacteria. Interestingly, in mouse studies at UCLA it was shown that mice could become more resilient to stress if the composition of the microbiome was changed.[33] Recent studies have associated risk of stress and depression with the gut microbiota.[34]

Research into the Psychological Effects of Stress

Clinical data show that having difficulty controlling your emotions plays an important role in the association between life stress, sleep disturbance, and depression symptoms. The part of the brain that controls these emotions is the prefrontal cortex, and its dysfunction during emotional regulation from negative life events is critical for the prevention of depression as well as sleep problems.[35]

Positive emotions are important for a happy daily life and are associated with a range of beneficial outcomes, including longevity, improved sleep quality, larger social networks, and increased pro-social behavior. Negative responses to chronic stress result in structural changes, like that in brain atrophy, and can lead to differential responses on cognition and memory depending on its severity and duration.[36] In milder cases, it can manifest itself as irritability or aggression, a feeling of loss of control, and insomnia. In more severe cases, it can lead to fatigue, exhaustion, concentration and memory problems, and depression. These physiological effects logically can result in psychological alterations in thinking too. Any new traumatic event can trigger a relapse to older stress events that can contribute to a lifetime stress disability. Since some aspects of stress are a matter of perception, the benefit from how you respond to a stress event is clearly evident in the outcome of its long-term effect on you both mentally and physically. The first step in managing stress is in identifying its cause and looking for ways to reduce it, if possible. Taking any concrete actions will reduce it.[37]

Tools for Managing Stress to Improve Health and Longevity

We have covered in detail some of the effects stress has on your mind and body. A lot of these effects can lead to negative consequences to your body and mind, and, in many cases, you don't have a lot of options in preventing this kind of stress from occurring. The research is clear, however, that how you respond to the stress has a lot to do with its negative consequences. First, you need to separate the good stress from the bad stress and develop healthy ways to manage it. Guidelines for stress management start with avoid, alter, adapt, or accept.[38] If you cannot avoid the stressor, then try to change your reaction to it. If you cannot alter the stressor, then accept the stressor and things you cannot change.

Summa Health offers seven healthy ways to manage your bad stress:

1. Eliminate stress where you can.
2. Accept there are events you can't control.
3. Think positive thoughts and look for the upside in the situation. Negative thoughts can lead to negative behavior, while a positive attitude can help offset difficult situations. Make an effort to think positively by looking for the upside in every situation, whether you learn from your mistakes or use major challenges as a time for personal growth. In addition, thinking about all the things you appreciate in your life, including your own positive qualities, can change your perspective.
4. Get support from family and friends or, if needed, from professionals. The process of sharing can be very helpful. These social relationships are very helpful for reducing stress.
5. Add relaxation techniques to your everyday routine such as exercise, meditation, or even yoga.
6. Stay healthy and fit. A well-balanced diet and staying active ensure your body is better prepared to fight stress. Exercise relaxes your body and mind. In fact, physical exercise has been proven to play a key role in preventing and reducing the effects of stress.
7. Get a good night's rest. Getting enough rest is important because it gives your body time to recover from stressful events and sets you up for the new challenges.

The key is identifying good stress from bad stress. As long as it's not chronic, good stress can be a positive addition to your life. Make an effort to reduce your chronic stress as much as possible and add positive activities to promote good stress. It creates a healthy balance and a better quality of life.[39] The Mayo Clinic recommends these five stress management strategies to reduce the overall day-to-day stress[40]:

1. Use guided meditation.
2. Practice deep breathing.

3. Maintain physical exercise and good nutrition.
4. Manage social media time.
5. Connect with others.

There are other kinds of recommendations from all kinds of sources, but the message is largely the same as these above. Do your best to not let the stress to make you sick from not coping with it in healthy ways.

Therapeutic Approaches for Treating Stress

There are no specific medications for stress but remember that many of the negative consequences of stress start in the brain. How the person responds to the stressors influences the severity of the patient's physiological responses. Doctors will first try non-drug ways to manage the symptoms. These recommendations will include meditation, physical exercise, mindfulness, and psychotherapy as described in the previous section. If that is not working, doctors will look to drugs for the brain that treat anxiety, depression, or have calming effects such as tranquilizers because they have anti-anxiety effects. Although they are not approved for anxiety, beta-blockers will be tried too.

Such drugs come with many side effects, so they should only be taken when really necessary. However, for the patient with severe and chronic stress symptoms, these drugs are beneficial and enable many patients to cope better with their stress.

CHAPTER 15

Hacking the Human Body to Improve Health and Longevity

Hacking the human body with electronic devices has long been an aspirational expectation for science fiction writers. The Borg in *Star Trek* were human–machine hybrid beings, and Lee Majors played the role of a much more pleasant machine–human hybrid (Col. Steve Austin) in the television show *The Six-Million Dollar Man* (ran from 1973 to 1978). There are many other examples in science fiction literature and films giving audiences great entertainment. Remarkably today "biohacking" is no longer science fiction.

Recent electronic advances enabled significant progress in developing electronics with microprocessors that are capable of the very complex device management and communication programs necessary for medical devices. The miniaturization of electronics and medical devices now makes it possible to consider using medical devices not just in hospitals or doctor's offices but also to address unmet medical needs on and within the human body. In this chapter, we will highlight a few of the many areas where miniaturized electronic devices are improving health and overcoming damaged functions in people. In the future, it will be quite likely that people will be living with multiple implanted devices to address medical issues that drugs and surgery alone cannot fix. This field is known as "bionics" and is associated with mechanical systems that function like parts of a person and repairs or corrects someone's physical limitations.[1]

Hacking the Nervous System

The brain, spinal cord, and peripheral nerves make up the nervous system. The brain can be viewed as an electrochemical organ that controls different regions of your body with each region focusing on managing a specific activity such as hearing, vision, memory, and so on. For example, the inner ear manages balance as well as hearing. The eye coordinates and communicates with the ear and brain to maintain proper balance by providing feedback to the brain about how well we are maintaining balance. In another example, even with the eyes closed, people know where hands are and, in their mind's eye, they can touch their nose with their eyes closed.[2] This last example is called proprioception, and it is an example of how the nervous system knows where your limbs are in 3D space without actually seeing them.

It is not as well recognized, but totally unsurprisingly the brain also directs many of the other things that go on throughout the entire body. It does so through release of various chemicals and hormones as well as sending "electrical" signals to specific organs via the nervous system to get the body to do what it is supposed to be doing.

Hacking Peripheral Nerves to Treat Back and Chronic Pain

It is estimated that about 20 percent of Americans suffer from chronic pain, and for 8 percent of them it is so severe that it limits life and work activities on a daily basis.[3] There are already a number of devices approved and used for pain management using skin or surface electrical stimulation. Transcutaneous Electrical Nerve Stimulation (TENS) devices are popular surface stimulators that send small, low-voltage electrical currents to targeted body parts in order to block the pain's source or its transmission to the brain. These devices are highly effective for some people depending on the severity of the pain and conditions being treated.

A TENS device is used for conditions such as bursitis, arthritis, and tendonitis where the muscles and nerves treated are close to the skin surface. For more severe chronic debilitating pain—such as in the lower back, leg (e.g., sciatica), or arm, various neuropathies, chest pain (angina), and nerve injuries—doctors might recommend a fully implanted spinal cord stimulator after nonsurgical options have failed.

A spinal cord stimulator is a fully implanted device that sends low levels of electricity into the spinal cord. These stimulators block the pain communication between the nerves and muscles at the pain's source and the brain. Spinal cord stimulators involve implanting a controller device in the chest where it manages the electronics and communications with the outside world and sends the programmed electrical stimulation impulses through the implanted electrode to the spinal cord.

Hacking the Heart—Pacemakers and Defibrillators

The heart, a muscle, is a marvelous machine. It beats at 60 to 70 beats a minute, even when resting, for an entire lifetime. An important feature of heart and other muscle tissues is that they will contract when given an electrical impulse. When you exercise, the heart beats faster but then slows down after exercise and resting. Despite all this continuous beating activity, the heart is still benefited by exercise. This may be counterintuitive for some. The exercise actually strengthens the heart muscle over time, and the strengthened heart will actually beat slower while performing the same amount of work. So, all in all, exercise is really good for the heart because it does the same work with fewer beats.

Why the Heart Might Need to Be Hacked

The heart has four chambers and pumps blood with a rhythm so that each chamber contracts to push the blood from one chamber into another or into a blood vessel. A proper sequence of heart contractions sends blood to the lungs for oxygenation or the oxygenated blood to the entire body. The rhythm is controlled, in part, by the brain's nervous system that sends stimuli to the heart muscle's control center where it stimulates a group of pacemaker cells. These cells, when stimulated, release a small current that stimulates the heart muscle to contract. Not surprisingly, there is active communication between the brain and the heart. When you are exercising, the brain tells the heart to beat faster. When you are stressed, sleeping, and so on, the heart gets different instructions to slow down or go faster. These instructions are important so that a normal person can respond relatively quickly to important situations in their life.

Keep in mind that there is a backup system for stimulating the heart muscle to pump blood. Heart muscle cells can self-initiate contraction under certain conditions from this backup system in the heart itself. Although it is not entirely "normal" beating without receiving the communication from the brain, the heart can continue to beat even if the nerve link is not functioning or severed. In these less-than-ideal situations, the backup system stimulates the heart muscle, and the heart continues to beat independently of the brain's signals.[4] With two systems that can both induce the heart to beat, there is a potential under diseased or other special conditions to cause a problem with one system miscommunicating with the other and causing near simultaneous contractions or other conflicts. A number of really undesirable situations arise when the heart muscle gets improperly timed signals. It becomes confused, and this condition can lead to tachycardias (an increased heart rate over normal rates), an irregular heart rhythm (arrhythmia), or ventricular fibrillation (an ineffectual heart muscle contraction that does not pump blood). If not resolved, these conditions can be fatal.

As you go through life, various other situations can occur to the heart that will cause it to malfunction. These include a heart attack when the heart muscle is torn, and the contractions may not work correctly. There may be a blood clot or blockage that starves the heart muscle of oxygen and causes some tissue to die and, if the patient recovers, the heart may not pump properly. To address some of these issues, doctors and scientists have taken advantage of the fact that the heart muscle responds to an electrical stimulation to override the body's "confusing" stimulating messages and "hack" this muscle. Using a pacemaker and/or defibrillator, medical devices can restore the heart muscle rhythm. These devices are implanted under the skin, and an electrical lead is placed on or near the heart muscle to stimulate muscle contraction according to the device's programming for pacemakers and to block inappropriate contractions for defibrillators.

Hacking the Pancreas and Diabetes with Devices

The brain and the nervous system play a major role in instructing all organs to maintain their function within the normal range in a process called homeostasis. The nervous system, therefore, must sense and integrate information and then tell the organ to increase or decrease its activities and secretions to maintain health. This can be challenging for the organ and brain when the changes can be rapid—such as when sugar levels rise following a meal or a sweet dessert. Abnormal sugar levels are dangerous. For the pancreas, it is especially challenging as it must control both the increase and decrease of blood insulin levels relatively quickly. If it is not done well or the pancreas is malfunctioning and not producing enough insulin on demand, blood glucose levels rise to abnormal levels, and the patient has diabetes.

Diabetes

For a type-1 diabetic, maintaining the correct sugar and insulin levels in the body/blood is complex. There is need for a certain level of insulin all the time just for normal body activities (basal insulin). Then, when the diabetic eats a meal, the body does not know what was eaten and how much it will change the blood sugar levels. The type-1 patient needs to estimate the glucose to be released from the meal relatively accurately. The diabetic must measure the blood glucose levels with a diagnostic tool, usually a drop of finger blood onto a sensor strip. Then they must guess how much insulin they need and then inject that amount of insulin into the body. The diabetic must check frequently to see if they did it right and keep the glucose blood levels within the normal range 24 hours a day. Failure to do this correctly will put the patient's health in danger. Researchers have developed insulin pumps for type-1's to maintain slow and steady delivery of insulin to maintain the necessary basal insulin (and proper glucose) concentrations. The pumps also have a button to give extra insulin following a meal. Over time, the pumps have become smarter, but they still don't know how much insulin is actually needed. Glucose diagnostics remain the main way diabetics determine their current glucose levels. In the last few years, smart sensors have been developed that are implanted on, in, and under the skin to continuously measure glucose levels to help the patient determine how much insulin is needed at any point in time. These are important improvements to be sure, but they are still not ideal.

A type-2 diabetic can manage this condition relatively well in the beginning with drugs, weight loss, diet, and exercise. In some cases, a type-2 diabetic may progress to a point where insulin needs to be given to maintain proper blood glucose levels. To be sure, there has been a lot of research and clinical attention given to how to make things better for type-2 diabetics, including via administration of drugs, so that continuous monitoring sensors and chronic insulin delivery pumps will not be as necessary.

The Artificial Pancreas

The "holy grail" for a diabetic is when a continuously monitoring glucose sensor can communicate to an insulin delivery system, such as a pump, directly or through a phone app, to tell the pump when insulin is needed and how much to deliver. In the case of diabetes, these devices are sometimes called an artificial pancreas.[5] Things are clearly better for diabetics now, but even with the convenience of these devices the mealtime sugar spikes remain a problem. The objective with these kinds of devices is to take the patient out of the loop and have the device determine how much insulin is needed at any specific time without the patient's involvement. Artificial pancreases are in advanced development where a sugar sensor will instruct a separate insulin pump to deliver the necessary insulin to enable glucose concentrations to stay within the normal range. Versions of this are already being used in man. However, the response time is still too slow, so the goal now is to improve them to have faster response times.[6]

Hacking the Ear—Cochlear Implants

The hearing organ in humans is a spiral-shaped organ, called the cochlea, that contains specialized cells called hair cells (not to be confused with hair cells that produce hair on your head and elsewhere) and the hearing nerves. The cochlea is found behind the eardrum and beyond the middle ear. When sound comes into the ear, it causes the eardrum to vibrate and then the little bones, called the hammer, anvil, and stirrups, in the middle ear, transmit and amplify that sound into the cochlea. When the sound finally comes into the cochlea, it moves the little "hair"-like cilia on the tips on each of these hair cells. The cochlea nerves then "report" they were stimulated to the hearing cortex of the brain that then interprets that sound stimulation as "hearing." The specific location of the hair cell stimulated in the cochlea is associated with a specific frequency. The hearing cortex in the brain then makes us aware of the sound at that frequency.

When these hearing hair cells are damaged by disease or very loud noises. they will die, and the affected person will have a hearing deficit at the sound frequency associated with that particular cell. If enough of these hair cells die, then the person will require a hearing aid to be able to hear sufficiently. If hearing gets even worse, then even hearing aids will not be good enough to restore adequate hearing. However, it is important to note that even though the hair cells have died, the nerves in the cochlea are still alive and waiting for input. When a cochlear nerve is in the vicinity of an electrode, the person hears a sound when the electrode fires. Enter the cochlear implant, a neuroprosthesis, that can restore hearing to the deaf. The cochlea implant is an electronic device with multiple electrodes that is inserted into the inner ear to stimulate the residual sound-sensing nerves. As described earlier in Chapter 10, this device is remarkably effective for deaf patients.

Hacking the Eye—Retinal Implants

The eye's optical system is designed to focus incoming light through the lens onto the retina, a very thin and nearly transparent sheet of neural tissues covering the back of the eyeball. Special cells called photoreceptors located at the back of the retina convert the light into neural signals that are relayed to the area of the brain called the visual cortex. Those signals form the basis for visual perception.

Vision also declines as people age. The lens of the eye becomes less flexible and less able to focus on close-up objects. While cataracts may develop to cloud an eye's lens, glasses or lens pre-placement surgery can address these conditions. There are diseases in which the retina detaches from the back of the eye and other diseases that destroy the ability to see.

Some of the most common diseases that primarily affect older patients include retinal degeneration and age-related macular degeneration (AMD). These diseases largely leave peripheral vision intact. Patients can navigate their surroundings but have difficulty reading, recognizing faces, and performing other tasks that require high visual acuity. A less common class of retinal degeneration, called retinitis pigmentosa (RP), originates from various genetic disorders and afflicts approximately 1 in 3,500 people. It typically affects patients in their 20s or 30s and leads to profound blindness.

Retinal Implants

Developing an electrical device to restore vision has some unique engineering and electrical challenges. Despite these many challenges over the past decade, retinal prostheses have emerged as a promising technology for restoring vision lost due to retinal degeneration. The FDA approved a first-generation device (Argus II) for RP by Second Sight Medical (now part of Vivani Medical, Inc.). Its 16-electrode (pixel) retinal chip effectively functions as artificial photoreceptors or even as artificial retinas. The system is composed of a wired retinal chip implanted inside the eyeball and tacked to the retina and back of the eyeball so that it is close enough to stimulate the nerve. The chip blocks light from hitting the retina. For this reason, the patient must wear special glasses fitted with a black-and-white camera that captures the image and sends the information to a computer. The computer then processes the images and sends instructions to the chip in the eye through the wires connected with the computer. These instructions quickly provide instructions for when to fire and stimulate the photoreceptor nerves in the right order and frequency to create an image in the patient's visual cortex in the brain. To be sure, a 16-pixel image is better than nothing and gives the patient some sense of seeing again.

But this first-generation device does not yet fully restore a patient's sight. The patient will need 20 to 30 times more pixels to be able to read a newspaper; however, these proof-of-concept devices are already demonstrating an ability to partially revive visual sensation, even in patients who've experienced decades of profound blindness. Next-generation devices will have more pixels and wireless chips that can communicate directly with the computer. One device under development is so small that the camera and chip will be placed entirely within the eyeball to eliminate the need to wear special glasses with an attached camera. While these next generation of devices are being developed, the Argus II is currently being studied for potential application to other optical diseases including glaucoma, diabetic retinopathy, and optic nerve injury.[7,8]

Sleep Apnea

Fortunately for us, we don't need to remember to breathe. It happens automatically, and, if you want, you can consciously take control of the process and "tell" the body to breathe. Your body has an oxygen sensor and a pH sensor that tell the brain that you need to breathe. Blood carbon dioxide (CO_2) changes the blood's pH. The change in pH is the trigger telling the brain to breathe. The brain then triggers the diaphragm pacer, a kind of muscle stimulator like the one in your heart, to fire and tell the breathing muscles in the diaphragm to contract and pull air into the lungs. When you sleep your body does this automatically.

Sleep apnea is a common condition in which your breathing is intermittently blocked many times while you sleep. This prevents your body, and especially your brain, from getting enough oxygen. It has many causes, but, in some cases, there is a part of your tongue that blocks the airway path. This is called obstructive sleep apnea. There are other cases called central sleep apnea that happens when your brain does not send the signals to the pacer to initiate breathing.[9] For people with sleep apnea, they can use a cPAP device at night which has a mask worn by the patient and provides elevated air pressure to aid breathing. For patients with obstructive sleep apnea or the cPAP device is not working well, there is an FDA-approved, fully implanted device (from Inspire, Inc.) that will electrically stimulate the tongue to move out of the breathing/air pathway.

Controlling Chronic Inflammation and Chronic Inflammatory Diseases

About three decades ago, Dr. Kevin Tracey accidentally discovered that the brain controls the immune system and communicates its instructions through the main nerve trunk called the vagus nerve and the so-stimulated organs' nerves respond back to the brain what they are "doing." It is a communications highway. The key here is, again, that the brain, as an "electrical" organ, communicates through nerves to the important systems throughout the body and those systems respond back. If for some reason the instructional signal is absent or wrong, the organ may malfunction, such as in the case of a chronic autoimmune disease like rheumatoid arthritis. For this reason, the electrical stimulation of a nerve may substitute for the missing or incorrect signal or initiate a new response. The stimulated nerve will forward the signal to the targeted organ, even if the brain did not originate it. Understanding this, Tracey subsequently discovered that vagal nerve electrical stimulation would turn off inflammation.[10] He then started a company (SetPoint Medical) with a specific mission to develop vagus and other nerve stimulation devices to specifically treat autoimmune diseases. SetPoint Medical has conducted several human trials since 2016 that confirmed that this kind of stimulation shows positive results for many patients against rheumatoid arthritis, psoriatic arthritis, Crohn's disease (a form of inflammatory bowel disease), ulcerative colitis, and multiple sclerosis (MS). The SetPoint products are still in development (just approved July 2025 by the FDA), but the early results support the conclusion that the electrical stimulation approach will benefit many, but perhaps not all, people with a variety of inflammatory diseases (autoimmune diseases). To be clear, it is not just SetPoint Medical working in this area. It is now an area of intense research by many investigators worldwide, as new applications are being identified for nerve stimulation not just of the vagal nerve itself, a main trunk nerve, but for some of the dedicated branches going just to a specific organs too. One reason this research is so exciting is that it uses the body's own nerves to control inflammatory diseases in a way that drugs cannot do and perhaps without the side effects of powerful drugs.

Hacking the Arm Muscles after Stroke: Vagal Nerve Stimulation

It is hard to overestimate the negative health consequences of stroke. Approximately 60 percent of the individuals who experience a stroke have a long-lasting upper-extremity dysfunction that hinders their activities of daily living (ADL) and compromises their mental well-being. In 2022, there were 101 million people living who had a stroke, and it has been predicted that, by 2050, the number of deaths from stroke will increase by 50 percent.[11] Standard rehabilitation therapy often cannot restore function after a stroke. Not surprisingly, there may be damage to the brain and its connections with the lower body through the vagus nerve. A number of human clinical studies have evaluated the benefits of vagal nerve skin (VNS) stimulation and transcutaneous (through skin) vagal nerve stimulation. Patients with fully implanted electrical stimulation devices are showing positive improvement when coupled with rehabilitation therapy.[12–14]

Hacking the Brain—Depression, Epilepsy, Dystonia, Schizophrenia, and More

Some brain-related diseases are caused by faulty (mutated) genes such as in Huntington's disease and multiple sclerosis (MS). As described earlier, degenerative diseases such as Parkinson's disease and Alzheimer's disease result when certain nerve cells are damaged or die. Epilepsy and related seizure disorders result when there are bursts of neurological signaling and sometimes contradictory signaling to produce the jerky muscle responses and seizures as the body tries to respond to this contradictory signaling from the brain. When something goes wrong with the brain, depending on the situation, you can have trouble not just with moving, speaking, breathing, and so on but also with your memory, senses, mood, and behavior. For many reasons, the brain has been a particularly difficult place to address diseases of mood, behavior, and memory. Some new therapies that now focus on diseases of mood and behavior can mitigate some of the symptoms of epilepsy, depression, bipolar disorder, schizophrenia, and many others. Despite the benefits of these medications to many, they are frequently associated with serious side effects. Drugs used to treat depression, bipolar disorder, and schizophrenia can also cause drowsiness, dizziness, blurred vision, hallucinations, suicidal thoughts and behaviors, or a sense of low energy.

To manage these side effects, patients on these therapies need to remain under the doctor's careful supervision. Patients with these issues may be subjected to a cocktail of one or multiple medications together with psychotherapy. When the patient is resistant to these therapies, it might require even more aggressive and invasive approaches such as electroconvulsive shock therapy (rebooting the brain), and even surgical procedures to remove focal brain regions related to the specific disease. Modern neurosurgery for movement disorders such as Parkinson's disease, essential tremor, and dystonia can involve surgical removal or killing brain cells in place with a hot tool targeting the initiating brain tissue. This "crude" form of therapy stops the source of the conflicting or inappropriate signals. It sounds desperate, but for some it helps. This kind of therapy permanently changes brain tissue. However, it must be a last resort, as it cannot be undone once done. Unfortunately, even after all this, about 20 percent of patients remain resistant to these usual therapies, and many others only have partial benefit. The new science of deep brain stimulation (DBS) tries to improve outcomes without such drastic measures. The results to date indicate that there is a real benefit to be gained from DBS for neurological diseases like depression, schizophrenia, and others.

Epilepsy

Epilepsy is a chronic neurological condition characterized by recurring seizures, or abnormal bursts of electrical activity in the brain that can trigger jerky movements, strange sensations or emotions, unusual behavior, and/or loss of consciousness. About 3.4 million people of all ages in the United States have this disorder.[15] Normally, brain electrical signals move between tissues in a steady and consistent pattern. An epileptic incident disrupts this pattern causing a large group of neurons to "flood" the brain with electrical activity and cause the brain to "seize" up the areas of the brain responsible for language, memory, emotion, and consciousness. Although there are about two-dozen anti-seizure medications available to help the majority of patients manage their epilepsy, a third or more receive little or no relief from these medical treatments. Some people resistant to standard medical therapy for epilepsy experience excellent outcomes with surgery to remove, kill the initiating brain cells with a hot probe or "disconnect" by cutting the brain tissue connections with other brain areas that initiate or propagate seizures. This surgical approach does help some patients, but it is not particularly practical, if there are multiple initiation sites, which is often the case in epilepsy.

It has become clear in recent decades that DBS can help regulate the brain's electrical activity or reset the neurological activity in a way similar to the way a pacemaker does for the heart. There are now several devices on the market that offer a more benign approach. The already marketed devices demonstrating benefits include SenTivaTM (from Vivism) for vagal nerve stimulation, the AspireSR (from LivaNova) that detects heart rate increases associated with brain activity and then targets the thalamus to disrupt the seizure, and the Percept PC (from Medtronic) that records brain activity to anticipate a coming seizure and then try to disrupt it before it becomes a clinical event. Patients implanted with DBS devices report less than half as many seizures.[16,17]

The best results come when the device can monitor brain activity associated with the initiation and propagation of a seizure and then send the DBS pulse to a specific location to interrupt the seizure at an early stage. Modern, smart devices can do this. In these cases, implantable neurostimulation devices offer an important additional alternative for improving the lives of epileptic patients without the use of drugs.[18]

Treating Tremor and Other Movement Disorders

Essential tremor is a neurological condition that causes people's hands to shake rhythmically and sometimes other parts of their body too. It is 5 to 10 times more common than Parkinson's disease. For essential tremor and other movement disorders, DBS may provide an opportunity for the body to repair itself over time. One research study reported by Lozano and colleagues showed that there are some essential tremor patients who get a very good benefit. For some of these patients, the tremors stop and do not return even when the DBS is discontinued. These patients are effectively "cured" of their tremor.[19]

In summary, hacking the brain is showing real progress in treating severe brain diseases not just with drugs but also with DBS. These observations suggest that in the future, better methods of DBS will provide not just additional therapy options for treating other brain diseases but may also provide for some patients a long-term cure. The benefits are huge because the brain is so important for a good quality of life and longevity.

Using the Brain to Drive Medical Devices—Prosthetic Limbs and Exoskeletons

As we noted in the beginning of this chapter, just a few decades ago using wearable exoskeletons (robotic suits), brain-controlled extra limbs, human mind–controlled computers, and other medical devices were found only in the imagination of science fiction writers. As already described earlier in this chapter, biomedical engineering and medical science are now able to address medical problems where drugs are not sufficient.

There is still another frontier to discuss—the brain–computer/device interface.[20] This is the science that explores how to get the brain to communicate with a computer or eventually with a medical device or an exoskeleton and so on. It is already possible for people to move a cursor on a computer screen by thinking about it.[21] From this capability, it is a relatively small technological jump for our minds to manage devices that can be computer-controlled.[22] Devices are already in active research that will respond to thought commands from the brain to manage a prosthetic device. The bionics may look impressively futuristic, but don't be fooled. Bionic limbs designed to restore function and provide people who have lost limbs with a better quality of life are already in use and, as we will show in the following two sections, how they will soon become much "smarter."[23]

Bion and IMES

The nervous system coming from the brain and spinal column has nerve endings in all the body's tissues and organs, including the muscles. When the appropriate nerve signal is received, the muscles contract or relax depending on the "brain's/nerve's instructions." Normal muscles maintain their strength, bulk, and fatigue resistance through exercise. Even when not exercising, the nervous system will send stimulatory contraction signals every now and then to the muscles, which helps maintain muscle tone but at a less frequent interval than when exercising. People do not notice most of these signals when not exercising. If an individual develops a medical problem that interrupts the brain's stimulatory communication (signaling), the muscles atrophy and become flabby. There are serious negative consequences from having atrophied muscles, including joint trauma, osteoporosis, and cardiorespiratory problems, just to name a few.

To prevent this muscle atrophy from occurring, doctors have been trying to electrically stimulate the relevant muscles through the skin or with electrodes that are placed on or just under the skin.[24,25] This approach works to a degree by causing the stimulated muscles to contract (twitch). The easiest way to do this is by using skin-surface electrodes to stimulate through the skin and to adjust the power to be sufficiently high so the stimulation will penetrate deeply enough into the tissue to get to the muscle(s) needing stimulating. The best results for skin-surface stimulation are for muscles near the surface and skin. To go deeper, wired electrodes must be placed through the skin and left under the skin imbedded within the targeted muscle. Modern miniaturized electronics now offer a much-improved solution—a wirelessly controlled, fully implanted electrical stimulating medical device that can work autonomously and/or through communication with an external controlling system. Accordingly, with modern micro-miniaturization, a small device implanted in a muscle, would stimulate specific muscles that are not functioning properly to improve muscle tone. In this way, it would overcome nerve damage or sense when the brain has sent a signal for something to happen. This still works when for medical reasons the muscle or tissue cannot or does not respond. In the next three sections, we will describe two examples where such devices have been developed and tested on people. First is a very small, implanted device that can provide the signals needed to restore some muscle function following a stroke that paralyzed the patient's arm with a microstimulator called a BION. In the second and third sections, we will describe how a very small sensor, called an IMES, can be used to detect the muscle's movement instructions and intuitively operate a prosthetic arm with the patient just thinking about what the patient wants the arm to do.[26]

Bion: Implanted Muscle Stimulator

In the late 1980s, researchers developed a single-channel fully implantable (non-wired) neurostimulator known as a BION, small enough that it could be injected into the tissue area needing stimulation.[27] The BION, about the size of a small piece of spaghetti (2.5 mm × 16.5 mm), is RF (radio frequency) powered. The version with an internal battery is slightly larger (3.3 mm × 27 mm). Each BION is a single-channel system and gives the patient control over a specific muscle. The BION is then injected to activate just one muscle. If multiple muscles need to be activated, then multiple Bions are injected—one into each muscle. The real achievement here is meeting the remarkable micro-miniaturized electronics requirements for a very small implanted fully functioning device. The BION has restored function to patients with a stroke-paralyzed arm in a small clinical study.

IMES—Intuitive Brain Controlled Prosthetic Limbs

There are around 2.1 million people in the United States living with limb loss, and that number is expected to double by 2050. There are over 1 million limb amputations globally every year. The most common causes of limb loss are vascular disease (54 percent) and trauma (45 percent). The number of amputations due to vascular disease will increase as the population ages and the incidence of diabetes and other vascular conditions continue to rise. Trauma amputations result mainly because of car accidents, work-related machinery accidents, and military service.[28,29]

The use of a prosthetic limb improves mobility, independence, and quality of life. For this reason, prosthetists try to get the patient to use one. The use of prosthetics, however, is not without its challenges, including skin irritation, discomfort, poor fit, the need to adjust the device during use, phantom limb pain/sensations, and the device's weight. Dissatisfaction with available prosthetics, including discomfort with the socket, have led to high rates of abandonment despite the benefits. The 20 to 30 percent of veterans who abandoned their prostheses altogether, gave device weight, discomfort with the socket, phantom pain, lack of functionality, and poor fit as their main reasons.[30] Even the most advanced upper-limb prosthetics with muscle-sensing and muscle-stimulating capabilities in their socket have high rejection rates. The clear need for improved prosthetic limbs has stimulated some important advances in new prosthetic limbs with computerized components and sensory feedback.

One example is Vessl Prosthetics, Inc.,[31] a Canadian company that is focused on making better prosthetic sockets that are more comfortable around the limb stump and will move and adjust as the patient and prosthetic moves. As more smart prosthetics are developed, the socket will be fitted with the necessary power, sensors, stimulators, and communication components to enable them to become more capable.

To understand how a person without, say, an arm could get a sense of touch or think and make a prosthetic limb do things, you need to understand some biological basics. In many cases, when a limb is lost for any reason, the nerves on the limb stump are still connected to the brain and continue to receive brain signals and, under certain circumstances, send messages back to the brain (e.g., phantom limb pain). The absence of the limb does not cause the associated nerves to die or the remaining muscles in the stump to die/atrophy. In healthy arms, it is possible to sense and measure the muscle's response or electrical activity in response to a nerve's stimulation of the muscle. This is called EMG (electromyography). In patients where the EMG is essentially normal, it is possible to "hack" the signal to operate a medical device or to communicate information back to the brain using a medical device. Advanced motorized prosthetic devices are currently controlled by EMG signals generated by residual muscles and recorded by surface electrodes on the skin. These surface recordings are often inconsistent and unreliable, leading to high prosthetic abandonment rates for individuals with upper-limb amputation. Surface electrodes are limited because of poor skin contact, socket rotation, or residual limb sweating. Additionally, their electronics can only record signals from superficial muscles, whose function frequently does not relate to the intended prosthetic function. This demonstration of potential is important, but it also shows the need to improve the prosthetic–patient interface with an implanted device (IMES) for this technology to move out of the lab and into broad application.

Thinking to Make the Hand and Wrist Prosthetic Move

The current state-of-the-art with prosthetic hands are generally single-degree-of-freedom (DoF) (opening and closing) devices. This is very different from the natural hand. In more complex prosthetics with multiple

DoF, the motorized mechanisms act linearly with one DoF change completed before the next one starts. This is slow and counterintuitive. Patients compare this kind of prosthetic with that of the natural hand, and, consequently, it fails to meet expectations.[32,33]

In the case of a hand and wrist amputation, not just the nerves but also some of the muscles that control the hand motion are still active in the forearm even though the wrist and hand are missing. For example, if a hand and wrist or a partial arm or leg prosthetic with enough DOF were developed that was managed by an external controller, it might function well enough. This is especially true for routine movements that are pre-programmed into the computer like for walking or opening a door. One company working in this area is Össur (www.ossur.com/en-us). It is a worldwide mobility company founded in Iceland focused on developing a wide variety of prosthetic arm, wrist and hand, and leg and foot devices, sockets, and sleeves, as well as other mobility-assisting devices. The most difficult challenges come when the patient needs some level of discretionary movement such as with a prosthetic hand and wrist picking up a glass of water and drinking from it without spilling. The prosthetic hand also cannot crush a paper cup or drop it from insufficient pressure, and so on. It is a complex set of decisions that need to be worked out very rapidly between the device and the brain for these actions to seem intuitive. Enter the IMES (short for Implanted MyoElectric Sensor). It is able to detect the signals from muscles when they "want" to contract/release. The IMES's electronics and communication designs prevent crosstalk with other IMES enabling the use of multiple IMES devices to simultaneously operate in close proximity but independently on different muscles. The IMES was tested for durability over four months implanted in cats and worked well.[34] The device was now ready for human testing.

For intuitive brain control to work, there needs to be an implanted sensor that detects the muscle and muscle nerve signals that are coming from the brain. How does the IMES work? The IMES also sends the detected muscle/nerve information to a nearby computer controller that then relays that information to the three DoF prosthetic wrist and hand being controlled. Second, the controllers need to be able to rapidly process up to 32 IMES sensors implanted in different muscles and remember the order that the signals are received and then forward that information to the prosthetic. The controller needs to tell the prosthetic when to close/release each of the fingers or rotate the wrist and so on. It also needs to tell it how long to do the specific task for each of the individual actions.

Finally, a very sophisticated mechanical prosthetic is needed with the ability to rapidly respond to the controller's instructions. Professor Richard Weir at Northwestern University, Phil Troyk at Sigenics, Inc., the Alfred Mann Foundation (now called huMannity Medtech), and colleagues have developed just such a sensor device, which they called IMES.[35] The IMES has also been tested in a man in a limited clinical study using an external controller in the prosthetic socket that communicates both with the IMES and with a three-DoF prosthetic hand and wrist device. An IMES needed to be implanted into each targeted muscle that will be used to control a function of the prosthetic arm. Two IMES devices are needed for each DoF. For example, one IMES device would control fingers' opening and another IMES device would control fingers' closing. Two others would be needed to control the wrist rotation left and right movements.[36] When tested in a man, it worked remarkably well to demonstrate the potential of this technology.

Summary—Hacking the Brain and Body

The development of modern electronics in the last 75 years or so, and the development of microminiaturized electronics, has led to the emergence of a new industry of wirelessly implanted medical devices. These devices are able to do things better than current drugs and offer alternative therapies, often without the side effects common with powerful drugs. The understanding of how foreign objects are rejected by the body has enabled these devices to avoid rejection by the immune system. The human body is innervated throughout and responds to electrical stimuli, and electronics are able to listen to these nerve signals too. If the malady can be addressed with electrical stimulation (such as with autoimmune suppression, depression, or epilepsy) or by listening to the muscle/nerves (in the case of the BION or IMES), then an implanted microelectronic device can be developed that will address it. It is still early days in the development of such devices. It is an exciting future with many potential applications, and there is a clear path for these devices to help extend health span and lifespan.

CHAPTER 16

Exercise to Increase Health Span and Lifespan

Whether it's from a social media influencer, a TV star who recently buffed up for a movie role, or from your friends, the exercise advice offered is usually anecdotal. In this chapter, we'll look at the latest medical research on this topic. It turns out that there are some significant findings when it comes to the relationship between exercise and both a healthier and a longer life. The research on the impact of exercise points to a significant decline in overall fitness as we age if we do not exercise. Starting in 30s, people lose between 3 and 8 percent of their muscle mass for each decade and at a faster rate after turning 60.[1]

The Health Span Benefits of Exercise

Everyone says exercise is good for you, but is that just anecdotal evidence or is there real medical proof? The answer can be found in several publications of Britain's National Health Service (NHS). Besides pointing to evidence that exercise can improve mental health, boost energy, and improve sleep quality, the NHS points to evidence that regular exercise can lower people's risk for coronary heart disease and stroke, type-2 diabetes, bowel and breast cancer, and hip fractures.[2–6]

The Amount of Exercise Time Required to Benefit

A few years ago, the U.S. Department of Health and Human Services came out with a series of recommendations, including 150 minutes of moderate-intensity aerobic exercise or 75 minutes of vigorous activity each week as well as two weekly strength training sessions targeting all major muscle groups. What if you can't allocate the 22 minutes for exercise every day? Research published in the *British Journal of Sports Medicine* indicate that a mere 11 minutes a day doing moderate-intensity exercise such as brisk walk is sufficient to lower the risk of heart disease, stroke, and a number of cancers.

Another study of 45,176 female nurses found that sedentary behavior was linked to reduced odds of healthy aging while light physical activity had the opposite effect and increased the odds of healthy aging. The study's conclusion was that light or moderate to vigorous physical activity is associated with decreased mortality and the suggestion that this exercise could bring about an increased lifespan and better overall health.[7–9]

The Benefits of Exercise Are More Than Skin Deep and Affect Longevity

Researchers have examined the biopsied tissues of rats during their exercise training to determine how exercise affects tissue-specific gene expression and, specifically, how the relationship between exercise adoption and gene expression impacts complex disease-associated genes. The results indicated that the exercise that stressed tissues with disease-associated genes appeared to reduce the chances of the various diseases manifesting themselves.

The National Institutes of Health sponsors an ongoing massive study of the underlying impact of exercise on a body's cells, tissues, and organs. Known as the Molecular Transducers of Physical Activity Consortium (MoTrPAC) project, scientists have been developing comprehensive molecular maps of how genes and proteins change after exercise in both rats and people. One significant finding is that a brisk walk of approximately one hour per day could protect against chronic diseases, including heart or blood vessel issues and type-2 diabetes.

Among the recent discoveries are how different tissues are affected by endurance exercise. Adrenal glands showed alterations in nearly half of mitochondria-associated genes following endurance training. Researchers also found gender differences in molecular responses across different tissues, particularly in white fat tissue. While the project is still in its early stages even after 10 years, these preliminary results show that someday it might be possible to develop personalized exercise programs that would be geared to a person's specific genetic and molecular makeup.

A recent medical journal article provided a significant review of the literature on the subject of exercise, health, and longevity pointed to one of the first research articles on the relationship between coronary heart disease and exercise using bus drivers and active train conductors as test subjects. The article also pointed to several studies validating the ability of exercise to improve the condition of diabetes patients and patients with mental health issues. Equally important, a study examined the relationship between maximum exercise capacity (VO_2 max) and mortality. It found that low estimated VO_2 max increases mortality 4.5-fold compared to high estimated VO_2 max.[10–12]

Is It Ever Too Late to Start Exercising?

Obviously, someone who has avoided exercise and suddenly decides to begin after decades needs to proceed slowly. It is encouraging that research shows that older people who begin exercising can still benefit significantly. Researchers studied two groups of adults, a group of 72-year-old Americans, and a group of 74-year-old Italians. The Americans took part in an exercise program for one year featuring aerobics, strength training, and flexibility, while the Italians remained sedentary. After that year the Americans showed marked improvement in their health while the Italians showed marked decline.[13]

The Link Between Exercise and a Healthy Brain

University of British Columbia researchers found that regular aerobic exercise boosted the size of the hippocampus, the part of the brain that is linked to verbal memory and learning. Exercise also causes the release of chemicals in the brain that cause the growth of new blood vessels and the survival of new brain cells. Besides the direct benefits of exercise on a healthy brain, researchers have long linked exercise to improved sleep and mood and the reduction in anxiety and stress.[14]

Stretching

Scandinavian researchers studied 3,000 people over a 13-year period and discovered that people with higher flexibility ranges tended to live longer than those with lower flexibility ranges. Another study on this subject conducted by Brazilian researchers discovered a direct link between flexibility and longevity. Women generally had a higher flexibility score than men, and people with higher flex index scores had a lower risk for mortality. While research on the relationship between stretching and longevity is relatively new, the Centers for Disease Control and Prevention's (CDC) statistics point to falling, particularly among the elderly, as a leading symptom and a leading cause of death. The lack of flexibility in older people leads to a variety of injuries. Older people who survive falls often find their health span shortened as they suffer mobility problems as a result of head injuries, fractured hips, broken legs, and so on.[15–18]

Conclusions

Recent research makes it clear that exercise programs that offer strength training, flexibility, and aerobic activity can increase participants' lifespans as well as improve their health spans and overall quality of life. It is encouraging that the research shows that even moderate exercise can have tangible positive effects in reducing the likelihood of heart disease, diabetes, and other major diseases. Exercise combined with stretching can pay dividends in reducing the likelihood of falls, a major source of death and loss of mobility among the elderly.

CHAPTER 17

Healthy Habits to Improve Health Span and Lifespan

Improving health span and lifespan requires the patient to adapt healthy habits and maintain an active partnership with the health care system. Doing so will not prevent all disease because your genetics cannot be ignored and nor can an external event. If you have a genetic mutation on a key gene, it might cause a disease. But as discussed in Chapter 6, CRISPR and other gene therapies may even cure a few genetic diseases now and far more in the future. If you are unfortunate, you may get cancer, arthritis, or an inflammatory disease, but researchers are increasingly improving early diagnosis and developing more effective therapies for many of these debilitating human diseases which will result in lexngthening people's heath span and lifespan.

Maintaining a Proper Weight or BMI (Body Mass Index)

A normal BMI is between 18.5 and 24.9. To calculate your BMI, you take your weight in pounds and multiply by 703 and divide that number by your height in inches twice. A BMI of 30 and higher is considered obese. The higher your BMI, the higher your risk of certain diseases such as heart disease, high blood cholesterol, high blood pressure, type-2 diabetes, breathing problems, and certain cancers and other diseases.[1] When you are obese, the extra fat in your body is deposited not just in your fat pads but also in many undesirable places and causes diseases such as fatty liver disease and clogged arteries that cause high blood pressure by restricting/blocking the flow of blood through the blood vessels. Fat deposits circulating in your blood make the pancreas work harder just to metabolize that fat. Fat may damage the kidney tissues to cause chronic kidney disease. These are just a few of the many problems caused by being overweight. The good news is that losing weight and getting to a better BMI result in clear benefits relatively quickly. Losing any amount weight and keeping it off have benefits. And if a healthy BMI is maintained for a long time, the improvements get better over time.[2] The best part is that the healthy habit benefits accrue at any age, when you maintain a normal BMI.

Physical Exercise

Throughout this book, we have been touting the importance of physical exercise and the health and mortality data that support it. Clearly, just being in good physical shape is so important for your general health as well as your general self-image and ability to perform activities of daily living (ADLs). The reasons go much deeper because physical exercise influences your health span and longevity. You naturally and involuntarily lose 3 to 8 percent muscle mass every decade after the age of 30, and this rate of decline is even higher after the age of 60. The loss of muscle mass (called sarcopenia) occurs more rapidly and more severely in older people, contributes to disability, and increases the risks of falling and injury. It is also associated with an accompanying increase in body fat, which also leads to increased insulin resistance and other negative metabolic consequences.[3] This muscle atrophy and the resultant decrease in general activity are very well known to severely reduce muscle mass and strength in the elderly. Hence, the focus is on physical activity for older people to maintain or reverse muscle mass loss.

Progressive weight (resistance) and aerobic exercise training have also been shown to induce muscle growth and increase strength in elderly and physically frail adults.[4,5] Aerobic exercise has been shown in several studies to improve oxygen saturation in blood, and physical activity reduces insulin sensitivity and energy expenditure in older individuals. Preliminary data suggest that aerobic exercise can also acutely increase muscle protein synthesis in healthy, independent older people. In summary, both resistance and aerobic exercise can counteract muscle mass loss and the associated metabolic alterations of the muscle.[6] Exercise as a healthy habit will indirectly result in improved health and longevity.

There is an association of muscle mass loss with weight loss too. Muscle loss occurs anytime you lose a substantial amount of weight, regardless of how it is done (i.e., diet, medications, or method). Weight-loss specialists explain that one-quarter to one-third of the weight lost is muscle. When calories are being restricted, the body turns to the energy stored in glycogen—the main source of energy that is primarily stored in the liver and muscles—and to fat and muscle to provide the fuel it needs during calorie restriction. A recent study showed that those taking Ozempic or any form of GLP-1 lost an average of 60 percent fat and 39 percent muscle mass. In another study that looked at those taking Zepbound (active ingredient GLP-1) showed that patients lost roughly 25 percent muscle and 75 percent fat during treatment.[7] Again, it is physical and aerobic exercise together with a proper diet with adequate amounts of protein maintains muscle mass or even reverses loss of muscle mass, if the person is diligent in physical activity. Importantly, this will change the ratio of fat loss to muscle loss. Finally, it is better to lose weight gradually than to do it quickly because it enables the body to adjust over time to the metabolic and fat-storage changes in tissues and muscles. Clearly, physical exercise is a healthy habit with clear benefits.

What We Learned from Blue Zones

The Mediterranean diet was first described in 1975 by Ancel and Margaret Keys who took inspiration from the eating habits of people living in Crete, Greece, and southern Italy in the early 1960s.[8] The diet actually can be traced back to the eating habits of the ancient Greeks and Romans. Their traditions offered a simple cuisine, but one rich in variety and taste, taking full advantage of all aspects of a healthy diet of available fruits and vegetables. The Mediterranean diet is also a "resource for sustainable development as it emphasizes the importance of local foods tied to the economic and identity culture of the region." What Keys showed was the correlation between cardiovascular disease and diet.[9] Keys also showed that there are blue zones in many places of the world following a study of heart disease and death around the world. The diet details from these different areas are similar but different in detail. The lifestyles emphasized fruits and vegetables, lots of fish, some poultry, and occasional red meat. In addition, they emphasized regular exercise and social inter-actions.[10] Those who had the highest adherence to a Mediterranean-type diet showed a 24 percent lower risk of cardiovascular disease and 23 per-cent lower risk of premature death compared with those who had the lowest adherence. A different study called the Nurses' Health Study stud-ied 10,670 women in the age range of 57 to 61 years and observed the effect of dietary patterns on aging. The study found that the women who followed a Mediterranean-type eating pattern were 46 percent more likely to age healthfully.[11]

As described in Chapter 12, the concept was enlarged in 1993 to en-compass a more general view of the importance of following an exercise regime based on a proper holistic combination of diet with daily phys-ical activity and socialization (socialization reads "mental health" here). The concept is that a food pyramid with exercise allows most foods from carbohydrates through red meat to be eaten but recommends that the frequency differ for the different foods based on their location on the pyramid. Furthermore, eating fruits, vegetables, nuts, and whole grains provide antioxidants that combat physiological stress and preserve telo-mere length, which, as we discussed earlier, is related to cell senescence and death when they get too short. The Mediterranean diet, perhaps, is better named the Blue Zone Lifestyle as the diet changes in different parts of the world, but the underlying concepts are the same in all blue zones. The Blue Zone Lifestyle is not a rigid prescription. Rather, it can be fol-lowed most of the time and allows some deviations and even "falling off the wagon" as long as it is followed most of the time over a lifetime. It is a healthy habit that improves health span and longevity.

Having a Stimulating Social Life Is Important Too

It goes without saying having an active and stimulating social life enriches your daily life by providing fun, entertainment, and education among other things. Having a good social system of friends and colleagues to share things with is critical to building emotional resilience. The bene-fits go well beyond just having fun with friends. Studies by Umberson and Montez show that "social relationships have short- and long-term effects on health, for better and for worse, and that these effects emerge in childhood and cascade throughout life to foster cumulative advantage or disadvantage in health."[12] According to a report from Steven Crane, a social engagement research scholar, "our relationship forms a lattice of support that constitutes the largest single factor in the overall well-being of most people." This is, in part, because when we don't engage in social relationships (or socialization) or nurture and maintain active bonds and regular communication and interaction with family and/or friends and relatives, loneliness and isolation can become chronic. Loneliness impacts mental health, combined with stress and behaviors that make the individuals more vulnerable to disease and early mortality. On the flipside, healthy networks of social connection do not just provide powerful protective health effects but also increase the odds for long-term survival by a remarkable 50 percent.[13] Conversely, detailed studies of social relationships have shown that the odds of early mortality increased by 91 percent among the socially isolated.[14] Supporting this research is other research that shows adults with a strong social life and social connections have a reduced risk of depression, high blood pressure, and an unhealthy BMI. By having friends to share life events with, a person has an increased sense of belonging and purpose, reduced stress, better ability to cope with traumas, and a source for encouragement to overcome unhealthy lifestyle habits.[15] In short, it is clear that having good social relationships and avoiding social isolation is a very important healthy habit that will improve your health and increase your longevity.

The Partnership Between the Patient and the Health Care System

A 1996 survey in the United States showed that about 70 percent of people in the United States had a medical checkup in the last year with people older than 70 years of age going more frequently.[16] What is most striking is the percentage of regular checkups vary widely between different countries. According to a Statista survey of 21 countries surveying 18-to-64-year-olds, Koreans had regular checkups 62 percent of the time while in Great Britain, Sweden, and the Netherlands only 30, 29, and 27 percent, respectively, had regular checkups. One reason it is higher in Korea is that it is mandatory for them to have a checkup every two years if they are part of the national health service.[17] This higher participation rate also, consequently, means improved health for participants taking part in the health checkups as it catches medical issues early. The downside for the Korean health care system is that the doctors and the health care system are overburdened by this high demand. More generally, there are many reasons that different countries have different rates of regular checkups.[18] But the data are quite convincing that getting regular medical checkups is clearly an important task for an individual to detect important disease markers and address any issues early.

The Importance of Regular Medical Checkups

The goal of these checkups is to detect disease early or trends that indicate future medical issues and thereby apply any intervention therapies to reduce disease impact. Many diseases do not come on suddenly like, say, a stroke or an inflammatory disease. They develop over time. For this reason, there is a benefit of longitudinal tracking of your health with diagnostics. There are many examples of this. Blood pressure is an example where it increases slowly giving the patient time to take medicine to control it. Type-2 diabetes is another where the hemoglobin A1c levels change over time and can be controlled with medicine to keep it within normal levels. Finally, another example is the tracking of prostate-specific antigen (PSA) levels in your blood to assess the growth of a man's prostate for benign prostate hyperplasia (BPH) and prostate cancer. These regular checkups and improving routine diagnostics for common aliments lead to improved health span and longevity by reducing the damage from treatable medical health issues. This is mainly because such health issues can be identified well ahead of time during regular checkups that help start a treatment regime in time and lead to either complete cure or minimize damage from such health issues to the lowest possible level. Getting regular medical checkups is clearly an important healthy habit.

Preventive Medicine and Prophylactic Drugs

Preventive medicine is a medical specialty that aims to prevent disease, disability, and death by promoting healthy behaviors over time. The hope for longevity is to prevent disease(s) that degrade your health and damage internal tissues. There is no lack of articles touting many remedies that will do that, but most are probably something akin to the "snake oil" salesmen in days of yore. However, modern medical research is clearly on the side of taking preventive actions to reduce your individual risk. Preventive medicine focuses on many of the things we have been discussing throughout this book. They include taking blood pressure, diabetes, and cholesterol medicine. Other aspects of preventive medicine are to conduct medical screenings on a regular basis (e.g., mammograms or colonoscopies), to eat right, and to have a healthy weight. Also, preventative medicine requires you to avoid things that damage your body, such as excessive alcohol and smoking. In the following sections, we will emphasize several ways to reduce risk through preventive medicine.

Vaccines and Prophylactic Drugs Have Huge Benefits

The real validated benefits of preventive medicine come from vaccines that prevent diseases like polio, measles, smallpox, and so on. Vaccines basically train your immune systems to identify a disease vector and then neutralize it. They provide lifetime immunity against many of these diseases. Unfortunately, some vaccines are only good for one season. Recent development of DNA and RNA vaccines are promising to provide permanent and medium-term immunity against a much wider variety of diseases. These newer kinds of vaccines using various DNA and RNA approaches work much faster and are much cheaper than the older methods of developing immunity. In addition, depending on their method of action, they can "highjack" the body's immune system or incorporate themselves into your immune cells to continue to make new anti-disease vectors for long periods of time.[19] These newer approaches to making vaccines are expected to improve their effectiveness.

Reduction of Inflammation Is an Essential Healthy Habit

As discussed in previous chapters, inflammation is a major cause of many human diseases and has a significant impact on aging. Some of the most widely used prophylactic drugs are anti-inflammatory drugs. Often inflammation is present in the background and not sufficiently debilitating to cause medical attention. As a result, many people just ignore its slow but relentless damage to the body's tissues and organs. This is not to minimize the chronic pain and associated debilitating effects from more advanced inflammatory diseases on the individual's quality of life. The medical therapy often consists of prescribing anti-inflammatory drugs that mostly come from two chemical classes—steroidal and nonsteroidal anti-inflammatory agents.

Steroidal drugs called corticosteroids are potent and are frequently prescribed to treat inflammation. As a class, steroidal drugs are quite effective when used properly and at the correct dosage. Examples of two steroidal anti-inflammatory drugs are prednisone and cortisone. Applications for these powerful drugs include rheumatological diseases like rheumatoid arthritis (RA), Crohn's disease, and lupus. Other applications can be for tennis elbow, asthma, COPD, and joint and muscle pain. One long-term use of these steroidal drugs is to prevent rejection in organ-transplant patients or in preterm delivery associated with fetal lung immaturity.[20] Steroidal drugs can come with side effects because as natural hormones they can affect other tissues in the body.[21] It is for this reason that anyone taking these drugs should be under a doctor's care.

Nonsteroidal anti-inflammatory drugs (NSAIDs) are used to reduce joint pain, postoperative pain, fever, and other types of inflammation, but, in general, they are not as powerful as steroids. Examples of NSAIDs include aspirin, naproxen, ibuprofen, celecoxib, and meloxicam. They can be used in low doses to reduce the risk of heart attack and stroke in high-risk patients. These drugs are commonly used and are effective for treating fever, mild pain, and other kinds of mild inflammation. They also have side effects common for anti-inflammatory drugs, including effects on your stomach, kidney, liver, and blood system especially at the higher doses and higher administration frequencies. As always, if the patient suspects a side-effect problem, they should contact a health care professional for advice on options.[22]

As part of the medical advances in biological understanding of the past few decades a number of new biotechnology-derived drugs are being introduced in the market. These include antibody drugs that block the action of tissue necrosis factor (TNF), a prominent component in the inflammatory process and its receptor. The advent of these powerful biologic drugs has markedly improved the management of autoimmune inflammatory diseases.[23] The disadvantage of these biologics is that up to 40 percent of patients do not respond to them.[24] It is still early days in the use of the anti-inflammatory, antibody-type, and biologic drugs. It is already clear that those who respond to these drugs have improved management of their disease. These drugs are more expensive than steroids and NSAIDs. However, they are more effective for some kinds of severe inflammatory diseases when these other approaches are insufficient to return the patient to a better state. One disadvantage of these biological drugs is that they have to be given by injection and cannot be self-administered chronically. Whereas the steroids and NSAIDs can be part of an active healthy habit and can be self-administered.

Non-healthy Habits

Looking for the fountain of youth is a lifelong quest for many people. For these people, two obviously harmful habits are smoking and drinking. If done to excess, they have a negative impact on one's lifespan and certainly one's health span. People who are clearly looking for ways to increase their health span and longevity are consequently willing to try some exotic and strange things in the hope that there will be a benefit. Most of these programs are outside of the medically studied areas and the person wanting to utilize them risk their safety, to say nothing about their effectiveness. In addition, they could be expensive.

Many people do lots of unnecessary testing for disease in the hopes of catching some disease very early. These tests include full body and brain imaging, whole genome sequencing (WGS) for genetic diseases, and epigenetic testing for markers of biological age. Other tests include microbiome sequencing, oral pathogen testing, nutritional testing, continuous glucose monitoring (when you don't have diabetes), and so many other things that could keep hypochondriacs really "busy."

Studies of People Who Live at High Altitudes

Humans require oxygen for life. The question is: "How much is the right amount? Pure oxygen therapy has been shown in recent years as useful for many things such as reducing stress, headache and migraine, energy levels, and improving mood. Scientists at the University of Colorado School of Medicine in partnership with Harvard found that people living at higher altitudes (less oxygen concentration in the air) have a lower chance of dying from ischemic heart disease and tend to live longer than others. The results are interesting. It is probably more complex than it seems on the surface, since Colorado is the leanest and fittest state as well as having, in general, fewer deaths from heart disease and a lower incidence of colon and lung cancer compared to other states.[25] Interestingly, there are studies of restricted oxygen in experimental animals showing they live longer. A study by Zou and colleagues in China reported a small benefit to life expectancy of about 0.15 years longer from restricted oxygen levels in humans with lung or hypoxic issues.[26] The positive results are interesting, but not large enough to be beyond the variability caused by the normal activities of daily living.

This kind of information has prompted studies for the benefits of both hyper-oxygen and oxygen-restriction therapies. An important oxygen application is the use of hyperbaric pure oxygen therapy for wound healing and burn treatments. In these cases, there may be some restriction of getting enough blood oxygen to the wound site to provide maximum healing.[27] If the patient has lung problems and the blood oxygen saturation levels are below normal, such as with COPD, emphysema, or sleep apnea, then oxygen supplementation therapy might be helpful to maintain healthy tissues and to provide the extra oxygen needed to prevent damage or to repair damaged tissues.[28]

These medical applications have prompted some healthy people to try hyperbaric pure oxygen therapy. From this has come the oxygen bars in malls and other locations.[29] Unfortunately, it is a salesman' dream, but there is little scientific evidence that it works. The sessions only last for a few minutes, and the person may feel invigorated by the session. However, the medical community has said that there is no evidence that a "shot" of pure oxygen has any benefits.[30]

Fad Diets

There are a huge number of diets continually talked about in the media that purport to have huge benefits to health span and longevity. Take, for example, smoothies. They are a great way to increase intake of fruit and vegetable juice and fiber in our diet, but they are loaded with unhealthy amounts of added sugars as well as natural sugars.[31] The fad diets are based on a variety of assumptions about health benefits of different foods, how they are prepared, and frequency of eating them. Most of these claims are not validated scientifically. To review these diets would take at least another book to cover them thoughtfully. The main point here is that diet and reduction of body weight do have an impact on health and longevity when done smartly. The healthy habit here recognizes that health is correlated with calorie intake. Reducing calorie intake has also been studied. A number of studies have shown that cutting caloric intake by 12 percent in lean or slightly overweight adults slowed the pace of aging by 2 to 3 percent. If maintained for 10 to 15 years, it may slow aging by 10 to 15 percent.[32] This is due to the reduction in metabolism rates in healthy, non-obese individuals. Kebbe and colleagues reviewed the impact of calorie restriction on health span and lifespan. They concluded that caloric restriction is an effective therapeutic approach for improving health span and biomarkers of lifespan.[33] This and other studies again reinforce the view that a normal body mass is important for longevity. The Kebbe and colleagues, however, pointed out in their study that the benefits from weight (fat) loss in obese individuals is good for the individual but it is a different biological response than the biological response resulting from a slowing metabolism induced by caloric restriction.

Calorie restriction can be dangerous to one's health, if taken too far or overdone. Even intermittent fasting is okay, if not taken too far and is balanced properly by a variety of healthy foods and vitamins to maintain an ideal body mass. The research showing the benefits supporting intermittent fasting is covered in Chapter 12. The effects of any single approach on increasing lifespan are difficult to assign to any one activity. Humans are physically very complex as we live a long time, are very genetically diverse, and have hugely different lifestyles and diets. Accordingly, it will be difficult for any one approach to be the key factor on a significant increase in longevity. From the guidance (described in this book) and from all the research cited, it is clear that a proper body weight provides a benefit in longevity regardless of how it is achieved.

There are two other areas related to diet that relate to "junk" foods and prepared, ultra-processed foods. As described in Chapter 12, there are data to support the view that unhealthy and unbalanced diets from eating too much of these junk and processed foods cause premature aging. Junk and ultra-processed foods are frequently high in calories, unhealthy fat, excess salt, food additives, and other chemicals that are used to make them acceptable for grocery store shelves and easy to eat. Often, they have little nutritional value. Another negative is that these foods substitute for healthy alternatives. In some cases, when eaten to excess, they can promote insulin resistance, diabetes, high blood pressure, and other metabolic diseases.[34] Junk foods are not a healthy habit unless done in moderation.

The last area to consider while discussing diet is eating out in restaurants. Generally, restaurant food is less healthy than home-prepared foods. They frequently have more salt, oil, saturated fat, sugar, and calories than the homemade versions. They are designed to have good taste and not to be particularly healthy. This, of course, does not refer to restaurants that offer food rich in whole grains, legumes, nuts, and seeds that are super-healthy foods. Eating out can be okay if you select healthy options of fruits and vegetables and watch your calories, oils, butter, and portion size.

Spas and Spa Health Treatments

One final area to discuss here is the benefits of spas and their health treatments. Spas are very popular, and, for many, they are a good place for a getaway to relax and reduce stress. In a 2006 survey, it was estimated that 57 million adults and 4 million teens have been to a spa. Going to a spa can be a healthy habit.[35] There are clear benefits from the various treatments that are available in spas. There are risks too in a small minority of spas especially in the treatments involving water. Studies of communal pools, saunas, and other water-related spa treatments show that they may have infectious organisms that are not killed by disinfectant chemicals like chlorine. The spa staff may not understand the risk of not changing the water often enough. If not maintained properly, there may be issues in inhaling organisms and developing skin problems. Other potential spa issues relate to manicures and pedicures, if the instruments are not properly cleaned. Other risks include infections or any unanticipated side effects from exotic treatments to "cleanse" your body, such as seaweed wraps, mud baths, and hot rocks; such treatments can be fun as long as the treatments are properly maintained.[36]

Postscript

In summary, the healthy habits described throughout this book are some of the best and, more importantly, tested and proven, ways (of course, with varying levels of efficacy depending on the health status of the individual prior to engaging in them) for an individual to improve their health span and longevity. Science and medicine are hard at work to cure diseases that degrade our bodies and health, and these new therapies will improve our health over time. Finally, the new fields of science and medicine dealing with the aging processes and how to modify or even roll them back are gaining steam and are expected to have a significant impact on our lives in many ways as new anti-aging drugs are shown to be effective on either aged organs or on our entire bodies. If we can live long enough for these new therapies to come online, then we can expect to live on average significantly longer than is now possible. It is an exciting time to be alive and share a future of improved health span and lifespan. For us and our descendants it will be an opportunity to live long and prosper!

Endnotes

Preface

1. "Health Disparities Overview" (2024).
2. "The State of Health Disparities in the United States" (2024).
3. "Eliminating Racial/Ethnic Disparities in Health Care: What Are the Options?" KFF.org (2008).
4. Gary Burtless (2016).
5. "The Equality of Opportunity Project" (n.d.).
6. Stephen H. Woolf et al. (2015).

Chapter 1

1. Johnson (2021a, xx).
2. Field and Cassel (1997).
3. Simonite (2023).
4. Sykes (2020).
5. Ohman and Gomez-Olivalencia (2018).
6. Adhiyaman and Chattopadhyay (2021).
7. Griffin (2008).
8. Washington Post Staff (2023).
9. Kaeberlein (2018).
10. Stibich (2022a).
11. Poulain and Pes (2004).
12. Buettner (2016)
13. See also Gerontology Research Group (n.d.).
14. Schoenhofen et al. (2006).
15. Gierman et al. (2014).
16. Garagnani et al. (2021).
17. D. G. Smith (2023).
18. Youmshajekian (2023).
19. Blagosklonny (2021).
20. Alter (2023).

Chapter 2

1. See a good general discussion of the various theories in Stibich (2022).
2. Perhaps the definitive medical journal article on this topic in Lopez-Otin et al. (2013).
3. Maugh II (1996).
4. Lakowski et al. (1996).
5. Stibich (2024).
6. Robbins et al. (2022, 112).
7. Takahashi et al. (2008).
8. See also a follow-up study: Liu et al. (2008).
9. Lu et al. (2020).
10. Burtner et al. (2010).
11. Hayasaki (2019).
12. Schumacher et al. (2021).
13. Yousefzadeh et al. (2021).
14. Costandi (2022).
15. Muñoz-Lorente et al. (2019).
16. Kimura et al. (2008).
17. Lopez-Otin et al. (2013).
18. von Kobbe et al. (2019).
19. C. Wang et al. (2009).
20. Dance et al. (2023).
21. Gonzales et al. (2023).
22. Chaib et al. (2022).
23. Hachmo et al. (2020).
24. Newman (2023).
25. Bratic (2013).
26. Benjamin et al. (2023).
27. Levine et al. (2018).
28. Zhang et al. (2023).
29. Wilmanski (2021).

Chapter 3

1. Reisch (2017).
2. Claus et al. (2016).
3. Shibagaki et al. (2017).
4. Sommer et al. (2013).
5. Gensollen et al. (2016).
6. Bull et al. (2014).

7. Zhao et al. (2023).
8. TG Oh et al. (2020).
9. Niu (2023).
10. Zhao et al. (2023).
11. Yu et al. (2017).
12. Tilg et al. (2018).
13. Baruch et al. (2021).
14. Davar et al. (2021).
15. Zheng et al. (2021).
16. Zhao et al. (2023).
17. Liu et al. (2021).
18. Inamura (2021).
19. Xu et al. (2019).
20. Bana et al. (2019).
21. Kirkendoll (2023).
22. Biagi et al. (2016).
23. Galkin et al. (2020).

Chapter 4

1. "About Dementia" (n.d.).
2. "Nutrition and the Brain" (n.d.).
3. Breit et al. (2018).
4. "First Patient Enrolled in Stage 2 of Pivotal Study of Setpoint Medical's Pioneering Technology for the Treatment of Rheumatoid Arthritis" (2022).
5. Emily Cronkleton (2021).
6. "Memory Problems, Forgetfulness, and Aging" (n.d.).
7. "Memory Problems, Forgetfulness, and Aging" (n.d.).
8. Poon et al. (2012).
9. Lindberg, "Focus" (2023b).
10. Lindberg "Brain Exercises" (2023a).
11. "How Music Can Improve Your Memory and Concentration" (2024).
12. "Keep Your Brain Young with Music" (n.d.).
13. Miranda (2023).
14. "Music as Medicine for Alzheimer's Disease and Dementia" (2022).
15. Phoenix (2023).
16. Jones (2021).
17. Jones (2025).
18. Jones (2025).
19. Jones (2021).
20. Ganz et al. (2018).

21. Jones (2021).
22. "Exercise Can Boost Your Memory and Thinking Skills" (2024).
23. Rauchman (2023).
24. Park and Bischof (2013).
25. Pacheco (n.d.).
26. "Brain Basics: Understanding Sleep" (n.d.).
27. Rasch and Born (2013).
28. "Brain Basics: Understanding Sleep" (n.d.).
29. DiGiulio (2017).
30. "Aging Changes in Sleep" (2022).
31. "Brain Basics: Understanding Sleep" (n.d.).
32. Spira et al. (2013).
33. Klein et al. (2017).
34. Perls (2004).
35. Peters (2006).
36. Effa (n.d.).
37. "Care in the Last Stages of Alzheimer's Disease" (n.d.).
38. Andersen-Ranberg et al. (2001).
39. Beker et al. (2021).
40. "Don't Buy into Brain Health Supplements" (2023).
41. "Brain Health Supplements Market Size 2022–2028" (n.d.).
42. Northrop (2024).
43. Williams (2019).
44. "Improving Health and Longevity Among People with Serious Mental Illness" (n.d.).
45. Chesney et al. (2014).
46. Ilyas et al. (2017).
47. Cook et al. (2014).

Chapter 5

1. Mayo Clinic Staff, "Stem Cells: What They Are and What They Do?"
2. Farr (2018).
3. Zhu et al. (2021).
4. Musial-Whysocka et al. (2019).
5. Kim et al. (2022).
6. Conger (2020).
7. "Scientists Identify a Method to Rejuvenate Old Stem Cells" (2023).
8. "Why We Age: Stem Cell Exhaustion" (2022).
9. Yamanaka (2007).
10. Buckberry et al. (2023).

11. Ullah and Sun (2018).
12. Evangelou (2022).

Chapter 6

1. Kozebek (2017).
2. Maryanovich et al. (2019).
3. Doudna (2024).
4. "What Is Huntington's Disease?" (n.d.).
5. Ekman et al. (2019).
6. Kaiser (2021).
7. Page (2021).
8. Houser (2022).
9. Foy et al. (2023).
10. Mullin. (2024).
11. Wang (2021).
12. Caobi et al. (2020).

Chapter 7

1. Ludwig and Elashoff (1972).
2. Conboy et al. (2005).
3. Zhang et al. (2023).
4. Kubala (2020).
5. Malík and Tlustoš (2022).
6. Brody (2024).
7. Veeresham (2012).
8. Williams (2019).
9. Gómez-Linton et al. (2019).
10. Bjørklund et al. (2022).
11. Chen et al. (2022).
12. Gómez-Linton et al. (2019).
13. Gómez-Linton et al. (2019).
14. "Centenarian Statistics" (2023).
15. Garay (2021). See also Gómez-Linton et al. (2019).
16. Arrieta et al. (2016). See also Wan et al. (2016).
17. Valenzano et al. (2006).
18. Blagosklonny (2019a).
19. Greene (2023).

20. Kirkland et al. (2020).
21. Breccia and Alimena (2011).
22. Yousefzadeh et al. (2018).
23. Kowald and Kirkwood (2021).

Chapter 8

1. "What You Need to Know About Blood Testing" (n.d.).
2. "Urinalysis."
3. "Colon Polyps" (n.d.).
4. "Eating, Diet, & Nutrition for Colon Polyps" (n.d.).
5. Healthline Editorial Staff (2019).
6. "Liquid Biopsy" (n.d.).
7. "Go Further with Cancer Screening" (n.d.).
8. Klein et al. (2021).
9. Klein et al. (2021).
10. "What Is FoundationOne Liquid CDX?" (n.d.).
11. Tamhane et al. (2019).
12. Alowais et al. (2023).
13. "Artificial Intelligence (AI) in Cardiovascular Medicine" (n.d.). See also Cheng et al. (2023).
14. Marino et al. (2023).
15. Apple, "Longevity Biomarkers" (n.d.).
16. Apple, "iPhone in Longevity Biomarkers LLC" (n.d.).
17. Google, "Longevity" (n.d.).
18. Murata et al. (2024).
19. Arai et al. (2015).
20. López-Otín et al. (2023).
21. López-Otín et al. (2013).
22. Schmauck-Medina et al. (2022).
23. Berman (2021).

Chapter 9

1. Sik (2022).
2. Johnson (2021b).
3. Mesko (2024).
4. Kwo (2021).
5. "Introduction to Medical 3D Printing" (n.d.).
6. Benichou et al. (2011).

7. Nawrat (2018).
8. Mesko (2024).
9. Barber (2023).
10. Pelc (2023).
11. Pleura (n.d.).
12. Gary Davis (2022).
13. Mesko (2022).
14. Hanaphy (2022).
15. Barber (2023).
16. Barber (2023).
17. Pleura (n.d.).
18. Chandak et al. (2019).
19. Global Data (2022).
20. Listek (2020).
21. Zein et al. (2013).
22. Barber (2023).
23. Barber (2023).
24. Mesko (2022).
25. Nawrat (2018).
26. Javaid et al. (2022).
27. "Want to 3D Print a Kidney?" (2022).
28. Bozkurt and Karayel (2021).

Chapter 10

1. Laricchia (2024).
2. Dehghani et al. (2018).
3. Consumer Reports Blog Fitness Tracker (2024).
4. Kang and Exworthy (2022).
5. "Continuous Glucose Monitoring" (n.d.).
6. "Artificial Pancreas" (n.d.).
7. "More Than Half of U.S. Adults" (2024).
8. "Cardiac Event Monitors" (n.d.).
9. Premier Cardiology Consultants (n.d.).
10. Hipp (2024).
11. Cunha (n.d.).
12. Digitale (2019).
13. Hossmann (1999).
14. "Overweight & Obesity Statistics" (n.d.).
15. Kritchevsky et al. (2015).
16. Godman (2021).

17. Cheatham et al. (2018).
18. Huang et al. (2023).
19. Brewster and Maitlin (2024).
20. Apple (2024).
21. Radel (2024).
22. Howley (2024).
23. De Raeve (2016).
24. Glassman. (2024).
25. Oliver (2020).
26. Zee (2021).
27. Apple, "Track Your Sleep on Apple Watch" (n.d.).
28. Rodrigues (2024).
29. Ates et al. (2021).

Chapter 11

1. "Preventing Cancer" (n.d.).
2. "What Is Cancer" (n.d.).
3. "Detect Cancers Early—National Cancer Plan" (n.d.).
4. Alix-Panabières et al. (2023).
5. Lennon et al. (2020).
6. "What Causes Cancer?" (n.d.).
7. "Age and Cancer" (n.d.).
8. "Cancer Growth Blockers" (n.d.).
9. "Are Telomeres the Key to Aging and Cancer" (n.d.).
10. Bretthauer and Kalager (2013).
11. City of Hope (2023b).
12. National Cancer Institute, "Immune Checkpoint Inhibitors" (n.d.).
13. "Cancer Cells Drain Energy from Immune Cells" (2021).
14. City of Hope (2023a).
15. City of Hope (2022).
16. "Aging and Health" (2024).
17. Stefanacci (2024).
18. Fontana and Hu (2014).
19. Oh et al.(2023).
20. Beauséjour et al. (2003).
21. Gail Dutton (2023).
22. Raffaele and Vinciguerra (2022).
23. Madison (2003).
24. Gilhar et al. (2004).
25. Gilchrest et al. (1979).
26. Tobin and Paus (2001).

27. Lunjani et al. (2021).
28. Mayo Clinic (n.d.).
29. American Cancer Society, "Skin Cancer Treatments" (n.d.).
30. Esteva et al. (2017).
31. Han et al. (2020).
32. Liu et al. (2020).
33. Wei et al. (2024).
34. Yakupu et al. (2023).
35. Li et al. (2020).
36. *Medical News Today* (n.d.).
37. Comfort Zone (n.d.).
38. López-Otín et al. (2023).
39. Qima Life Sciences (n.d.).
40. The Skin Network (n.d.).
41. Lawton (2023).
42. Marshall (2024).
43. Blagosklonny (n.d.).
44. Blagosklonny (2019b).
45. Blagosklonny (2018).
46. Blagosklonny (2006).
47. Novelle et al. (2016).
48. Senior Healthcare (n.d.).
49. USCDornsife (2024).

Chapter 12

1. "Evolution of USDA Food Guides" (2015).
2. Paulas (2015).
3. Smallwood (2013).
4. Anahad O'Connor (2024b).
5. Fazzino et al. (2023).
6. Saavedra et al. (2023).
7. Singh et al. (2024).
8. Li et al. (2023).
9. Brown University Health Blog Team (2024).
10. Pretzel (2024).
11. Pretzel (2024).
12. Mammoser (2024).
13. Poole et al. (2018).
14. Loftfield et al. (2015).
15. Makiso et al. (2023).
16. Korat et al. (2024).

17. Korat et al. (2024).
18. C. Li et al. (2024).
19. Naghshi et al. (2020).
20. Melnick (2023).
21. Landry et al. (2023).
22. "Intermittent Fasting: How It Works and 4 Types Explained" (2022).
23. Richard Joseph (2022). See also de Cabo and Mattson (2019).
24. Sutton et al. (2018).
25. O'Connor (2024a).
26. Bluezones.com
27. LeBlanc (2023).
28. Prater (2023).
29. Tor-Roca et al. (2023).
30. Amenabar (2024).
31. Calvo-Malvar et al. (2021).
32. Mishra et al. (2023).
33. Wei et al. (2017).
34. Lee et al. (2021).
35. Fadus et al.(2017).
36. Mirzavandi et al. (2020).
37. Satidpitakul (2023).
38. Shade (2020).
39. Learn (2024).
40. Harrison et al. (2009).
41. Smith (2024).
42. Chai et al. (2011).
43. Barcelos and Haas (1996).
44. Madeo et al. (2019).
45. Wirth et al. (2021).

Chapter 13

1. "Getting Good Sleep Could Add Years to Your Life" (2023).
2. Memar and Faradji (2018).
3. Patel et al. (2024).
4. "Brain Basics: Understanding Sleep" (n.d.).
5. Schildhouse (2024).
6. "Brain Basics: Understanding Sleep" (n.d.).
7. Robbins et al. (2021).
8. Xie et al.(2013).
9. "Understanding the Connection Between Sleep and Dementia" (2021).

10. "Brain Basics: Understanding Sleep" (n.d.).
11. Zhou et al. (2019).
12. "What Is Narcolepsy?" (n.d.).
13. "Narcolepsy" (n.d.).
14. Makiso et al. (2023).
15. "Melatonin for Sleep: Does It Work?" (n.d.).
16. Bauer (n.d.).
17. "Melatonin for Sleep: Does It Work?" (n.d.).
18. Wiginton (2023).
19. Drake et al. (2013).
20. "Caffeinated or Not, Coffee Linked with Longer Life" (2018).
21. Park et al. (2015).
22. Stanborough (n.d.).
23. Hirotsu et al. (2015).
24. Serrano (2024).
25. Akerstedt and Fröberg (1979).
26. Chung et al. (2024).
27. Cribb et al.(2023).
28. "Getting Good Sleep Could Add Years to Your Life" (2023).
29. Hublin et al. (2007).
30. H. Li et al. (2024).
31. X. Wang et al., "Day-to-Day Deviations" (2023).
32. Robbins et al. (2021).
33. Sun et al. (2023).
34. Sun et al. (2023).
35. Glass et al. (2005).

Chapter 14

1. Monk (2023).
2. "Stress Management" (2021).
3. "Stress Management" (2021).
4. Khansari et al.(1990).
5. Dantzer and Kelley (1989).
6. Lupien et al.(2009).
7. Bremner (1999).
8. Schwabe et al. (2010).
9. Yaribeygi et al.(2017).
10. Dhabhar (2018).
11. "Acute Stress Primes Brain" (2013).
12. Lucassen et al. (2015).

13. "The Effects of Stress on Your Body" (2024).
14. LeMoult et al.(2023).
15. Mayo Clinic Staff, "Chronic Stress Puts Your Health at Risk" (n.d.).
16. "Stress Effects on the Body" (2024).
17. Kessler et al. (1995).
18. "How Stress Affects Your Health" (2024).
19. Segal (2010).
20. Bremner (2006).
21. Branan (2007).
22. Malberg et al. (2000).
23. Pavlov and Tracey (2012).
24. "Vagus Nerve" (n.d.).
25. Reiche et al. (2004).
26. Reiche et al. (2004).
27. Khansari et al. (1990).
28. Pavlov and Tracey (2012).
29. Molina-Torres et al. (2019).
30. Qin et al. (2010).
31. Cryan and Dinan (2012). See also Karl et al. (2018).
32. An et al. (2024).
33. Neufeld et al. (2011).
34. Mohajeri et al.(2018).
35. Lee et al.(2022).
36. Lupien et al. (2009).
37. Red Cross Blogger (2020).
38. "Stress? What Stress???" (n.d.).
39. "Stress Management: How to Tell the Difference Between Good and Bad Stress" (2021).
40. Hessler (n.d.).

Chapter 15

1. "Bionic Limbs" (n.d.).
2. EO Johnson et al. (2008).
3. Dahlhamer et al. (2018).
4. Soattin et al. (2021).
5. AG Gonzales et al. (2020).
6. Templer (2022).
7. "Revolutionizing the Treatment of Chronic Disease" (n.d.).
8. "Dynamic Stimulation of Visual Cortex Lets Blind People 'See' Shapes" (2020).

9. "The Dangers of Uncontrolled Sleep Apneia" (n.d.).
10. Borovikova et al. (2000).
11. World Stroke Organization (n.d.). See also Feigin et al. (2023).
12. Wang X, Ding Q, et al . (2023).
13. George et al . (2000).
14. Slomski (2021).
15. "Epilepsy Basics" (n.d.).
16. "Vagus Nerve Stimulation (VNS) Therapy" (n.d.).
17. "A New Hope for Patients with Epilepsy" (2021).
18. "Brain Stimulation Therapies for Epilepsy" (n.d.).
19. Lozano (n.d.).
20. Willmer (2022).
21. Mullin (2023).
22. "Brain-Computer Interface Guide" (n.d.) ".
23. "Bionic Limbs" (n.d.).
24. Teoli et al. (2024).
25. "Pain Treatments" (n.d.).
26. MJ Kane et al. (2011).
27. Loeb et al . (2001).
28. Ziegler-Graham et al. (2008).
29. "29 Limb Loss Statistics, Facts & Demographics" (n.d.).
30. McFarland et al. (2010).
31. "A Whole New Way to Wear a Prosthetic Leg" (n.d.).
32. Dhillon and Horch (2005).
33. Atkins et al. (1996).
34. Weir et al. (2009).
35. Weir et al. (2009).
36. "Implantable MyoElectric Sensors (IMES…)" (2018).

Chapter 16

1. Friedman (2023).
2. "Overview: Alzheimer's Disease" (n.d.).
3. "Bowel Cancer" (n.d.).
4. "Breast Cancer in Women" (n.d.).
5. "Overview: Osteoarthritis" (n.d.).
6. "Broken Hip" (n.d.).
7. Fairbank (2023).
8. Rogers (2023).
9. Shi et al. (2024).
10. Vetr and Gay (2024).

11. Fan (2024).
12. Booth and Ruegegger (2018).
13. Manning et al. (2024).
14. Godman (2014).
15. Araújo et al.(2024).
16. Watts (2024).
17. "About Older Adult Fall Prevention" (2024).
18. Vaishya and Vaish (2020).

Chapter 17

1. "Accessing Your Weight and Health Risk" (n.d.).
2. "Health Risks of Overweight & Obesity" (n.d.).
3. Volpi et al. (2004).
4. Fiatarone et al. (1994).
5. Jozsi et al. (1999).
6. Tracy et al. (1999).
7. Baton Rouge General (2024).
8. "Mediterranean Diet" (n.d.).
9. A. B. Keys and M. Keys (1975).
10. A. B. Keys (1980).
11. "Diet Review: Mediterranean Diet" (n.d.).
12. Umberson and Montez (2010).
13. Carly Smith (2023).
14. Holt-Lunstad et al. (2010).
15. Mayo Clinic Staff, "Friendships: Enrich Your Life and Improve Your Health" (n.d.).
16. Culica et al. (2002).
17. H. T. Kang (2022).
18. Fleck (2024).
19. Leitner et al. (1999).
20. Yasir et al. (2023).
21. D. Liu et al. (2013).
22. Ghlichloo and Gerriets (2023).
23. Meier et al. (2013).
24. Roda et al. (2016).
25. "Keys to Long Life? Not What You Might Expect" (2011).
26. Zou et al. (2023).
27. M. Gupta and J. Rathored (2024).
28. "Hyperbaric Oxygen Therapy" (n.d.).
29. Santos-Longhurst (2019).

30. "The Rise of Oxygen Bars" (n.d.).
31. Smoothies—Helpful or Harmful?" (n.d.).
32. "Cutting Calories May Slow the Pace of Aging in Healthy Adults"Cutting Calories May Slow Aging in Healthy Adults (2023)".
33. Kebbe et al. (2021).
34. Mititelu et al. (2023).
35. Bouchez (2007).
36. Bouchez (2007).

Bibliography

"29 Limb Loss Statistics, Facts & Demographics." promedeast.com. Accessed December 14, 2024. https://promedeast.com/limb-loss-statistics/.

"About Dementia." Alzheimer Society. Accessed December 30, 2024. https://alzheimer.ca/en/about-dementia/do-i-have-dementia/differences-between-normal-aging-dementia.

"About Older Adult Fall Prevention." CDC, May 16, 2024, https://www.cdc.gov/falls/about/index.html#:~:text=Falls%20among%20adults%2065%20and,injury%20death%20for%20that%20group.

"Accessing Your Weight and Health Risk." National Heart, Lung, and Blood Institute. Accessed December 15, 2024. https://www.nhlbi.nih.gov/health/educational/lose_wt/risk.htm#:~:text=The%20higher%20your%20BMI%2C%20the,breathing%20problems%2C%20and%20certain%20cancers.

"Acute Stress Primes Brain for Better Cognitive and Mental Performance." *Science Daily*, April 1, 2013, https://www.sciencedaily.com/releases/2013/04/130416204546.htm#:~:text=Chronic%20stress%20is%20known%20to,improved%20cognitive%20and%20mental%20performance.

Adhiyaman, V., and I. Chattopadhyay. "Is It Appropriate to Link 'Old Age' to Certain Causes of Death on the Medical Certificate of Cause of Death?" *Future Healthcare Journal* 8, no. 3 (2021): e686–e688. https://pmc.ncbi.nlm.nih.gov/articles/PMC8651340/.

"Age and Cancer." cancerresearchuk.org. Accessed December 12, 2024. https://www.cancerresearchuk.org/about-cancer/causes-of-cancer/age-and-cancer#:~:text=Often%20our%20body%20repairs%20the,up%2C%20making%20cancer%20more%20likely.

"Aging and Health." World Health Organization, October 1, 2024. https://www.who.int/news-room/fact-sheets/detail/ageing-and-health#:~:text=Common%20health%20conditions%20associated%20with,%2C%20diabetes%2C%20depression%20and%20dementia.

"Aging Changes in Sleep." MedlinePlus, July 21 2022. https://medlineplus.gov/ency/article/004018.htm#:~:text=Sleep%20patterns%20tend%20to%20change,to%207%20hours%20per%20night.

Akerstedt, T., and J. E. Fröberg. "Sleep and Stressor Exposure in Relation to Circadian Rhythms in Catecholamine Excretion." *Biological Psychology* 8, no. 1 (1979): 69–80. https://pubmed.ncbi.nlm.nih.gov/465621/.

Alix-Panabières, C., D. Marchetti, and Julie E. Lang. "Liquid Biopsy: From Concept to Clinical Application." *Scientific Reports* 13 (2023): 21685. https://www.nature.com/articles/s41598-023-48501-x.

Alowais, S. A., S. S. Alghamdi, N. Alsuhebany, et al. "Revolutionizing Healthcare: The Role of Artificial Intelligence in Clinical Practice." *BMC Medical Education* 23 (2023): 689. https://doi.org/10.1186/s12909-023-04698-z.

Alter, C. "The Man Who Thinks He Can Live Forever." *Time*, September 20, 2023. https://time.com/6315607/bryan-johnsons-quest-for-immortality/?u…&utm_content=+++20230920+++body&et_rid=241208574&lctg=241208574.

Amenabar, T. "What's the Atlantic Diet? A Variation on Mediterranean Eating Shows Benefits." *Washington Post*, February 19, 2024. https://www.washingtonpost.com/wellness/2024/02/19/atlantic-diet-mediterranean-differences/.

American Cancer Society. "Skin Cancer Treatments." Accessed March 6, 2025. https://www.cancer.org/content/dam/cancer-org/cancer-control/en/booklets-flyers/skin-cancer-treatments.pdf.

"A New Hope for Patients with Epilepsy." yalemedicine.org., March 21, 2021. https://www.yalemedicine.org/news/epilepsy-deep-brain-stimulation#:~:text=Now%20they%20may%20have%20found,reduce%20the%20frequency%20of%20seizures.

An, E., D. R. Delgadillo, J. Yang, et al. "Stress-Resilience Impacts Psychological Wellbeing: Evidence from Brain–Gut Microbiome Interactions." *Nature Mental Health* 2, no. 8 (2024): 935–950. https://pubmed.ncbi.nlm.nih.gov/39620114/.

Andersen-Ranberg, K., L. Vasegaard, and B. Jeune. "Dementia Is Not Inevitable: A Population-Based Study of Danish Centenarians." *Journals of Gerontology: Series B* 56, no. 3 (2001): P152–P159. https://pubmed.ncbi.nlm.nih.gov/11316833/.

Apple. "Apple Introduces Groundbreaking Health Features to Support Conditions Impacting Billions of People." *Apple Newsroom*, September 9, 2024. https://www.apple.com/newsroom/2024/09/apple-introduces-groundbreaking-health-features/.

Apple. "Longevity Biomarkers." Apple App Store. Accessed December 11, 2024. https://apps.apple.com/us/app/longevity-biomarkers/id1553911832.

Apple. "iPhone in Longevity Biomarkers LLC." Apple App Store Preview. Accessed December 10, 2024. https://apps.apple.com/us/developer/longevity-biomarkers-llc/id1553911834.

Apple. "Track Your Sleep on Apple Watch and Use Sleep on iPhone." support.apple.com. Accessed December 10, 2024. https://support.apple.com/en-us/108906.

Arai, Y., C. M. Martin-Ruiz, M. Takayama, et al. "Inflammation, but not Telomere Length, Predicts Successful Ageing at Extreme Old Age: A Longitudinal

Study of Semi-Supercentenarians." *EBioMedicine* 2, no. 10 (2015): 1549–1558. https://pubmed.ncbi.nlm.nih.gov/26629551/.

Araújo, C., C. de Souza e Silva, S. K. Kunutsor, et al. "Reduced Body Flexibility Is Associated with Poor Survival in Middle-Aged Men and Women: A Prospective Cohort Study." *Scandinavian Journal of Medicine & Science in Sports* 34 (2024): e14708. https://pubmed.ncbi.nlm.nih.gov/39165228/.

"Are Telomeres the Key to Aging and Cancer" learn.genetics.utah.edu. Accessed December 12, 2024. https://learn.genetics.utah.edu/content/basics/telomeres/.

Arrieta, O., E. Varela-Santoyo, E. Soto-Perez-de-Celis, et al. "Metformin Use and Its Effect on Survival in Diabetic Patients with Advanced Non-Small Cell Lung Cancer." *BMC Cancer* 16 (2016): 633. https://pubmed.ncbi.nlm.nih.gov/27519177/.

"Artificial Intelligence (AI) in Cardiovascular Medicine." Mayoclinic.org. Accessed December 9, 2024. https://www.mayoclinic.org/departments-centers/ai-cardiology/overview/ovc-20486648.

"Artificial Pancreas." National Institute of Diabetes and Digestive and Kidney Diseases. Accessed December 10, 2024 https://www.niddk.nih.gov/health-information/diabetes/overview/managing-diabetes/artificial-pancreas.

Ates, H., A. Yetisen, F. Güder, and C. Dincer. "Wearable Devices for the Detection of COVID-19." *Nature Electronics* 4, no. 1 (2021): 13–14. https://www.nature.com/articles/s41928-020-00533-1.

Atkins, D. J., D. C. Y. Heard, and W. Donovan. "Epidemiologic Overview of Individuals with Upper-Limb Loss and Their Reported Research Priorities." *Journal of Prosthetics and Orthotics* 8, no. 1 (1996): 2–11. https://www.semanticscholar.org/paper/Epidemiologic-Overview-of-Individuals-with-Loss-and-Atkins-Heard/c40c7ca9f4ad2c78425b7eaf18d0fdf4f0927a0b.

"A Better Way to Wear a Prosthetic Leg." vesslpro.com. Accessed December 14, 2024. https://www.vesslpro.com.

Bana, B., and F. Cabreiro. "The Microbiome and Aging." *Annual Review of Genetics*, 53 (2019): 239–261. https://pubmed.ncbi.nlm.nih.gov/31487470/.

Barber, C. "3D-Printed Organs May Soon Be a Reality." *Fortune Well*, August 2, 2023, https://fortune.com/well/2023/02/15/3d-printed-organs-may-soon-be-a-reality.

Barcelos, I. P., and R. H. Haas. "CoQ10 and Aging." *Biology (Basel)* 8, no. 2 (1996): 28. https://pubmed.ncbi.nlm.nih.gov/31083534/.

Baruch, E. N., I. Youngster, G. Ben-Betzalel, et al. "Fecal Microbiota Transplant Promotes Response in Immunotherapy-Refractory Melanoma Patients." *Science* 371 (2021): 602–609. https://pubmed.ncbi.nlm.nih.gov/33303685/.

Baton Rouge General. "Does Ozempic Make You Lose More Muscle?" brgeneral. org., June 2024. https://www.brgeneral.org/news-blog/2024/june/does-ozempic-make-you-lose-more-muscle-/#:~:text=A%20recent%20study%20showed%20that,fat%20and%2039%25%20muscle%20mass.

Bauer, Brent. "Is Melatonin a Helpful Sleep Aid—And What Should I Know About Melatonin Side Effects?" Mayoclinic.org. Accessed December 13, 2024. https://www.mayoclinic.org/healthy-lifestyle/adult-health/expert-answers /melatonin-side-effects/faq-20057874#:~:text=The%20hormone%20 melatonin%20plays%20a,from%20insomnia%20and%20jet%20lag.

Beauséjour, C. M., A. Krtolica, F. Galimi, et al. "Reversal of Human Cellular Senescence: Roles of the p53 and p16 Pathways." *EMBO Journal* 22, no. 16 (2003): 4212–4222. https://pubmed.ncbi.nlm.nih.gov/12912919/.

Beker, N., A. Ganz, M. Hulsman, et al. "Association of Cognitive Function Trajectories in Centenarians with Postmortem Neuropathology, Physical Health, and Other Risk Factors for Cognitive Decline." *JAMA Network Open* 4, no. 1 (2021): e2031654. https://pubmed.ncbi.nlm.nih.gov/33449094/.

Benichou, G., Y. Yamada, S.-H. Yun, C. Lin, M. Fray, and G. Tocco. "Immune Recognition and Rejection of Allogeneic Skin Grafts." *Immunotherapy* 3, no. 6 (2011): 757–770. https://pubmed.ncbi.nlm.nih.gov/21668313/.

Benjamin, D. I., J. O. Brett, P. Both, et al. "Multiomics Reveals Glutathione Metabolism as a Driver of Bimodality During Stem Cell Aging." *Cell Metabolism* 35 (2023): 472–486.e6. https://www.sciencedirect.com/science/article /pii/S1550413123000372.

Berman, Robby. "New Study Finds Unusual Genetic Difference in People Who Live to 105." BigThink.com, May 11, 2021. https://bigthink.com/health /semi-supercentenarians-dna-repair/.

Biagi, E., C. Franceschi, S. Rampelli, et al. "Gut Microbiota and Extreme Longevity." *Current Biology* 26 (2016): 1480–1485. https://pubmed.ncbi .nlm.nih.gov/27185560/.

"Bionic Limbs." Australian Academy of Science. Accessed December 14, 2024. https://www.science.org.au/curious/people-medicine/bionic-limbs.

Bjørklund, G., M. Shanaida, R. Lysiuk, et al. "Natural Compounds and Products from an Anti-Aging Perspective." *Molecules* 27, no. 20 (2022): 7084. https:// www.mdpi.com/1420-3049/27/20/7084.

Blagosklonny, M. V. "No Limit to Maximal Lifespan in Humans: How to Beat a 122-Year-Old Record." *Oncoscience* 8 (2021): 110–119. https://www .oncoscience.us/article/547/text/.

Blagosklonny, M. V. "Fasting and Rapamycin: Diabetes versus Benevolent Glucose Intolerance." *Cell Death & Disease* 10, no. 8 (2019a): 607. https:// pubmed.ncbi.nlm.nih.gov/31406105/.

Blagosklonny, M. V. "Rapamycin for the Aging Skin." *Aging (Albany NY)* 11, no. 24 (2019b): 12822–12826. https://pmc.ncbi.nlm.nih.gov/articles/PMC6949048/.

Blagosklonny, M. V. "Methods and Compositions for Preventing or Treating Age-Related Diseases." WO2008022256A2. Accessed March 6, 2025. https:// patents.google.com/patent/WO2008022256A2/en.

Blagosklonny, M. V. "Rapamycin, Proliferation and Geroconversion to Senescence." *Cell Cycle* 17 (2018): 2655–2665. https://pubmed.ncbi.nlm .nih.gov/30541374/.

Blagosklonny, M. V. "Aging and Immortality: Quasi-Programmed Senescence and Its Pharmacologic Inhibition." *Cell Cycle* 5 (2006): 2087–2102. https:// pubmed.ncbi.nlm.nih.gov/17012837/.

Blue Zones. "Food Guidelines." https://www.bluezones.com/recipes/food -guidelines/.

Booth, F. W., and G. N. Ruegegger. "Health Benefits of Exercise." *Cold Spring Harbor Perspectives in Medicine* 8, no. 7 (2018): a029694. https://pubmed .ncbi.nlm.nih.gov/28507196/.

Borovikova, L. V., S. Ivanova, M. Zhang, et al. "Vagus Nerve Stimulation Attenuates the Systemic Inflammatory Response to Endotoxin." *Nature* 405, no. 6785 (2000): 458–462. https://www.nature.com /articles/35013070.

Bouchez, Colette. "Spas: The Risks and Benefits." webmd.com, June 21, 2007. https://www.webmd.com/beauty/features/spas-the-risks-and-benefits.

"Bowel Cancer." www.nhs.uk. Accessed December 14, 2024.

Bozkurt, Y., and E. Karayel. "3D Printing Technology; Methods, Biomedical Applications, Future Opportunities and Trends." *Journal of Materials Research and Technology* 14 (2021): 1430–1450. https://www.sciencedirect .com/science/article/pii/S2238785421007134.

"Brain Basics: Understanding Sleep." National Institute of Neurological Disorders and Stroke. Accessed December 9, 2024. https://www.ninds.nih.gov/health -information/public-education/brain-basics/brain-basics-understanding -sleep#:~:text=In%20fact%2C%20your%20brain%20and,biological%20 purpose%20remains%20a%20mystery.

"Brain-Computer Interface Guide." Emotiv.com. Accessed December 24, 2024. https://www.emotiv.com/blogs/glossary/brain-computer-interface -guide#:~:text=A%20subject%20wearing%20an%20EEG,the%20 robotic%20arm%20will%20wave.

"Brain Health Supplements Market Size 2022–2028." Stratview Research. Accessed December 9, 2024. https://www.stratviewresearch.com/3114 /brain-health-supplements-market.html.

"Brain Stimulation Therapies for Epilepsy." National Institute of Neurological Disorders and Stroke. Accessed December 14, 2024. https://www.ninds.nih.gov /about-ninds/what-we-do/impact/ninds-contributions-approved-therapies /brain-stimulation-therapies-epilepsy.

Branan, Nicole. "Stress Kills Brain Cells Off." Scientificamerican.com, June 1, 2007. https://www.scientificamerican.com/article/stress-kills-brain -cells/.

Bratic, A., and N.-G. Larsson. "The Role of Mitochondria in Aging." *Journal of Clinical Investigation* 123, no. 3 (2013): 951–957. https://pmc.ncbi.nlm.nih.gov/articles/PMC3582127/.

"Breast Cancer in Women." www.nhs.uk. Accessed December 14, 2024. https://www.nhs.uk/conditions/breast-cancer-in-women/.

Breccia, M., and G. Alimena. "Activity and Safety of Dasatinib as Second-Line Treatment or in Newly Diagnosed Chronic Phase Chronic Myeloid Leukemia Patients." *BioDrugs* 25, no. 3 (2011): 147–157. https://pubmed.ncbi.nlm.nih.gov/21528941/.

Breit, S., A. Kupferberg, G. Rogler, and G. Hasler. "Vagus Nerve as Modulator of the Brain-Gut Axis in Psychiatric and Inflammatory Disorders." *Frontiers in Psychiatry* 13, no. 90 (2018): 44. https://pubmed.ncbi.nlm.nih.gov/29593576/.

Bremner, J. D., "Does Stress Damage the Brain?" *Biological Psychiatry* 45 (1999): 797–805. https://pubmed.ncbi.nlm.nih.gov/10202566/.

Bremner, J. D. "Stress and Brain Arophy." *CNS & Neurological Disorders—Drug Targets* 5, no. 5 (2006): 503–512. https://pubmed.ncbi.nlm.nih.gov/17073653/.

Bretthauer, M., and M. Kalager. "Principles, Effectiveness and Caveats in Screening for Cancer." *British Journal of Surgery* 100, no. 1 (2013): 55–65. https://pubmed.ncbi.nlm.nih.gov/23212620/.

Brewster, K. K., and C. Maitlin. "The Effect of Hearing Aids on Mortality." *Lancet Healthy Longevity* 5, no. 1 (2024):e10–e11. https://pubmed.ncbi.nlm.nih.gov/38183991/.

Brody, Barbara. "What Are Nootropics?" *WebMD*, May 22, 2024. https://www.webmd.com/vitamins-and-supplements/features/nootropics-smart-drugs-overview.

"Broken Hip." www.nhs.uk. Accessed December 14, 2024. https://www.nhs.uk/conditions/broken-hip/.

Brown University Health Blog Team. "Inflammaging: What You Should Know About Inflammation and Aging." Brownhealth.org, March 14, 2024. https://www.brownhealth.org/be-well/inflammaging-what-you-should-know-about-inflammation-and-aging.

Buckberry, S., X. Liu, D. Poppe, et al. "Transient Naive Reprogramming Corrects hiPS Cells Functionally and Epigenetically." *Nature* 620, no. 7975 (2023): 863–872. https://pubmed.ncbi.nlm.nih.gov/37587336/.

Buettner, D. "Power 9: Reverse Engineering Longevity." Accessed January 3, 2025. https://www.bluezones.com/2016/11/power-9/.

Bull, M. J., N. T. Plummer. "Part 1: The Human Gut Microbiome in Health and Disease." *Integrative Medicine (Encinitas)* 13, no. 6 (2014): 17–22. https://pubmed.ncbi.nlm.nih.gov/26770121/.

Burtless, Gary. "The Growing Life-Expectancy Gap Between Rich and Poor." Brookings.edu, February 22, 2016. https://www.brookings.edu/articles/the -growing-life-expectancy-gap-between-rich-and-poor/#:~:text=Researchers %20have%20long%20known%20that,efforts%20to%20protect%20 Social%20Security.

Burtner, C. R., and B. K. Kennedy. "Progeria Syndromes and Ageing: What Is the Connection?" *Nature Reviews Molecular Cell Biology* 11, no. 8 (2010): 567–578. https://pubmed.ncbi.nlm.nih.gov/20651707/.

"Caffeinated or Not, Coffee Linked with Longer Life." T. H. Chan School of Public Health, July 5, 2018. https://hsph.harvard.edu/news/coffee -longer-life/#:~:text=People%20who%20drink%20up%20to,or%20 decaf%2C%20brewed%20or%20instant.

Calvo-Malvar, M., A. J. Benitez-Estevez, J. Sánchez-Castro, R. Leis, and F. Gude. "Effects of a Community-Based Behavioral Intervention with a Traditional Atlantic Diet on Cardiometabolic Risk Markers: A Cluster Randomized Controlled Trial ('The GALIAT Study')." *Nutrients* 13, no. 4 (2021): 1211. https://www.mdpi.com/2072-6643/13/4/1211.

"Cancer Cells Drain Energy from Immune Cells." NIH Research Matters, December 7, 2021. https://www.nih.gov/news-events/nih-research-matters /cancer-cells-drain-energy-immune-cells#:~:text=Cancer%20cells%20 must%20evade%20the,these%20proteins%20with%20immune%20cells.

"Cancer Growth Blockers." cancerresearchuk.org. Accessed December 12, 2024. https://www.cancerresearchuk.org/about-cancer/treatment/targeted-cancer -drugs/types/cancer-growth-blockers#:~:text=Tyrosine%20kinase%20 inhibitors&text=Tyrosine%20kinases%20help%20to%20send,kinase%20 are%20called%20multi%20TKIs.

Caobi, A., R. K. Dutta, L. D. Garbinski, et al. "The Impact of CRISPR-Cas9 on Age-Related Disorders: From Pathology to Therapy." *Aging and Disease* 11, no. 4 (2020): 895–915. https://pubmed.ncbi.nlm.nih.gov/32765953/.

"Cardiac Event Monitors." MedlinePlus.gov. Accessed December 10, 2024. https://medlineplus.gov/ency/article/007700.htm.

"Care in the Last Stages of Alzheimer's Disease." National Institute on Aging. Accessed December 9, 2024. https://www.nia.nih.gov/health /alzheimers-caregiving/care-last-stages-alzheimers-disease#:~:text=With%20 dementia%2C%20a%20person%27s%20body,choices%20about%20 their%20health%20care.

"Centenarian Statistics." Chobanian and Avedisian School of Medicine, January 1, 2023. https://www.bumc.bu.edu/centenarian/statistics/#:~:text=A%20 Human%20Model%20of%20Exceptional%20Longevity%20and%20 Aging%20Well&text=Centenarians%20are%20models%20of%20 aging,we%20call%20them%20.

Chai, W., R. V. Cooney, A. A. Franke, et al. "Plasma Coenzyme Q10 Levels and Prostate Cancer Risk: The Multiethnic Cohort Study." *Cancer Epidemiology, Biomarkers & Prevention* 20, no. 4 (2011): 708–710. https://pubmed.ncbi .nlm.nih.gov/21297042/.

Chaib, S., T. Tchkonia, and J. L. Kirkland. "Cellular Senescence and Senolytics: The Path to the Clinic." *Nature Medicine* 28 (2022): 1556–1568. https:// www.nature.com/articles/s41591-022-01923-y.

Chandak, P., N. Byrne, A. Coleman, et al. "Patient-Specific 3D Printing: A Novel Technique for Complex Pediatric Renal Transplantation." *Annals of Surgery* 269 (2019): e18–e23. https://pubmed.ncbi.nlm.nih .gov/30247323/.

Cheatham, S. W., K. R. Stull, M. Fantigrassi, and I. Motel. "The Efficacy of Wearable Activity Tracking Technology as Part of a Weight Loss Program: A Systematic Review." *Journal of Sports Medicine and Physical Fitness* 58, no. 4 (2018): 534–548. https://pubmed.ncbi.nlm.nih.gov/28488834/.

Chen, Y., S. Hamidu, X. Yang, et al. "Dietary Supplements and Natural Products: An Update on Their Clinical Effectiveness and Molecular Mechanisms of Action During Accelerated Biological Aging." *Frontiers in Genetics* 13 (2022): 880421. https://pubmed.ncbi.nlm.nih.gov/35571015/.

Cheng, Chi-Yung, C.-C. Wu, and H.-C. Chen, et al. "Development and Validation of a Deep Learning Pipeline to Measure Pericardial Effusion in Echocardiography." *Frontiers Cardiovascular Medicine* 10, (2023): 1–10. https://doi.org/10.3389/fcvm.2023.1195235;   https://www.frontiersin.org /journals/cardiovascular-medicine/articles/10.3389/fcvm.2023.1195235/full.

Chesney, E., G. M. Goodwin, S. Fazel, et al. "Risks of All-Cause and Suicide Mortality in Mental Disorders: A Meta-Review." *World Psychiatry* 13 (2014): 15360. https://pubmed.ncbi.nlm.nih.gov/24890068/.

Chung, J., M. O. Goodman, T. Huang, et al. "Objectively Regular Sleep Patterns and Mortality in a Prospective Cohort: The Multi-Ethnic Study of Atherosclerosis." *Journal of Sleep Research* 33, no. 1 (2024): e14048. https:// pubmed.ncbi.nlm.nih.gov/37752591/.

City of Hope. "CAR T-Cell Therapy." cancercenter.com, January 12, 2023a. https://www.cancercenter.com/treatment-options/precision-medicine/ immunotherapy/car-t-cell-therapy.

City of Hope. "What's Driving the Improvement in U.S. Cancer Survival Rates?" cancercenter.com, January 26, 2023b. https://www.cancercenter.com/community /blog/2023/01/cancer-survival-rates-are-improving#:~:text=The%20 country's%20cancer%20death%20rate,Cancer%20Society%20(ACS)%20 report.

City of Hope. "Chemotherapy." cancercenter.com, June 1, 2022. https://www .cancercenter.com/treatment-options/chemotherapy.

Claus, S. P., H. Guillou, S. Ellero-Simatos, et al. "The Gut Microbiota: A Major Player in the Toxicity of Environmental Pollutants?" *NPJ Biofilms and Microbiomes* 2 (2016): 16003. https://www.nature.com/articles/npjbiofilms20163.

"Colon Polyps." Mayoclinic.org. Accessed December 9, 2024. https://www.mayoclinic.org/diseases-conditions/colon-polyps/symptoms-causes/syc-20352875.

Comfort Zone. "Understanding Skin Longevity: The Science of Aging Well." Accessed March 6, 2025. https://world.comfortzoneskin.com/blogs/blog/understanding-skin-longevity-the-science-of-aging-well.

Conboy, I. M., M. J. Conboy, A. J. Wagers, E. R. Girma, I. L. Weissman, and T. A. Rando. "Rejuvenation of Aged Progenitor Cells by Exposure to a Young Systemic Environment." *Nature* 433, no. 7027 (2005): 760–764. https://pubmed.ncbi.nlm.nih.gov/15716955/.

Conger, K. "Old Human Cells Rejuvenated with Stem Cell Technology." News Center/Stanford Medicine, March 24, 2020. https://med.stanford.edu/news/all-news/2020/03/old-human-cells-rejuvenated-with-stem-cell-technology.html.

Consumer Reports Blog Fitness Tracker. 2024. https://www.consumerreports.blog/best-fitness-tracker/?utm_source=google&utm_medium=cpc&utm_id=22023431410&utm_content=173642314762&utm_term=fitness%20watch&creativeId=725161974678&adgroupid=173642314762&targetid=kwd-160607678&gad_source=1&gbraid=0AAAAA-BrLGOTsK6cWM7MbSEbyvE-yQ_-n&gclid=Cj0KCQiAs5i8BhDmARIsAGE4xHyyjv-0sOE1yNPt-XDMqigeAgLJAzp1u6IDZUP1JH5RSGvgPrndacIaAnOTEALw_wcB.

"Continuous Glucose Monitoring." National Institute of Diabetes and Digestive and Kidney Diseases. Accessed December 10, 2024. https://www.niddk.nih.gov/health-information/diabetes/overview/managing-diabetes/continuous-glucose-monitoring.

Cook, B., G. Wayne, E. N. Kafali, Z. Liu, C. Shu, and M. Flores. "Trends in Smoking Among Adults with Mental Illness and Association Between Mental Health Treatment and Smoking Cessation." *JAMA* 311 (2014): 172–182. https://pubmed.ncbi.nlm.nih.gov/24399556/.

Costandi, M. "'SuperAgers' with Super Memory Have Super Neurons." BigThink, November 1, 2022. https://bigthink.com/neuropsych/superagers-with-super-memory-have-super-neurons/.

Cribb, L., R. Sha, S. Yiallourou, et al. "Sleep Regularity and Mortality: A Prospective Analysis in the UK Biobank." *eLife* 12 (2023): RP88359. https://elifesciences.org/articles/88359.

Cronkleton, Emily. "Vagus Nerve Stimulation: Benefits, Risks, and More." Medicalnewstoday.com, October 14, 2021. https://www.medicalnewstoday.com/articles/vagus-nerve-stimulation.

Cryan, J. F., and T. G. Dinan. "Mind-Altering Microorganisms: The Impact of the Gut Microbiota on Brain and Behaviour." *Nature Reviews Neuroscience* 13, no. 10 (2012): 701–712. https://pubmed.ncbi.nlm.nih.gov/22968153/.

Culica, D., J. Rohrer, M. Ward, P. Hilsenrath, P. Pomrehn. "Medical Checkups: Who Does Not Get them? *American Journal of Public Health* 92, no. 1 (2002): 88–91.

Cunha, John. "What Is a Good Oxygen Rate by Age?" emedicinehealth. com. Accessed December 10, 2024. https://www.emedicinehealth.com /what_is_a_good_oxygen_rate_by_age/article_em.htm.

"Cutting Calories May Slow the Pace of Aging in Healthy Adults." National Institute on Aging, December 28, 2023. https://www.nia.nih.gov/news /cutting-calories-may-slow-pace-aging-healthy-adults.

Dahlhamer, J., J. Lucas, C. Zelaya, et al. "Prevalence of Chronic Pain and High-Impact Chronic Pain Among Adults—United States 2016." *MMWR—Morbidity and Mortality Weekly Report* 67 (2018): 1001–1006. https://www .cdc.gov/mmwr/volumes/67/wr/mm6736a2.htm.

Dance, A. "Could Getting Rid of Old Cells Turn Back the Clock on Aging?" Big Think, January 12, 2023. https://bigthink.com/health/cell-aging/.

Dantzer, R., and K. W. Kelley. "Stress and Immunity: An Integrated View of Relationships Between the Brain and the Immune System." *Life Sciences* 44 (1989): 1995–2008. https://pubmed.ncbi.nlm.nih.gov/2568569/.

Davar, D., A. K. Dzutsev, J. A. McCulloch, et al. "Fecal Microbiota Transplant Overcomes Resistance to Anti-PD-1 Therapy in Melanoma Patients." *Science* 371 (2021): 595–602. https://pubmed.ncbi.nlm.nih.gov/33542131/.

Davis, G. "Top 5 Medical Applications of 3D Printing." Intelligent Living, August 19, 2022, https://www.intelligentliving.co/top-5-medical-applications -of-3d-printing/.

de Cabo, R., and M. P. Mattson. "Effects of Intermittent Fasting on Health, Aging, and Disease." *New England Journal of Medicine* 381, no. 26 (2019): 2541–2551. https://pubmed.ncbi.nlm.nih.gov/31881139/.

Dehghani, M. A., K. J. Kim, and R. M. Dangelico. "Will Smartwatches Last? Factors Contributing to Intention to Keep Using Smart Wearable Technology." *Telematics and Informatics* 35, no. 2 (2018): 480–490. https://www.researchgate .net/publication/322910768_Will_smartwatches_last_Factors_contributing_ to_intention_to_keep_using_smart_wearable_technology.

De Raeve. "Cochlear Implants in Belgium: Prevalence in Paediatric and Adult Cochlear Implantation." *European Annals of Otorhinolaryngology, Head and Neck Diseases* 133, no. suppl. 1: (2016): S57–S60. https://doi.org/10.1016/j .anorl.2016.04.018.

"Detect Cancers Early—National Cancer Plan." nationalcancerplan.cancerd.gov. Accessed December 10, 2024. https://nationalcancerplan.cancer.gov/goals /detect-cancers-early.

Dhabhar, F. S., "The Short-Term Stress Response—Mother Nature's Mechanism for Enhancing Protection and Performance Under Conditions of Threat, Challenge, and Opportunity." *Frontiers in Neuroendocrinology* 49 (2018): 175–192. https://pubmed.ncbi.nlm.nih.gov/29596867/.

Dhillon, G. S., and K. W. Horch. "Direct Neural Sensory Feedback and Control of a Prosthetic Arm." *IEEE Transactions on Neural Systems and Rehabilitation Engineering* 13, no. 4 (2005): 468–472. https://pubmed.ncbi.nlm.nih.gov/16425828/.

"Diet Review: Mediterranean Diet." Nutrition Source. Accessed December 15, 2024. https://nutritionsource.hsph.harvard.edu/healthy-weight/diet-reviews/mediterranean-diet/#:~:text=%5B6%5D%20Those%20who%20had%20the,who%20had%20the%20lowest%20adherence.&text=Another%20Nurses'%20Health%20Study%20following,of%20dietary%20patterns%20on%20aging.

Digitale, Erin. "New Research Links Brain Injury from Low Oxygen to Specific Cells." med.Stanford.edu, May 6, 2019. https://med.stanford.edu/news/all-news/2019/05/research-links-brain-injury-from-low-oxygen-to-specific-cells.html.

DiGiulio, Sarah. "What Happens in Your Body and Brain While You Sleep." *NBC News*, October 10, 2017. https://www.nbcnews.com/better/health/what-happens-your-body-brain-while-you-sleep-ncna805276.

"Don't Buy into Brain Health Supplements." Harvard Health Publishing, August 8, 2023. https://www.health.harvard.edu/mind-and-mood/dont-buy-into-brain-health-supplements.

Doudna, Jennifer. "Gene Editing Needs to Be for Everyone." *Wired Magazine*, January 8, 2024. https://www.wired.com/story/gene-editing-needs-to-be-for-everyone/.

Drake, C., T. Roehrs, J. Shambroom, and T. Roth. "Caffeine Effects on Sleep Taken 0, 3, or 6 Hours Before Going to Bed." *Journal of Clinical Sleep Medicine* 9, no. 11 (2013): 1195–2000. https://pubmed.ncbi.nlm.nih.gov/24235903/.

Dutton, Gail. "Removing Senescent Cells May Slow, Halt, or Reverse Diseases of Aging." genengnews.com, March 2, 2023. https://www.genengnews.com/topics/drug-discovery/removing-senescent-cells-may-slow-halt-or-reverse-diseases-of-aging/#:~:text=Senolytics%2C%20drugs%20that%20remove%20senescent,to%20prior%20levels%20of%20function.

"Dynamic Stimulation of Visual Cortex Lets Blind People 'See' Shapes." Physicsworld.com June 3, 2020. https://physicsworld.com/a/dynamic-stimulation-of-visual-cortex-lets-blind-people-see-shapes/.

"Eating, Diet, & Nutrition for Colon Polyps." National Institute of Diabetes and Digestive and Kidney Diseases." Accessed December 9, 2024. https://www.niddk.nih.gov/health-information/digestive-diseases/colon-polyps/eating

-diet-nutrition#:~:text=Research%20suggests%20that%20eating%20
less,hot%20dogs%2C%20and%20lunch%20meats.

Effa, Cecilia. "How Long Does Dementia Last? Duration and Life Expectancy." medicalnewstoday.com. Accessed December 31, 2024. https://www.medicalnewstoday.com/articles/how-long-does-dementia-last#life-expectancy.

Ekman, F. K., D. S. Ojala, M. M. Adil, P. A. Lopez, D. V. Schaffer, and T. Gaj. "CRISPR-Cas9-Mediated Genome Editing Increases Lifespan and Improves Motor Deficits in a Huntington's Disease Mouse Model." *Molecular Therapy Nucleic Acids* 17 (2019): 829–839. https://pubmed.ncbi.nlm.nih.gov/31465962/.

"Eliminating Racial/Ethnic Disparities in Health Care: What Are the Options?" October 20, 2008. https://www.kff.org/racial-equity-and-health-policy/issue-brief/eliminating-racialethnic-disparities-in-health-care-what/.

"Epilepsy Basics." Accessed December 24, 2024. https://www.cdc.gov/epilepsy/about/?CDC_AAref_Val=https://www.cdc.gov/epilepsy/about/fast-facts.htm#.

Esteva, A., B. Kuprel, R. A. Novoa, et al. "Dermatologist-Level Classification of Skin Cancer with Deep Neural Networks." *Nature* 542 (2017): 115–118. https://pubmed.ncbi.nlm.nih.gov/28117445/.

Evangelou, C. "Using Stem Cells to Reverse Aging?" Longevity Technology, May 10, 2022. https://longevity.technology/news/using-stem-cells-to-reverse-aging/.

"Evolution of USDA Food Guides to Today's MyPlate." Riley Children's Health, February 23, 2015. https://www.rileychildrens.org/connections/evolution-of-usda-food-guides-to-todays-myplate.

"Exercise Can Boost Your Memory and Thinking Skills." Harvard Health, August 26, 2024. https://www.health.harvard.edu/mind-and-mood/exercise-can-boost-your-memory-and-thinking-skills.

Fadus, M. C., C. Lau, J. Bikhchandani, and H. T. Lynch. "Curcumin: An Age-Old Anti-Inflammatory and Anti-Neoplastic Agent." *Journal of Traditional and Complementary Medicine* 7, no. 3 (2017): 339–346. https://pubmed.ncbi.nlm.nih.gov/28725630/.

Fairbank, R. "You Can Do This 10-Minute Workout at Home with No Equipment." *New York Times*, January 11, 2023. https://www.nytimes.com/2023/01/11/well/move/bodyweight-strength-workout.html.

Fan, Shelly. "A Massive Study Is Revealing Why Exercise Is So Good for Our Health." Singularityhub.com, May 6, 2024. https://singularityhub.com/2024/05/06/a-massive-study-is-revealing-why-exercise-is-so-good-for-our-health/.

Farr, C. "Tech Workers Are Paying $7,000 to Freeze Their Stem Cells in Hope of Extending Life." CNBC.com, May 4, 2018. https://www.cnbc

.com/2018/05/04/tech-workers-are-paying-forever-labs-7000-to-freeze -stem-cells.html.

Fazzino, T. L., D. Jun, L. Chollet-Hinton, and K. Bjorlie. "US Tobacco Companies Selectively Disseminated Hyper-Palatable Foods into the US Food System: Empirical Evidence and Current Implications." *Addiction* 119, no. 1 (2023): 62–71. https://doi.org/10.1111/add.16332.

Feigin, V. L., M. O. Owolabi, on Behalf of the World Stroke Organization—Lancet Neurology Commission. "Pragmatic Solutions to Reduce the Global Burden of Stroke: A World Stroke Organization-*Lancet Neurology* Commission." *Lancet Neurology Commissions* 22, no. 12 (2023): P1160–P1206. https://www .thelancet.com/journals/laneur/article/PIIS1474-4422(23)00277-6/fulltext.

Fiatarone, M. A., E. F. O'Neill, N. D. Ryan, et al. "Exercise Training and Nutritional Supplementation for Physical Frailty in Very Elderly People." *New England Journal of Medicine* 330 (1994): 1769–1775. https://pubmed .ncbi.nlm.nih.gov/8190152/.

Field, M. J., C. K. Cassel, eds. *Approaching Death: Improving Care at the End of Life.* National Academies Press (US), 1997. https://www.ncbi.nlm.nih.gov/books /NBK233601/#:~:text=A%20century%20ago%2C%20communicable%20 diseases,et%20al.%2C%201970.

"First Patient Enrolled in Stage 2 of Pivotal Study of Setpoint Medical's Pioneering Technology for the Treatment of Rheumatoid Arthritis." Setpoint Medical, October 10, 2022. https://setpointmaistg.wpengine.com/first-patient -enrolled-in-stage-2-of-pivotal-study-of-setpoint-medicals-pioneering -technology-for-the-treatment-of-rheumatoid-arthritis/#header-blog.

Fleck, Anna. "Which Cultures Normalize Regular Health Check-Ups?" Statista.com, September 17, 2024. https://www.statista.com/chart/33078 /respondents-who-undergo-regular-medical-check-ups/.

Fontana, L., and F. B. Hu. "Optimal Body Weight for Health and Longevity: Bridging Basic, Clinical, and Population Research." *Aging Cell* 13, no. 3 (2014): 391–400. https://pubmed.ncbi.nlm.nih.gov/24628815/.

Foy, S. P., K. Jacoby, D. A. Bota, et al. "Non-Viral Precision T-Cell Receptor Replacement for Personalized Cell Therapy." *Nature* 615 (2023): 687–696. https://www.nature.com/articles/s41586-022-05531-1.

Friedman, D. "How You Should Change Your Workout Once You Hit 40." *New York Times*, August 1, 2023, Updated August 4, 2023. https://www.nytimes .com/2023/08/01/well/move/workout-fitness-over-40.html.

Galkin, F., P. Mamoshina, A. Aliper, et al. "Human Gut Microbiome Aging Clock Based on Taxonomic Profiling and Deep Learning." *iScience* 23, no. 6 (2020): 101199. https://pubmed.ncbi.nlm.nih.gov/32534441/.

Ganz, A. B., N. Beker, M. Hulsman, et al. "Neuropathology and Cognitive Performance in Self-Reported Cognitively Healthy Centenarians." *Acta*

Neuropathologica Communications 6, no. 1 (2018): 64. https://pubmed.ncbi .nlm.nih.gov/30037350/.

Garagnani, P., J. Marquis, M. Delledonne, et al. "Whole-Genome Sequencing Analysis of Semi-Supercentenarians." *eLife* 10 (2021): e57849. https:// elifesciences.org/articles/57849.

Garay, R. P. "Recent Clinical Trials Registered in ClinicalTrials.gov and clinicaltrialsregister.eu." *Expert Opinion on Investigational Drugs* 30, no. 7 (2021): 749–758. https://eurekamag.com/research/091/393/091393090.ph p?srsltid=AfmBOoq4dQV4Elf1yCYgoO-H1yjmM2wZE6YbtXHFLluMg V5Wr5DVMz4-.

Gensollen, T., S. S. Iyer, D. L. Kasper, and R. S. Blumberg. "How Colonization by Microbiota in Early Life Shapes the Immune System." *Science* 352, no. 6285 (2016): 539–544. https://pubmed.ncbi.nlm.nih.gov/27126036/.

George, M. S., H. A. Sackeim, A. J. Rush, et al. "Vagus Nerve Stimulation: A New Tool for Brain Research and Therapy." *Biological Psychiatry* 47, no. 4 (2000): 287–295. https://pubmed.ncbi.nlm.nih.gov/10686263/.

Gerontology Research Group. "Supercentenarians." Accessed January 3, 2025. https://grg.org/sc/scindex.html.

"Getting Good Sleep Could Add Years to Your Life." American College of Cardiology, February 23, 2023. https://www.acc.org/About-ACC /Press-Releases/2023/02/22/21/35/Getting-Good-Sleep-Could-Add-Years -to-Your-Life.

Ghlichloo, I., and V. Gerriets. "Nonsteroidal Anti-Inflammatory Drugs (NSAIDS)." ncbi.nlm.nih.gov, May 1, 2023. https://www.ncbi.nlm.nih .gov/books/NBK547742/#:~:text=NSAIDs%20are%20a%20class%20 of,points%20for%20providers%20regarding%20NSAIDs.

Gierman, H. J., K. Fortney, J. C. Roach, et al. "Whole-Genome Sequencing of the World's Oldest People." *PLoS One* 9, no. 11 (2014):e112430. https:// journals.plos.org/plosone/article?id=10.1371/journal.pone.0112430.

Gilchrest, B. A., F. B. Blog, and G. Szabo. "Effects of Aging and Chronic Sun Exposure on Melanocytes in Human Skin." *Journal of Investigative Dermatology* 73 (1979): 141–143. https://pubmed.ncbi.nlm.nih.gov/88488/.

Gilhar, A., Y. Ullmann, R. Karry, et al. "Ageing of Human Epidermis: The Role of Apoptosis, Fas and Telomerase." *British Journal of Dermatology* 150 (2004): 56–63. https://pubmed.ncbi.nlm.nih.gov/14746617/.

Glass, J., K. L. Lanctôt, N. Herrmann, B. A. Sproule, and U. E. Busto. "Sedative Hypnotics in Older People with Insomnia: Meta-Analysis of Risks and Benefits." *BMJ* 331, no. 7526 (2005): 1169. https://pubmed.ncbi.nlm.nih.gov/16284208/.

Glassman, Suzie. "Your Guide to the Best TV Hearing Devices." Forbes.com, February 12, 2024. https://www.forbes.com/health/hearing-aids/best -tv-hearing-devices/#:~:text=Wireless%20headphones%20and%20 Bluetooth%20hearing,captioning%20as%20a%20free%20alternative.

Global Data. "3D-Printed Organs and Their Affordability." Medical Device Network, June 15, 2022. https://www.medicaldevice-network.com/analyst -comment/3d-printed-organs-affordability/.

"Go Further with Cancer Screening." Galleri.com. Accessed December 9, 2024. https://www.galleri.com.

Godman, H., "Regular Exercise Changes the Brain to Improve Memory, Thinking Skills." Harvard Health Blog, April 9, 2014, https://www.health. harvard.edu/blog/regular-exercise-changes-brain-improve-memory-thinking -skills-201404097110

Godman, Heidi. "Wearable Fitness Trackers May Aid Weight-Loss Efforts." health. harvard.edu, July 1, 2021. https://www.health.harvard.edu/staying-healthy /wearable-fitness-trackers-may-aid-weight-loss-efforts.

Gómez-Linton, D. R., S. Alavez, A. Alarcón-Aguilar, N. E. López-Diazguerrero, M. Konigsberg, and L. J. Pérez-Flores. "Some Naturally Occurring Compounds That Increase Longevity and Stress Resistance in Model Organisms of Aging." *Biogerontology* 20, no. 5 (2019): 583–603. https:// pubmed.ncbi.nlm.nih.gov/31187283/.

Gonzales, A. G., R. Etienne-Cummings, and P. Georgiou. "Closed-Loop Bioelectronic Medicine for Diabetes Management." *Bioelectronic Medicine* 6 (2020): 11. https:// bioelecmed.biomedcentral.com/articles/10.1186/s42234-020-00046-4.

Gonzales, M. M., V. R. Garbarino, E. Marques Zilli, et al. "Senolytic Therapy to Modulate the Progression of Alzheimer's Disease (SToMP-AD)—Outcomes from the First Clinical Trial of Senolytic Therapy for Alzheimer's Disease." *Research Square* [Preprint]. 24 (2023): rs.3.rs-2809973. https://pubmed.ncbi .nlm.nih.gov/35098970/.

Google. "Longevity." Google Play. Accessed December 10, 2024. https://play.google .com/store/apps/details?id=com.netpulse.mobile.longevitynetwork&hl=en_US.

Greene, Karima. "A Longevity Expert Who Studied People Who Live to 110 on How Humanity and AI Will Master Aging." CNBC.com, March 7, 2023. https://www.cnbc.com/2023/03/06/stanford-expert-on-the-super-old-on -how-humans-and-ai-will-beat-aging.html#:~:text=We%20use%20AI%20 and%20machine,help%20everyone%20age%20more%20successfully.

Griffin, J. "Changing Life Expectancy Throughout History." *Journal of the Royal Society of Medicine* 101, no. 12 (2008): 577. https://journals.sagepub.com/ doi/10.1258/jrsm.2008.08k037.

Gupta, M., and J. Rathored. "Hyperbaric Oxygen Therapy: Future Prospects in Regenerative Therapy and Anti-Aging." *Aging*, May 1, 2024. https://www .frontiersin.org/journals/aging/articles/10.3389/fragi.2024.1368982/full.

Hachmo, Y., A. Hadanny, R. A. Hamed, et al. "Hyperbaric Oxygen Therapy Increases Telomere Length and Decreases Immunosenescence in Isolated Blood Cells: A Prospective Trial." *Aging (Albany NY)* 18, no. 12 (2020): 22445–22456. https://pubmed.ncbi.nlm.nih.gov/33206062/.

Han, S. S., I. Park, S. E. Chang, et al. "Augmented Intelligence Dermatology: Deep Neural Networks Empower Medical Professionals in Diagnosing Skin Cancer and Predicting Treatment Options for 134 Skin Disorders." *Journal of Investigative Dermatology* 40 (2020): 1753–1761. https://pubmed.ncbi.nlm. nih.gov/32243882/.

Hanaphy, P. "Collplant to Trial 3D Bioprinted Breast Implants in Breakthrough Animal Study." 3Dprintingindustry.com, March 31, 2022. https://3dprintingindustry.com/news/collplant-to-trial-3d-bioprinted -breast-implants-in-breakthrough-animal-study-207127/.

Harrison, D., R. Strong, Z. D. Sharp, et al. "Rapamycin Fed Late in Life Extends Lifespan in Genetically Heterogeneous Mice." *Nature* 460 (2009): 392–395. https://pmc.ncbi.nlm.nih.gov/articles/PMC2786175/.

Harvard Health Publishing Staff. "Intermittent Fasting: The Positive News Continues." Health.Harvard.edu, February 28, 2021, https://www.health .harvard.edu/blog/intermittent-fasting-surprising-update-2018062914156.

Hayasaki, E. "Has This Scientist Found the Fountain of Youth?" *MIT Technology Review*, August 8, 2019. https://www.technologyreview.com /2019/08/08/65461/scientist-fountain-of-youth-epigenome/.

"Health Disparities Overview." ncsl.org. Accessed December 30, 2024. https://www .ncsl.org/health/health-disparities-overview#:~:text=For%20example%2C%20 Black%20people%20have,more%20likely%20to%20suffer%20strokes.

"Health Risks of Overweight & Obesity." National Institute of Diabetes and Digestive and Kidney Diseases. Accessed December 15, 2024. https:// www.niddk.nih.gov/health-information/weight-management/adult -overweight-obesity/health-risks.

Healthline Editorial Staff. "Colonic (Colorectal) Polyps." Healthline, September 4, 2019. https://www.healthline.com/health/colorectal-polyps.

Hessler, Brian. "5 Tips to Manage Stress." Mayoclinichealthsystem.org. Accessed December 14, 2024. https://www.mayoclinichealthsystem.org /hometown-health/speaking-of-health/5-tips-to-manage-stress.

Hipp, Deb. "Normal Resting Heart Rate by Age (Chart)." Forbes.com, March 28, 2024. https://www.forbes.com/health/wellness/normal-heart-rate-by-age/.

Hirotsu, C., S. Tufik, and M. L. Andersen. "Interactions Between Sleep, Stress, and Metabolism: From Physiological to Pathological Conditions." *Sleep Science* 8, no. 3 (2015): 143–152. https://pubmed.ncbi.nlm.nih.gov/26779321/.

Holt-Lunstad, J., T. B. Smith, and J. B. Layton. "Social Relationships and Mortality Risk: A Meta-Analytic Review." *PLoS Medicine* 7, no. 7 (2010):e1000316. https://pubmed.ncbi.nlm.nih.gov/20668659/.

Hossmann, K. A. "The Hypoxic Brain: Insights from Ischemia Research." *Advances in Experimental Medicine and Biology* 474 (1999): 155–169. https:// pubmed.ncbi.nlm.nih.gov/10635000/.

Houser, K. "New CRISPR Cancer Treatment Tested in Humans for First Time." November 19, 2022. https://www.freethink.com/health/crispr-cancer-treatment.

"How Music Can Improve Your Memory and Concentration." Twelve Tone Music School, September 26, 2024. https://www.twelvetonemusicschool .com/how-music-can-improve-your-memory-and-concentration/how-music -can-improve-your-memory-and-concentration/#:~:text=Music%20can%20 also%20influence%20our,or%20has%20a%20personal%20meaning.

"How Stress Affects Your Health." apa.org, October 21, 2024. https://www.apa .org/topics/stress/health.

Howley, Daniel. "Apple's Big Health Updates Are Impressive and Meant to Keep Users Coming Back for Years." finance.yahoo.com, September 14, 2024. https://finance.yahoo.com/news/apples-big-health-updates-are-impressive -and-meant-to-keep-users-coming-back-for-years-212623985.html#.

Huang, A. R., K. Jiang, F. R. Lin, J. A. Deal, and N. S. Reed. "Hearing Loss and Dementia Prevalence in Older Adults in the US." *JAMA* 329 (2023): 171–173. https://pubmed.ncbi.nlm.nih.gov/36625819/.

Hublin, C., M. Partinen, M. Koskenvuo, and J. Kaprio. "Sleep and Mortality: A Population-Based 22-Year Follow-Up Study." *Sleep* 30, no. 10 (2007): 1245–1253. https://academic.oup.com/sleep/article-abstract/30/10/1245/2 696836?redirectedFrom=fulltext.

"Hyperbaric Oxygen Therapy." hopkinsmedicine.org. Accessed December 16, 2024. https://www.hopkinsmedicine.org/health/treatment-tests-and-therapies /hyperbaric-oxygen-therapy#.

Ilyas, A., E. Chesney, and R. Patel. "Improving Life Expectancy in People with Serious Mental Illness: Should We Place More Emphasis on Primary Prevention?" *British Journal of Psychiatry* 211, no. 4 (2017): 194–197. https:// pubmed.ncbi.nlm.nih.gov/28882826/.

"Immune Checkpoint Inhibitors." National Cancer Institute. Accessed December 12, 2024. https://www.cancer.gov/about-cancer/treatment/types /immunotherapy/checkpoint-inhibitors.

"Implantable MyoElectric Sensors (IMES) for Prosthetic Control in Transhumeral Amputees (TH-IMES)." clinicaltrials.gov, August 23, 2018. https://clinicaltrials.gov/study/NCT03644394.

"Improving Health and Longevity Among People with Serious Mental Illness." Johns Hopkins Alacrity Center for Health and Longevity in Mental Illness. Accessed December 9, 2024. https://publichealth.jhu.edu/alacrity -center-for-health-and-longevity-in-mental-illness#:~:text=People%20 with%20serious%20mental%20illness%20currently%20die%20 10%2D20,earlier%20than%20the%20overall%20population.

Inamura, K. "Gut Microbiota Contributes Towards Immunomodulation Against Cancer: New Frontiers in Precision Cancer Therapeutics." *Seminars in Cancer*

Biology 70 (2021): 11–23. https://www.sciencedirect.com/science/article/pii /S1044579X20301425.

"Intermittent Fasting Explained: Benefits and How to Do It Safely." Cleveland Clinic, August 9, 2024; https://health.clevelandclinic.org/intermittent -fasting-4-different-types-explained/.

"Introduction to Medical 3D Printing: What Is Actually Possible?" Sculpteo. com. Accessed December 10, 2024. https://www.sculpteo.com /en/3d-learning-hub/applications-of-3d-printing/medical-3d-printing/.

Javaid, M., A. Haleem, R. P. Singh, and R. Suman. "3D Printing Applications for Healthcare Research and Development." *Global Health Journal* 6, no. 4 (2022): 217–226. https://www.sciencedirect.com/science/article/pii /S2414644722000744.

Johnson, E. O., G. C. Babis, K. C. Soultanis, and P. N. Soucacos. "Functional Neuroanatomy of Proprioception." *Journal of Surgical Orthopaedic Advances* 17, no. 3 (2008): 159–164. https://pubmed.ncbi.nlm.nih.gov/18851800/.

Johnson, Jon. "What to Know About Vascular Dementia." *Medical News Today*, February 6, 2020. https://www.medicalnewstoday.com/articles /vascular-dementia.

Johnson, S. *Extra Life: A Short History of Living Longer.* Riverhead Books, 2021a.

Johnson, S. "The 3D Printed Bionic Arm That Is Disrupting the Prosthetics Industry." *Big Think*, August 18, 2021b. https://bigthink.com/the-present /bionic-arm/.

Jones, Julie Floyd. "How to Exercise for Better Brain Health, According to Experts." EatingWell, June 22, 2021. https://www.yahoo.com/lifestyle/ exercise-better-brain-health-according-181716432.html.

Jones, Julie Floyd. "What Happens to Your Brain When You Exercise, According to Doctors." EatingWell, 2025. https://www.eatingwell.com/ why-exercise-is-good-for-your-brain-8778043

Joseph, Richard. "Should You Try Intermittent Fasting for Weight Loss?" health.harvard.edu, July 28, 2022. https://www.health.harvard.edu/blog /should-you-try-intermittent-fasting-for-weight-loss-202207282790.

Jozsi, A. C., W. W. Campbell, L. Joseph, S. L. Davey, and W. J. Evans. "Changes in Power with Resistance Training in Older and Younger Men and Women." *Journals of Gerontology, Series A: Biological Sciences and Medical Sciences* 54 (1999): M591–M596. https://pubmed.ncbi.nlm.nih.gov/10619323/.

Kaeberlein, M. "How Healthy Is the Healthspan Concept?" *Geroscience* 40, no. 4 (2018): 361–364. https://pubmed.ncbi.nlm.nih.gov/30084059/.

Kaiser, J. "Gene Therapy Beats Premature-aging Syndrome in Mice." *Science* 371, no. 6525 (2021):114. https://doi.org/10.1126/science.371.6525.114.

Kaiser, J. "'Incredible' Gene-Editing Result in Mice Inspires Plans to Treat Premature-Aging Syndrome in Children." *Science* (January 6, 2021).

https://jaivikshastram.com/2021/01/incredible-gene-editing-result-in
-mice-inspires-plans-to-treat-premature-aging-syndrome-in-children
-sciencemagazine-jaivikshastram/

Kane, M. J., P. P. Breen, F. Quondamatteo, and G. ÓLaighin. "BION Microstimulators: A Case Study in the Engineering of an Electronic Implantable Medical Device." *Medical Engineering & Physics* 33, no. 1 (2011): 7–16. https://pubmed.ncbi.nlm.nih.gov/21087890/.

Kang, H. T. "Current Status of the National Health Screening Programs in South Korea." *Korean Journal of Family Medicine* 43, no. 3 (2022): 168–173. https://pmc.ncbi.nlm.nih.gov/articles/PMC9136500/.

Kang, H. S., and M. Exworthy. "Wearing the Future-Wearables to Empower Users to Take Greater Responsibility for Their Health and Care: Scoping Review." *JMIR mHealth and uHealth* 10, no. 7 (2022): e35684. https://mhealth.jmir.org/2022/7/e35684.

Karl, J. P., A. M. Hatch, S. M. Arcidiacono, et al. "Effects of Psychological, Environmental and Physical Stressors on the Gut Microbiota." *Frontiers in Microbiology* 9 (2018): 2013. https://pmc.ncbi.nlm.nih.gov/articles/PMC6143810/.

Kebbe, M., J. R. Sparks, E. W. Flanagan, and L. M. Redman. "Beyond Weight Loss: Current Perspectives on the Impact of Calorie Restriction on Healthspan and Lifespan." *Expert Review of Endocrinology & Metabolism* 16 (2021): 95–108. https://pubmed.ncbi.nlm.nih.gov/33957841/.

"Keep Your Brain Young with Music." Johns Hopkins Medicine. Accessed December 9, 2024. https://www.hopkinsmedicine.org/health/wellness-and-prevention/keep-your-brain-young-with-music#:~:text=It%20provides%20a%20total%20brain,%2C%20mental%20alertness%2C%20and%20memory.

Kessler, R. C., A. Sonnega, E. Bromet, M. Hughes, and C. B. Nelson. "Posttraumatic Stress Disorder in the National Comorbidity Survey." *Archives of General Psychiatry* 52, no. 12 (1995): 1048–1060. https://pubmed.ncbi.nlm.nih.gov/7492257/.

Keys, A. B. *Seven Countries: A Multivariate Analysis of Death and Coronary Heart Disease.* Harvard University Press, 1980.

Keys, A. B., and M. Keys. *How to Eat Well and Stay Well, the Mediterranean Way.* Doubleday, 1975. https://www.amazon.com/How -eat-well-stay-Mediterranean/dp/0385009062.

"Keys to Long Life? Not What You Might Expect." sciencedaily.com, March 12, 2011. https://www.sciencedaily.com/releases/2011/03/110311153541 .htm#google_vignette. https://www.sciencedaily.com/releases/2011/03/1103 w25151643.htm#:~:text=In%20one%20of%20the%20most,to%20live%20 longer%20than%20others.

Khansari, D. N., A. J. Murgo, and R. E. Faith. "Effects of Stress on the Immune System." *Immunology Today* 11 (1990): 170–175. https://pubmed.ncbi.nlm.nih.gov/2186751/.

Kim, K. L., W. S. Lee, J.-H. Kim, J.-K. Bae, and W. Jin. "Safety and Efficacy of the Intra-Articular Injection of Mesenchymal Stem Cells for the Treatment of Osteoarthritic Knee: A 5-Year Follow-Up Study." *Stem Cells Translational Medicine* 11, no. 6 (2022): 586–596. https://pubmed.ncbi.nlm.nih.gov/35567774/.

Kimura, M., J. V. Hjelmborg, J. P. Gardner, et al. "Telomere Length and Mortality: A Study of Leukocytes in Elderly Danish Twins." *American Journal of Epidemiology* 167, no. 7 (2008): 799–806. https://pubmed.ncbi.nlm.nih.gov/18270372/.

Kirkendoll, Shantell M. "Gut Microbiome May Hold the Key to Healthy Aging." Duke University School of Medicine, March 28, 2023. https://medschool.duke.edu/news/gut-microbiome-may-hold-key-healthy-aging.

Kirkland, J. L., and T. Tchkonia. "Senolytic Drugs: From Discovery to Translation." *Journal of Internal Medicine* 288, no. 5 (2020): 518–536. https://pubmed.ncbi.nlm.nih.gov/32686219/.

Klein, E. A., D. Richards, A. Cohn, et al. "Clinical Validation of a Targeted Methylation-Based Multi-Cancer Early Detection Test Using an Independent Validation Set." *Annals of Oncology* 32, no. 9 (2021): 1167–1177. https://pubmed.ncbi.nlm.nih.gov/34176681/.

Klein, L., T. Gao, N. Barzilai, and S. Milman. "Association Between Sleep Patterns and Health in Families with Exceptional Longevity." *Frontiers in Medicine* 4 (2017): 214. https://pmc.ncbi.nlm.nih.gov/articles/PMC5727046/.

Korat, A. V. A., M. K. Shea, P. F. Jacques, et al. "Dietary Protein Intake in Midlife in Relation to Healthy Aging—Results from the Prospective Nurses' Health Study Cohort." *American Journal of Clinical Nutrition* 199, no. 2 (2024): 271–282. https://pubmed.ncbi.nlm.nih.gov/38309825/.

Kowald, A., and T. B. L. Kirkwood. "Senolytics and the Compression of Late-Life Mortality." *Experimental Gerontology* 155 (2021): 111588. https://pubmed.ncbi.nlm.nih.gov/34637949/.

Kozebek, J. "How Gene Editing Could Ruin Human Evolution." *Time*, January 9, 2017. https://time.com/4626571/crispr-gene-modification-evolution/.

Kritchevsky, S. B., K. M. Beavers, M. E. Miller, et al. "Intentional Weight Loss and All-Cause Mortality: A Meta-Analysis of Randomized Clinical Trials." *PLoS One* 10 (2015): e0121993. https://pubmed.ncbi.nlm.nih.gov/25794148/.

Kubala, Jillian. "Can You Overdose on Vitamins?" Healthline, January 20, 2020. https://www.healthline.com/nutrition/can-you-overdose-on-vitamins.

Kwo, L. "Contributed: Top 8 Healthcare Uses for 3D Printing." *Mobile Health News*, October 25, 2021. https://www.mobihealthnews.com/news/contributed-top-8-healthcare-uses-3d-printing.

Lakowski, B., and H. Siegfried. "Determination of Life-Span in Caenorhabditis Elegans by Four Clock Genes." *Science* 272, no. 5264 (1996): 1010–1013. https://pubmed.ncbi.nlm.nih.gov/8638122/.

Landry, M. J., C. P. Ward, K. M. Cunanan, et al. "Cardiometabolic Effects of Omnivorous vs Vegan Diets in Identical Twins: A Randomized Clinical Trial." *JAMA Network Open* 6, no. 11 (2023): e2344457. https://jamanetwork.com /journals/jamanetworkopen/fullarticle/2812392.

Laricchia, Federica. "Wearables Unit Shipments Worldwide by Vendor from 1st Quarter 2014 to 1st Quarter 2024." Statista.com, October 8, 2024. https://www.statista.com/statistics/435933/quarterly-wearables-shipments -worldwide-by-vendor/.

Lawton, G. "The Radical New Theory That Wrinkles Actually Cause Ageing." NewScientist, March 28, 2023. https://www.newscientist.com /article/2366093-the-radical-new-theory-that-wrinkles-actually-cause-ageing/.

Learn, J. R. "What You Should Know About Rapamycin and If It Can Really Slow Aging." *Discover Magazine*, August 29, 2024. https://www. discovermagazine.com/health/what-you-should-know-about-rapamycin -and-if-it-can-really-slow-aging.

LeBlanc, Kelly. "Blue Zone Diet of Costa Rica." health, usnews.com, May 25, 2023. https://health.usnews.com/wellness/food/articles/blue-zone-diet-of-costa-rica.

Lee, K. H., H. Y. Lee, I. Park, et al. "Life Stress, Sleep Disturbance and Depressive Symptoms: The Moderating Role of Prefrontal Activation During Emotion Regulation." *Australian & New Zealand Journal of Psychiatry* 56, no. 6 (2022): 709–720. https://pubmed.ncbi.nlm.nih.gov/34254527/.

Lee, M. B., C. M. Hill, A. Bitto, and M. Kaeberlein. "Antiaging Diets: Separating Fact from Fiction." *Science* 274 (2021): eabe7365. https://pubmed.ncbi.nlm. nih.gov/34793210/.

Leitner, W. W., H. Ying, and N. P. Restifo. "DNA and RNA-Based Vaccines: Principles, Progress and Prospects." *Vaccine* 18, nos. 9–10 (1999): 765–777. https://pubmed.ncbi.nlm.nih.gov/10580187/.

LeMoult, J., A. M. Battaglini, B. Grocott, E. Jopling, K. Rnic, and L. Yang. "Advances in Stress and Depression Research." *Current Opinion in Psychiatry* 36, no. 1 (2023): 8–13. https://pubmed.ncbi.nlm.nih.gov/36194148/.

Lennon, Anne-Marie, Adam H. Buchanan, I. Kinde, et al. "Feasibility of Blood Testing Combined with PET-CT to Screen for Cancer and Guide Intervention." *Science* 369, no. 6499 (2020). https://www.science.org /doi/10.1126/science.abb9601.

Levine, M. E., A. T. Lu, A. Quach, et al. "An Epigenetic Biomarker of Aging for Lifespan and Healthspan." *Aging (Albany NY)* 10, no. 4 (2018): 573–591. https://pubmed.ncbi.nlm.nih.gov/29676998/.

Li, C., T. R. P. Bishop, F. Imamura, et al. "Meat Consumption and Incident Type 2 Diabetes: An Individual-Participant Federated Meta-Analysis of

1·97 Milion Adults with 100 000 Incident Cases from 31 Cohorts in 20 Countries." *Lancet Diabetes & Endocrinology* 12, no. 9 (2024): 619–630. https://pubmed.ncbi.nlm.nih.gov/39174161/.

Li, H., F. Qian, L. Han, et al. "Association of Healthy Sleep Patterns with Risk of Mortality and Life Expectancy at Age of 30 Years: A Population-Based Cohort Study." *QJM* 117, no. 3 (2024): 177–186. https://pubmed.ncbi.nlm.nih.gov/37831896/.

Li, X., C. Li, W. Zhang, Y. Wang, P. Qian, and H. Huang. "Inflammation and Aging: Signaling Pathways and Intervention Therapies." *Signal Transduction and Targeted Therapy* 8 (2023): 239. https://www.nature.com/articles/s41392-023-01502-8.

Li, Z., X. Bai, T. Peng, et al. "New Insights into the Skin Microbial Communities and Skin Aging." *Frontiers in Microbiology* 11 (2020): 565549. https://pubmed.ncbi.nlm.nih.gov/33193154/.

Lindberg, Sara. "'Brain Exercises.' in '13 Brain Exercises to Help Keep You Mentally Sharp.'" *Healthline*, February 17, 2023a. https://www.healthline.com/health/mental-health/brain-exercises#Brain-exercises.

Lindberg, Sara. "'Focus' in '13 Brain Exercises to Help Keep You Mentally Sharp.'" *Healthline*, February 17, 2023b. https://www.healthline.com/health/mental-health/brain-exercises#focus.

"Liquid Biopsy." Cleveland Clinic.org. Accessed December 9, 2024. https://my.clevelandclinic.org/health/diagnostics/23992-liquid-biopsy.

Listek, V. "Top 10 Bioprinting Stories of 2020: Paving the Way to Future Organ Transplants." 3Dprint.com, December 23, 2020. https://3dprint.com/276967/top-10-bioprinting-stories-of-2020-paving-the-way-to-future-organ-transplants/.

Liu, D., A. Ahmet, L. Ward, et al. "A Practical Guide to the Monitoring and Management of the Complications of Systemic Corticosteroid Therapy." *Allergy, Asthma & Clinical Immunology* 9, no. 1 (2013): 30. https://pubmed.ncbi.nlm.nih.gov/23947590/.

Liu, X., J. Huang, T. Chen, et al. "Yamanaka Factors Critically Regulate the Developmental Signaling Network in Mouse Embryonic Stem Cells." *Cell Research* 18, no. 12 (2008): 1177–1189. https://pubmed.ncbi.nlm.nih.gov/19030024/.

Liu, Y., Y. Baba, H. Tsutsuki, et al. "*Fusobacterium Nucleatum* Confers Chemoresistance by Modulating Autophagy in Oesophageal Squamous Cell Carcinoma." *British Journal of Cancer* 124 (2021): 963–974. https://www.nature.com/articles/s41416-020-01198-5.

Liu, Y., A. Jain, C. Eng, et al. "A Deep Learning System for Differential Diagnosis of Skin Diseases." *Nature Medicine* 26 (2020): 900–908. https://pubmed.ncbi.nlm.nih.gov/32424212/.

Loeb, G. E., R. A. Peck, W. H. Moore, and K. Hood. "BION System for Distributed Neural Prosthetic Interfaces." *Medical Engineering & Physics* 23 (2001): 9–18. https://pubmed.ncbi.nlm.nih.gov/11344003/.

Loftfield, E., M. S. Shiels, B. I. Graubard, et al. "Associations of Coffee Drinking with Systemic Immune and Inflammatory Markers." *Cancer Epidemiology, Biomarkers & Prevention* 24, no. 7 (2015): 1052–1060. https://pubmed.ncbi .nlm.nih.gov/25999212/.

López-Otín, C., M. A. Blasco, L. Partridge, M. Serrano, and G. Kroemer. "Hallmarks of Aging: An Expanding Universe." *Cell* 186, no. 2 (2023): 243–278. https://www.cell.com/cell/fulltext/S0092-8674(22)01377-0.

López-Otín, C., M. A. Blasco, L. Partridge, M. Serrano, and G. Kroemer. "The Hallmarks of Aging." *Cell* 153, no. 6 (2013): 1194–1217. https://www.cell .com/cell/fulltext/S0092-8674(13)00645-4.

Lozano, Andres. "Deep Brain Stimulation: Challenges to Integrating Stimulation Technology with Human Neurobiology, Neuroplasticity, and Neural Repair." *Journal of Rehabilitation Research & Development* 38, no. 6 (2001): x–xix.

Lu, Y., B. Brommer, X. Tian, et al. "Reprogramming to Recover Youthful Epigenetic Information and Restore Vision." *Nature* 588 (2020): 124–129. https://www.nature.com/articles/s41586-020-2975-4.

Lucassen, P. J., C. A. Oomen, E. F. G. Naninck, et al. "Regulation of Adult Neurogenesis and Plasticity by (Early) Stress, Glucocorticoids, and Inflammation." *Cold Spring Harbor Perspectives in Biology* 7, no. 9 (2015): a021303. https://pmc.ncbi.nlm.nih.gov/articles/PMC4563706/.

Ludwig, F. C., and R. M. Elashoff. "Mortality in Syngeneic Rat Parabionts of Different Chronological Age." *Transactions of the New York Academy of Sciences* 34, no. 7 (1972): 582–587. https://pubmed.ncbi.nlm.nih.gov/4507935/.

Lunjani, N., S. Ahearn-Ford, F. S. Dube, C. Hlela, and L. O'Mahony. "Mechanisms of Microbe-Immune System Dialogue Within the Skin." *Genes & Immunity* 22 (2021): 276–288. https://pubmed.ncbi.nlm.nih.gov/33993202/.

Lupien, S. J., B. S. McEwen, M. R. Gunnar, and C. Heim. "Effects of Stress Throughout the Lifespan on the Brain, Behaviour and Cognition." *Nature Reviews Neuroscience* 10 (2009): 434–445. https://www.nature.com/articles/nrn2639.

Madeo, F., M. A. Bauer, D. Carmona-Gutierrez, and G. Kroemer. "Spermidine: A Physiological Autophagy Inducer Acting as an Anti-Aging Vitamin in Humans?" *Autophagy* 15, no. 1 (2019): 165–168. https://pubmed.ncbi.nlm .nih.gov/30306826/.

Madison, K. C. "Barrier Function of the Skin: 'La Raison d'Etre' of the Epidermis." *Journal of Investigative Dermatology* 121 (2003): 231–241. https://pubmed .ncbi.nlm.nih.gov/12880413/.

Makiso, M. U., Y. B. Tola, O. Ogah, and F. L. Endale. "Bioactive Compounds in Coffee and Their Role in Lowering the Risk of Major Public Health

Consequences: A Review." *Food Science & Nutrition* 12, no. 2 (2023): 734–764. https://pubmed.ncbi.nlm.nih.gov/38370073/.

Malberg, J. E., A. J. Eisch, E. J. Nestler, and R. S. Duman. "Chronic Antidepressant Treatment Increases Neurogenesis in Adult Rat Hippocampus." *Journal of Neuroscience* 20, no. 24 (2000): 9104–9110. https://pubmed.ncbi.nlm.nih.gov/11124987/.

Malík, M., and P. Tlustoš. "Nootropics as Cognitive Enhancers: Types, Dosage and Side Effects of Smart Drugs." *Nutrients* 14, no. 16 (2022): 3367. https://pmc.ncbi.nlm.nih.gov/articles/PMC9415189/.

Mammoser, G. "Eating a Healthy Diet with Less Sugar May Slow Signs of Biological Aging." healthline.com, July 31, 2024. https://www.healthline.com/health-news/healthy-diet-less-sugar-biological-aging.

Manning, K. M., K. S. Hall, R. Sloane, et al. "Longitudinal Analysis of Physical Function in Older Adults: The Effects of Physical Inactivity and Exercise Training." *Aging Cell* 23, no. 1 (2024): e13987. https://pubmed.ncbi.nlm.nih.gov/37681737/. (See also Vaishya and Vaish)

Marino, N., G. Putignano, S. Cappilli, et al. "Towards AI-Driven Longevity Research: An Overview." *Frontiers in Aging* 4 (2023): 1057204. https://www.frontiersin.org/journals/aging/articles/10.3389/fragi.2023.1057204/full.

Marshall, M. "The Unexpected Ways Your Skin Impacts Your Health and Longevity." *NewScientist*, February 28, 2024. https://www.newscientist.com/article/mg26134802-900-the-unexpected-ways-your-skin-impacts-your-health-and-longevity/.

Maryanovich, M., A. H. Zahalka, H. Pierce, et al. "Author Correction: Adrenergic Nerve Degeneration in Bone Marrow Drives Aging of the Hematopoietic Stem Cell Niche." *Nature Medicine* 25, no. 4 (2019): 701. Erratum for: *Nature Medicine* 24, no. 6 (2018): 782–791. https://pubmed.ncbi.nlm.nih.gov/30903101/.

Maugh, T. A., II "Researchers Alter Genes to Extend Worm's Life Span." *Los Angeles Times*, May 17, 1996. https://www.latimes.com/archives/la-xpm-1996-05-17-mn-5275-story.html.

Mayo Clinic. "Melanoma." Accessed April 6, 2025. https://www.mayoclinic.org/diseases-conditions/melanoma/symptoms-causes/syc-20374884.

Mayo Clinic Staff. "Chronic Stress Puts Your Health at Risk." mayoclinic.org. Accessed December 13, 2024. https://www.mayoclinic.org/healthy-lifestyle/stress-management/in-depth/stress/art-20046037.

Mayo Clinic Staff. "Friendships: Enrich Your Life and Improve Your Health." Accessed December 16, 2024 https://www.mayoclinic.org/healthy-lifestyle/adult-health/in-depth/friendships/art-20044860#:~:text=Adults%20with%20strong%20social%20connections,body%20mass%20index%20(BMI).

Mayo Clinic Staff. "Stem Cells: What They Are and What They Do?" Accessed December 9, 2024. https://www.mayoclinic.org/tests-procedures/bone-marrow-transplant/in-depth/stem-cells/art-20048117.

McFarland, L. V., S. L. H. Winkler, A. W. Heinemann, M. Jones, and A. Esquenazi. "Unilateral Upper-Limb Loss: Satisfaction and Prosthetic-Device Use in Veterans and Servicemembers from Vietnam and OIF/OEF Conflicts." *Journal of Rehabilitation Research and Development* 47, no. 4 (2010): 299–316. https://pubmed.ncbi.nlm.nih.gov/20803400/.

Mears, M., D. V. Coonrod, R. Curtis Bay, T. E. Mills, and M. C. Watkins. "Routine History as Compared to Audio Computer-Assisted Self-Interview for Prenatal Care History Taking." *Journal of Reproductive Medicine* 50, no. 9 (2005): 701–706. https://pubmed.ncbi.nlm.nih.gov/16363759/.

Medical News Today. "Healthy Microbiome Plays a Role in Healthy Skin Aging, Reaearchers Say." Accessed March 6, 2025. https://www.medicalnewstoday.com/articles/microbiome-reveals-clues-about-skin-aging#How-does-the-microbiome-affect-skin-health.

"Mediterranean Diet." Wikipedia.org. Accessed December 15, 2024. https://en.wikipedia.org/wiki/Mediterranean_diet#:~:text=The%20Mediterranean%20diet%20is%20a,formulated%20in%20the%20early%201960s.

Meier, F., M. Freix, W. Hermann, and U. M. Muller-Ladner. "Current Immunotherapy in Rheumatoid Arthritis." pubmet.ncbi.nim.nih.gov., September 5, 2013. https://pubmed.ncbi.nlm.nih.gov/23998731/.

"Melatonin for Sleep: Does It Work?" Johns Hopkins Medicine. Accessed December 13, 2024. https://www.hopkinsmedicine.org/health/wellness-and-prevention/melatonin-for-sleep-does-it-work.

Melnick, K. "Scientists Studied Twins' Diets: Those Who Ate Vegan Saw Fast Results." *Washington Post*, December 6, 2023. https://www.washingtonpost.com/nation/2023/12/06/twin-diet-study-vegan-stanford/.

Memar, P., and F. A. Faradji. "A Novel Multi-Class EEG-Based Sleep Stage Classification System." *IEEE Transactions on Neural Systems and Rehabilitation Engineering* 26, no. 1 (2018): 84–95. https://pubmed.ncbi.nlm.nih.gov/29324406/.

"Memory Problems, Forgetfulness, and Aging." National Institute on Aging. Accessed December 9, 2024. https://www.nia.nih.gov/health/memory-loss-and-forgetfulness/memory-problems-forgetfulness-and-aging#:~:text=These%20changes%20are%20usually%20signs,other%20factors%20beyond%20normal%20aging.

Mesko, B. "3D Bioprinting: Eradicating Transplantation Waiting Lists and Testing Drugs on Living Tissues." MedicalFuturist.com, May 19, 2022. https://medicalfuturist.com/3d-bioprinting-overview/.

Mesko, B. "3D Printing in Medicine and Healthcare—The Ultimate List." *Medical Futurist*, May 31, 2024. https://medicalfuturist.com /3d-printing-in-medicine-and-healthcare/.

Miranda, Daniel R. "How Playing Music Stops Brain Shrinkage and Boost Memory: Swiss Study." NAD.Com, May 24, 2023. https://www.nad.com /news/how-playing-music-affects-brain-memory.

Mirzavandi, F., M. Mollahosseini, A. Salehi-Abargouei, E. Makiabadi, and H. Mozaffari-Khosravi. "Effects of Garlic Supplementation on Serum Inflammatory Markers: A Systematic Review and Meta-Analysis of Randomized Controlled Trials." *Diabetes & Metabolic Syndrome: Clinical Research & Reviews* 14, no. 5 (2020): 1153–1161. https://pubmed.ncbi.nlm .nih.gov/32673835/.

Mishra, A., M. Fanti, X. Ge, et al. "Fasting Mimicking Diet Cycles Versus a Mediterranean Diet and Cardiometabolic Risk in Overweight and Obese Hypertensive Subjects: A Randomized Clinical Trial." *NPJ Metabolic Health and Disease* 1 (2023): 1. https://www.nature.com/articles/s44324-023-00002-1.

Mititelu, M., C. N. Oancea, S. M. Neacşu, et al. "Evaluation of Junk Food Consumption and the Risk Related to Consumer Health Among the Romanian Population." *Nutrients* 15, no. 16 (2023): 3591. https://pubmed .ncbi.nlm.nih.gov/37630781/.

Mohajeri, M. H., G. La Fata, R. E. Steinert, and P. Weber. "Relationship Between the Gut Microbiome and Brain Function." *Nutrition Reviews* 76, no. 7 (2018): 481–496. https://pubmed.ncbi.nlm.nih.gov/29701810/.

Molina-Torres, G., M. Rodriguez-Arrastia, P. Roman, N. Sanchez-Labraca, and D. Cardona. "Stress and the Gut Microbiota-Brain Axis." *Behavioural Pharmacology* 30, nos. 2 and 3-Spec Issue (2019): 187–200. https://pubmed .ncbi.nlm.nih.gov/30844962/.

Monk, Alice. "The Positive Effects of Stress: How Stress Can Actually Be Beneficial to Your Wellbeing." allhealthmatters.co.uk, November 14, 2023. https://www.allhealthmatters.co.uk/post/the-positive-effects-of-stress-how -stress-can-actually-be-beneficial-to-your-wellbeing.

"More Than Half of U.S. Adults Don't Know Heart Disease Is Leading Cause of Death, Despite 100-Year Reign." *American Heart Association Newsroom*, January 24, 2024. https://newsroom.heart.org/news/more-than-half-of-u-s-adults-dont -know-heart-disease-is-leading-cause-of-death-despite-100-year-reign.

Mullin, E. "A Gene-Edited Pig Liver Was Attached to a Person—And Worked for 3 Days." *Wired Magazine*, January 18, 2024. https://www.wired.com/story /gene-edited-liver-attached-to-person/.

Mullin, E. "The Race to Put Brain Implants in People Is Heating Up." *Wired Magazine*, December 23, 2023. https://www.wired.com/story/the-race-to-put-brain-implants -in-people-is-heating-up/?bxid=5dba1f56954fcf042f795516&cndid=590634

46&esrc=bounceXmulti&source=Email_0_EDT_WIR_NEWSLETTER_0
_DAILY_ZZ&utm_brand=wired&utm_campaign=aud-dev&utm
_content=WIR_Daily_122323&utm_mailing=WIR_Daily_122323&utm
_medium=email&utm_source=nl&utm_term=P3.

Muñoz-Lorente, M. A., A. C. Cano-Martin, and M. A. Blasco. "Mice with Hyper-Long Telomeres Show Less Metabolic Aging and Longer Lifespans." *Nature Communications* 10 (2019): 4723. https://www.nature.com/articles /s41467-019-12664-x.

Murata, S., M. Ebeling, A. C. Meyer, K. Schmidt-Mende, N. Hammar, and K. Modig. "Blood Biomarker Profiles and Exceptional Longevity: Comparison of Centenarians and Non-Centenarians in a 35-Year Follow-Up of the Swedish AMORIS Cohort." *GeroScience* 46 (2024): 1693–1702. https:// pubmed.ncbi.nlm.nih.gov/37726432/.

Musial-Whysocka, A., M. Kot, and M. Majka, et al. "The Pros and Cons of Mesenchymal Stem Cell-Based Therapies." *Cell Transplantation* 28, no. 7 (2019): 801–812. https://pubmed.ncbi.nlm.nih.gov/31018669/.

"Music as Medicine for Alzheimer's Disease and Dementia." *Northwestern Medicine*, July 2022. https://www.nm.org/healthbeat/healthy-tips/emotional-health /music-as-medicine-alzheimers-dementia#:~:text=Music%20evokes%20 emotions%20and%20memories,improve%20communication%20and%20 caregiver%20relationships.

Naghshi, S., O. Sadeghi, W. C. Willett, and A. Esmaillzadeh. "Dietary Intake of Total, Animal, and Plant Proteins and Risk of All Cause, Cardiovascular, and Cancer Mortality: Systematic Review and Dose-Response Meta-Analysis of Prospective Cohort Studies." *BMJ*, 370 (2020). https://pubmed.ncbi.nlm .nih.gov/32699048/.

"Narcolepsy." National Institute of Neurological Disorders and Stroke. Accessed December 13, 2024. https://www.ninds.nih.gov/health-information/disorders /narcolepsy.

National Cancer Institute. "Immune Checkpoint Inhibitors." Accessed March 6, 2025. https://www.cancer.gov/about-cancer/treatment/types/immunotherapy /checkpoint-inhibitors#:~:text=Immune%20checkpoints%20engage%20 when%20proteins,signal%20to%20the%20T%20cells.

Nawrat, A. "3D Printing in the Medical Field: Four Major Applications Revolutionising the Industry." medicaldevicenetwork.com, August 7, 2018. https://www.medicaldevice-network.com/features/3d-printing-in-the-medical -field-applications/?cf-view.

Neufeld, K. M., N. Kang, J. Bienenstock, and J. A. Foster. "Reduced Anxiety-Like Behavior and Central Neurochemical Change in Germ-Free Mice." *Neurogastroenterology & Motility* 23, no. 3 (2011): 255–264. https://pubmed .ncbi.nlm.nih.gov/21054680.

Newman, T. "What Are Mitochondria?" *Medical News Today*, June 14, 2023. https://www.medicalnewstoday.com/articles/320875.

Niu, C., Y. Tu, Q. Jin, et al. "Mapping the Human Oral and Gut Fungal Microbiota in Patients with Metabolic Dysfunction-Associated Fatty Liver Disease." *Frontiers in Cellular and Infection Microbiology* 26, no. 13 (2023): 1157368. https://pubmed.ncbi.nlm.nih.gov/37180439/.

Northrop, Alyssa. "Your Guide to the Best Brain Supplements." *Forbes*, January 18, 2024. https://www.forbes.com/health/supplements/best-brain-supplements/.

Novelle, M. G., A. Ali, C. Diéguez, M. Bernier, and R. de Cabo. "Metformin: A Hopeful Promise in Aging Research." *Cold Spring Harbor Perspectives in Medicine* 6, no. 3 (2016): a025932. https://pubmed.ncbi.nlm.nih.gov/26931809/.

"Nutrition and the Brain." University of Washington. Accessed January 4, 2025. http://faculty.washington.edu/chudler/nutr.html#:~:text=Your%20brain%20also%20needs%20special,can%20be%20converted%20to%20glucose.

O'Connor, Anahad. "Intermittent Fasting Trend May Pose Risks to Your Heart." *Washington Post*, March 18, 2024a. https://www.washingtonpost.com/wellness/2024/03/18/intermittent-fasting-time-restricted-eating/.

O'Connor, Anahad. "Many of Today's Unhealthy Foods Were Brought to You by Big Tobacco." *Washington Post*, September 19, 2024b. https://www.washingtonpost.com/wellness/2023/09/19/addiction-foods-hyperpalatable-tobacco/.

Oh, T. G., S. M. Kim, C. Caussy, et al. "A Universal Gut-Microbiome-Derived Signature Predicts Cirrhosis." *Cell Metabolism* 32, no. 5 (2020): 878–888.e6. https://pubmed.ncbi.nlm.nih.gov/32610095/.

Oh, H. S. H., J. Rutledge, D. Nachun, et al. "Organ Aging Signatures in the Plasma Proteome Track Health and Disease." *Nature* 624 (2023): 164–172. https://www.nature.com/articles/s41586-023-06802-1.

Ohman, J., and A. Gomez-Olivalencia. "Neanderthals Cared for Each Other and Survived into Old Age"—New Research, *Conversation*, April 5, 2018. https://theconversation.com/neanderthals-cared-for-each-other-and-survived-into-old-age-new-research-93110.

Oliver, James. "Night Watch: How Do Sleep Trackers Work?" Newscientist.com, March 25, 2020. https://www.newscientist.com/lastword/mg24532751-300-night-watch-how-do-sleep-trackers-work/#:~:text=The%20sleep%20tracker%2C%20like%20most,the%20stage%20you%20are%20in.

"Overview: Alzheimer's Disease." www.nhs.uk. Accessed December 14, 2024. https://www.nhs.uk/conditions/alzheimers-disease/.

"Overview: Osteoarthritis." www.nhs.uk. Accessed December 14, 2024. https://www.nhs.uk/conditions/osteoarthritis/.

"Overweight & Obesity Statistics." National Institute of Diabetes and Digestive and Kidney Diseases." Accessed December 10, 2024. https://www.niddk.nih.gov /health-information/health-statistics/overweight-obesity#:~:text=the%20 above%20table-,Nearly%201%20in%203%20adults%20(30.7%25)%20 are%20overweight.,9.2%25)%20have%20severe%20obesity.

Pacheco, Beatriz. "Neuroplasticity and Longevity." cenie.eu. Accessed December 9, 2024. https://cenie.eu/en/blogs/technology-and-longevity /neuroplasticity-and-longevity.

Page, M. L. "CRISPR Doubles Lifespan of Mice with Rapid Ageing Disease Progeria." *New Scientist,* January 6, 2021. https://www.newscientist.com /article/2264168-crispr-doubles-lifespan-of-mice-with-rapid-ageing-disease -progeria/.

"Pain Treatments." bioventus.com. Accessed December 24, 2024. https://www .bioventus.com/products/paintreatments/.

Park, D. C., and G. N. Bischof. "The Aging Mind: Neuroplasticity in Response to Cognitive Training." *Dialogues in Clinical Neuroscience* 15, no. 1 (2013): 109–119. https://pubmed.ncbi.nlm.nih.gov/23576894/.

Park, S. Y., M. K. Oh, B.-S. Lee, et al. "The Effects of Alcohol on Quality of Sleep." *Korean Journal of Family Medicine* 36, no. 6 (2015): 294–299. https:// pmc.ncbi.nlm.nih.gov/articles/PMC4666864/.

Patel, Aakash K., Vamsi Reddy, K. R. Shumway, and J. F. Araujo. *Physiology, Sleep Stages.* StatPearls Publishing, January 26, 2024. https://www.ncbi.nlm.nih .gov/books/NBK526132/#:~:text=Approximately%2075%25%20of%20 sleep%20is,roughly%2090%20to%20110%20minutes.

Paulas, R. "Revisiting the Evils of the Food Pyramid." pbssocal.org, January 26, 2015. https://www.pbssocal.org/food-discovery/food /revisiting-the-evils-of-the-food-pyramid.

Pavlov, V. A., and K. J. Tracey. "The Vagus Nerve and the Inflammatory Reflex— Linking Immunity and Metabolism." *Nature Reviews Endocrinology* 8, no. 12 (2012): 743–754. https://pmc.ncbi.nlm.nih.gov/articles/PMC4082307/.

Pelc, C. "A Look at the Possible Uses of 3D Printers for Eye Care." MedicalNewsToday.com, June 7, 2023. https://www.medicalnewstoday .com/articles/a-look-at-the-possible-uses-of-3d-printers-for-eye-care.

Perls, T. "Centenarians Who Avoid Dementia." *Trends in Neurosciences* 27 (2004): 633–636. https://pubmed.ncbi.nlm.nih.gov/15374676/.

Peters, R. "Ageing and the Brain." *Postgraduate Medical Journal* 82, no. 964 (2006): 84–88. https://pubmed.ncbi.nlm.nih.gov/16461469/.

Phoenix, Kaitlyn. "10 Easy Brain Exercises to Improve Your Memory." Good Housekeeping, February 25, 2023. https://www.goodhousekeeping.com /health/wellness/a43068545/brain-exercises-for-memory/.

Pleura, K. "The Most Promising 3D Printed Organs Projects (2021 Update)." Accessed December 10, 2024. https://www.sculpteo.com/blog/2019/10/16 /the-most-promising-3d-printed-organs-projects/.

Poole, R., O. J. Kennedy, and P. Roderick, J. A. Fallowfield, P. C. Hayes, and J. Parkes. "Coffee Consumption and Health: Umbrella Review of Meta-Analyses of Multiple Health Outcomes." *BMJ* 360 (2018): k194. https:// www.bmj.com/content/360/bmj.k194.

Poon, L. W., J. L. Woodard, L. S. Miller, et al. "Understanding Dementia Prevalence Among Centenarians." *Journals of Gerontology, Series A: Biological Sciences and Medical Sciences* 67, no. 4 (2012): 358–365. https://pubmed. ncbi.nlm.nih.gov/22389466/.

Poulain, M., G. M. Pes, C. Grasland, et al. "Identification of a Geographic Area Characterized by Extreme Longevity in the Sardinia Island: The AKEA Study." *Experimental Gerontology* 39, no. 9 (2004): 1423–1429. https:// pubmed.ncbi.nlm.nih.gov/15489066/.

Prater, E. "A New Study on the Mediterranean Diet Offers the Strongest Proof Yet That It's Associated with Healthy Brain Aging." *Fortune*, November 24, 2023. https://fortune.com/well/2023/11/24/mediterannean -diet-lowers-alzheimers-dementia-risk-study/.

Premier Cardiology Consultants. "Is It Anxiety or a Heart Problem?" Premiercar-diology.com. Accessed December 10, 2024. https://www.premiercardiology. com/blog/is-it-anxiety-or-a-heart-problem#:~:text=This%20can%20be%20 done%20with,first%2C%20anxiety%20or%20abnormal%20beats.

Pretzel, J. "The Foods That Fight Inflammation." *New York Times*, September 18, 2024. https://www.nytimes.com/2024/09/18/well/eat/inflammation-food -diet.html.

"Preventing Cancer." Siteman Cancer Center. Accessed December 10, 2024. https://siteman.wustl.edu/prevention/preventing-cancer/.

Qima Life Sciences. "Ageless Beauty: The Pursuit of Skin Longevity." Accessed March 6, 2025. https://qima-lifesciences.com/blog/blog-cosmetics/skin -longevity-aging/.

Qin, J., R. Li, J. Raes, et al. "A Human Gut Microbial Gene Catalogue Established by Metagenomic Sequencing." *Nature* 464, no. 7285 (2010): 59–65. https:// www.nature.com/articles/nature08821.

Racine, Vanessa. "The Impact of Stress on Your Mental Health." redcross.ca. Accessed December 14, 2024. https://www.redcross.ca/blog/2020/10 /the-impact-of-stress-on-your-mental-health.

Radel, Felicia. "iPhone 16, New Watch and AirPods Are Coming: But Is Apple Thinking Differently Enough?" usatoday.com, September 13, 2024. https://www .usatoday.com/story/tech/2024/09/13/iphone-16-watch-airpods-hearing-aid /75152109007/.

Raffaele, M., and M. Vinciguerra. "The Costs and Benefits of Senotherapeutics for Human Health." *Lancet Healthy Longevity* 3, no. 1 (2022): e67–e77. https://pubmed.ncbi.nlm.nih.gov/36098323/.

Rasch, B., and J. Born. "About Sleep's Role in Memory." *Physiological Reviews* 93, no. 2 (2013): 681–766. https://doi.org/10.1152/physrev.00032.2012.

Rauchman, Brianna. "Neuroplasticity and Healthy Aging: What You Need to Know." Pacific Neuroscience Institute, March 28, 2023. https://www.pacificneuroscienceinstitute.org/blog/brain-health/neuroplasticity-and-healthy-aging-what-you-need-to-know/.

Red Cross Blogger. "The Impact of Stress on Your Mental Health." Red Cross Talks, October 2, 2020. https://www.redcross.ca/blog/2020/10/the-impact-of-stress-on-your-mental-health.

Reisch, M. "The Microbiome Comes to Cosmetics." *Chemical & Engineering News*, May 8, 2017, 30–34. https://www.researchgate.net/publication/318772008_The_microbiome_comes_to_cosmetics.

Reiche, E. M. V., S. O. V. Nunes, and H. K. Morimoto. "Stress, Depression, the Immune System, and Cancer." *Lancet Oncology* 5 (2004): 617–625. https://pubmed.ncbi.nlm.nih.gov/15465465/.

"Revolutionizing the Treatment of Chronic Disease." vivani.com. Accessed December 14, 2024. https://vivani.com/portfolio/.

Robbins, R., S. F. Quan, M. D. Weaver, G. Bormes, L. K. Barger, and C. A. Czeisler. "Examining Sleep Deficiency and Disturbance and Their Risk for Incident Dementia and All-Cause Mortality in Older Adults Across 5 Years in the United States." *Aging (Albany NY)* 13 (2021): 3254–3268. https://pubmed.ncbi.nlm.nih.gov/33570509/.

Robbins, T., and P. H. Diamandis. *Life Force: How New Breakthroughs in Precision Medicine Can Transform Your Life and Those You Love.* Simon & Schuster, 2022. https://www.simonandschuster.com/books/Life-Force/Tony-Robbins/9781982121709

Roda, G., B. Jharap, N. Neeraj, and J.-F. Colombel. "Loss of Response to Anti-TNFs: Definition, Epidemiology, and Management." *Clinical and Translational Gastroenterology* 7 (2016): e135. https://pubmed.ncbi.nlm.nih.gov/26741065/.

Rodrigues, Jodhaira. "Worth It: Oura Ring Generation 3." consumerreports.org, August 2, 2024. https://www.consumerreports.org/electronics/wearable-technology/oura-ring-generation-3-review-a5538901516/#:~:text=What%20Does%20the%20Oura%20Ring,temperature%2C%20activity%2C%20and%20sleep.

Rogers, K. "11 Minutes of Daily Exercise Could Have a Positive Impact on Your Health, Large Study Shows." CNN, March 1, 2023. https://www.cnn.com/2023/02/28/health/moderate-physical-activity-cancer-death-risk-wellness/index.html.

Saavedra, D., A. L. Añé-Kourí, N. Barzilai, et al. "Aging and Chronic Inflammation: Highlights from a Multidisciplinary Workshop." *Immunity & Ageing* 20 (2023): 25. https://pubmed.ncbi.nlm.nih.gov/37291596/.

Santos-Longhurst, Adrienne. "Are Oxygen Bars Safe? Benefits, Risks, and What to Expect." healthline.com, March 25, 2019. https://www.healthline.com/health/oxygen-bar.

Satidpitakul, K. S. "Omega 3: Health Benefits of Nutrition." medparkhospital.com, June 17, 2023, https://www.medparkhospital.com/en-US/lifestyles/omega-3-health-benefits-of-nutrition#:~:text=is%20omega%203?-,Omega%203%20is%20a%20polyunsaturated%20fatty%20acid%20(PUFA)%20with%20abundant,heart%20disease%20and%20ischemic%20stroke.

Schildhouse, Jill. "The #1 Habit You Should Start to Live Longer, According to Health Experts." Eatingwell.com, January 16, 2024. https://www.eatingwell.com/sleep-and-longevity-8430567#:~:text=The%20most%20important%20habit%20to.

Schmauck-Medina, T., A. Molière, S. Lautrup, et al. "New Hallmarks of Ageing: A 2022 Copenhagen Ageing Meeting Summary." *Aging (Albany NY)* 14, no. 16 (2022): 6829–6839. https://www.aging-us.com/article/204248/text.

Schoenhofen, E. A., D. F. Wyszynsi, S. Andersen, et al. "Characteristics of 32 Supercentenarians." *Journal of the American Geriatrics Society* 54 (2006): 1237–1240. https://pmc.ncbi.nlm.nih.gov/articles/PMC2895458/.

Schumacher, B., J. Pothof, J. Vijg, and J. H. J. Hoeijmakers. "The Central Role of DNA Damage in the Ageing Process." *Nature* 592, no. 7856 (2021): 695–703. https://pubmed.ncbi.nlm.nih.gov/33911272/.

Schwabe, L., O. T. Wolf, and M. S. Oitzl. "Memory Formation Under Stress: Quantity and Quality." *Neuroscience & Biobehavioral Reviews* 34, no. 4 (2010): 584–591. https://doi.org/10.1016/j.neubiorev.2009.11.015. Epub 2009 Nov 30. PMID: 19931555. https://pubmed.ncbi.nlm.nih.gov/19931555/.

"Scientists Identify a Method to Rejuvenate Old Stem Cells." UCLA Health, February 27, 2023. https://www.uclahealth.org/news/release/scientists-identify-method-rejuvenate-old-stem-cells

Segal, D. *Diagnostic and Statistical Manual of Mental Disorders* (DSM-IV-TR), American Psychiatric Press, 2010. https://doi.org/10.1002/9780470479216.corpsy0271.

Senior Healthcare. "Can Ozempic Slow Aging?" Accessed March 6, 2025. https://seniorhealthcaresolutions.com/blog/can-ozempic-slow-aging/#:~:text=Some%20studies%20have%20indicated%20that,process%20at%20a%20cellular%20level.

Serrano, Jamie F. "What's the Least Amount of Sleep You Need to Get?" *Time Magazine*, July 2, 2024. https://time.com/6994478/how-much-sleep-do-you-need/.

Shade, C. "The Science Behind NMN-A Stable, Reliable NAD+Activator and Anti-Aging Molecule." *Integrative Medicine (Encinitas)* 19, no. 1 (2020): 12–14. https://pmc.ncbi.nlm.nih.gov/articles/PMC7238909/.

Shi, H., F. B. Hu, T. Huang, et al. "Sedentary Behaviors, Light-Intensity Physical Activity, and Healthy Aging." *JAMA Network Open* 7, no. 6 (2024):e2416300. https://jamanetwork.com/journals/jamanetworkopen/fullarticle/2819832.

Shibagaki, N., W. Suda, C. Clavaud, et al. "Aging-Related Changes in the Diversity of Women's Skin Microbiomes Associated with Oral Bacteria." *Scientific Reports* 7, no. 1 (2017): 10567. https://pubmed.ncbi.nlm.nih .gov/28874721/.

Sik, W. M. "7 Stunning Use Cases for 3D Printing in Medical Field." novusls. com, February 14, 2022. https://www.novusls.com/post/7-use-cases -for-medical-3d-printing.

Simonite, T. "The Search for a Pill That Can Help Dogs–and Humans—Live Longer." *Wired Magazine*, October 13, 2023. https://www.wired.com/story /the-search-for-a-pill-for-dog-and-human-longevity/.

Singh, A., S. H. Schurman, A. Bektas, et al. "Aging and Inflammation." *Cold Spring Harbor Perspectives in Medicine* 14, no. 6 (2024): a041197. https:// pubmed.ncbi.nlm.nih.gov/38052484.

Slomski, A. "Vagus Nerve Stimulation Restores Arm Function Years After Stroke." *JAMA* 325, no. 24 (2021): 2427. https://pubmed.ncbi.nlm.nih .gov/34156410/.

Smallwood, K. "Who Invented the Food Pyramid?" Today I Found Out— todayIfoundout.com, September 27, 2013. http://www.todayifoundout .com/index.php/2013/09/invented-food-pyramid/.

Smith, Carly. "How Social Connection Supports Longevity." longevity.stanford. edu, December 18, 2023. https://longevity.stanford.edu/lifestyle/2023/12/18/ how-social-connection-supports-longevity/#:~:text=The%20researchers%20 estimate%20that%20having,longevity%20by%20roughly%2050%20percent.

Smith, D. G. "Anti-Aging Enthusiasts Are Taking a Pill to Extend Their Lives: Will It Work?" *New York Times*, September 24, 2024. https://www.nytimes. com/2024/09/24/well/live/rapamycin-aging-longevity-benefits-risks.html.

Smith, D. G. "What's Your 'Biological Age'?" *New York Times*, December 19, 2023. https://www.nytimes.com/2023/12/19/well/live/biological-age-testing.html.

"Smoothies—Helpful or Harmful?" extensionusu.edu. Accessed December 16, 2024. https://extension.usu.edu/nutrition/research/smoothies-helpful-or -harmful.

Soattin, L., Z. Borbas, J. Caldwell, et al. "Structural and Functional Properties of Subsidiary Atrial Pacemakers in a Goat Model of Sinus Node Disease." *Frontiers in Physiology* 12 (2021): 592229. https://pubmed.ncbi.nlm.nih. gov/33746765/.

Sommer, F., and F. Bäckhed. "The Gut Microbiota—Masters of Host Development and Physiology." *Nature Reviews Microbiology* 11, no. 4 (2013): 227–238. https://www.nature.com/articles/nrmicro2974.

Spira, A. P., A. A. Gamaldo, A. Yang, et al. "Self-Reported Sleep and β-Amyloid Deposition in Community-Dwelling Older Adults." *JAMA Neurology* 2013, no. 12 (70): 1537–1543. https://pubmed.ncbi.nlm.nih.gov/24145859/.

Stanborough, Rebecca J. "How Does Cortisol Affect Your Sleep?" Healthline. com. Accessed December 13, 2024.

Stefanacci, Richard G. "Disorders in Older Adults." Merc Manual Consumer Version, April 2024. https://www.merckmanuals.com/home /older-people's-health-issues/the-aging-body/disorders-in-older-adults.

Stibich, M. "Healthy Life Expectancy and How It's Calculated." VeryWell Health, April 20, 2022a. https://www.verywellhealth.com/ understanding-healthy-life-expectancy-2223919.

Stibich, M. "Why Do You Age?" verywellhealth.com, May 31, 2022b. https://www. verywellhealth.com/why-we-age-theories-and-effects-of-aging-2223922.

Stibich, M. "What Is the Genetic Theory of Aging? How Genes Affect Aging and How You May 'Alter' Your Genes." verywellhealth.com May 25, 2023. Updated 2024. https://www.verywellhealth.com/the-genetic-theory-of-aging-2224222.

"Stress Effects on the Body." Apa.org, October 21, 2024. https://www.apa.org /topics/stress/body.

"Stress Management: How to Tell the Difference Between Good and Bad Stress." summahealth.org, January 18, 2021. https://www.summahealth.org/flourish /entries/2021/01/stress-management-how-to-tell-the-difference-between -good-and-bad-stress#:~:text=A%20little%20bit%20of%20stress,vital%20 for%20a%20healthy%20life.

"Stress? What Stress???" ars.usda.gov. Accessed December 14, 2024. https://www .ars.usda.gov/ARSUserFiles/ODEO/stress%20management.pdf.

Summer, J., and A. Rehman. "Does Benadryl Make You Sleepy?" Sleepfoundation. org, May 9, 2023. https://www.sleepfoundation.org/sleep-aids/does-benadryl -make-you-sleepy.

Sun, Y., M. K. Tsai, and C.-P. Wen. "Association of Sleep Duration and Sleeping Pill Use with Mortality and Life Expectancy: A Cohort Study of 484,916 Adults." *Sleep Health* 9, no. 3 (2023): 354–362. https://www. sleephealthjournal.org/article/S2352-7218(23)00030-X/abstract.

Sutton, E. F., R. Beyl, K. S. Early, W. T. Cefalu, E. Ravussin, and C. M. Peterson. "Early Time-Restricted Feeding Improves Insulin Sensitivity, Blood Pressure, and Oxidative Stress Even Without Weight Loss in Men with Prediabetes." *Cell Metabolism* 27, no. 6 (2018): 1212–1221.e3. https://pubmed.ncbi.nlm.nih .gov/29754952/.

Sykes, R. *Kindred: Neanderthal Life, Love, Death and Art.* Bloomsbury, 2020. https://www.bloomsbury.com/us/kindred-9781472937490/.

Takahashi, K., and S. Yamanaka. "Induction of Pluripotent Stem Cells from Mouse Embryonic and Adult Fibroblast Cultures by Defined Factors." *Cell* 126 (2006): 663–676. https://www.cell.com/fulltext/S0092-8674(06)00976-7.

Tamhane, M., S. Cabrera-Ghayouri, G. Abelian, and V. Viswanath. "Review of Biomarkers in Ocular Matrices: Challenges and Opportunities." *Pharmaceutical Research* 36, no. 3 (2019): 40. https://pubmed.ncbi.nlm.nih.gov/30673862/.

Templer, S. "Closed-Loop Insulin Delivery Systems: Past, Present, and Future Directions." *Frontiers in Endocrinology (Lausanne)* 13 (2022): 919942. https://pubmed.ncbi.nlm.nih.gov/35733769/.

Teoli, D., A. Dua, and J. An. "Transcutaneous Electrical Nerve Stimulation." March 20, 2024. In: *StatPearls* [Internet]. StatPearls Publishing. 2024 January. https://pubmed.ncbi.nlm.nih.gov/30725873/.

"The Dangers of Uncontrolled Sleep Apnea." Johnshopkinsmedicine.org. Accessed December 14, 2024. https://www.hopkinsmedicine.org/health /wellness-and-prevention/the-dangers-of-uncontrolled-sleep-apnea.

"The Effects of Stress on Your Body." WebMD.com, February 29, 2024. https://www .webmd.com/balance/stress-management/effects-of-stress-on-your-body.

"The Equality of Opportunity Project." The Equality of Opportunity Project. Accessed January 3, 2025. http://www.equality-of-opportunity.org /health/#:~:text=The%20richest%20American%20men%20live,are%20 growing%20rapidly%20over%20time.

"The Rise of Oxygen Bars." WebMD.com. Accessed December 16, 2024. https:// www.webmd.com/balance/features/rise-of-oxygen-bars.

The Skin Network. "How Your Skin Affects Health and Longevity." Accessed March 6, 2025. https://www.skincarenetwork.co.uk/dermatology-news /skin-health-and-longevity/#:~:text=Research%20findings%20suggest%20 that%20skin,will%20reduce%20body%20wide%20deterioration.

The State of Health Disparities in the United States. ncbi.nlm.nih.gov. Accessed December 30, 2024. https://www.ncbi.nlm.nih.gov/books/NBK425844/#:~:text= Heart%20disease%20and%20cancer%20are,HHS%2C%202016b%2Cd.

Tilg, H., T. E. Adolph, R. R. Gerner, and A. R. Moschen. "The Intestinal Microbiota in Colorectal Cancer." *Cancer Cell* 33 (2018): 954–964. https:// pubmed.ncbi.nlm.nih.gov/29657127/.

Tobin, D. J., and R. Paus. "Graying: Gerontobiology of the Hair Follicle Pigmentary Unit." *Experimental Gerontology* 36 (2001): 29–54. https:// pubmed.ncbi.nlm.nih.gov/11162910/.

Tor-Roca, A., A. Sánchez-Pla, A. Korosi, et al. "A Mediterranean Diet-Based Metabolomic Score and Cognitive Decline in Older Adults: A Case–Control Analysis Nested Within the Three-City Cohort Study." *Molecular Nutrition & Food Research* 68, no. 13 (2023): 2300271. https://doi.org/10.1002/mnfr.202300271.

Tracey, K. "The Inflammatory Reflex." *Nature* 420 (2002): 853–859. https:// pubmed.ncbi.nlm.nih.gov/12490958/.

Tracy, B. L., F. M. Ivey, D. Hurlbut, et al. "Muscle Quality. II. Effects of Strength Training in 65- to 75-yr-old Men and Women." *Journal of Applied Physiology* 86 (1999): 195–201. https://pubmed.ncbi.nlm.nih.gov/9887131/.

Ullah, M., and Z. Sun. "Stem Cells and Anti-Aging Genes: Double-Edged Sword—Do the Same Job of Life Extension." *Stem Cell Research & Therapy* 9 (2018): 3. https://stemcellres.biomedcentral.com/articles/10.1186/s13287-017-0746-4.

Umberson, D., and J. K. Montez. "Social Relationships and Health: A Flashpoint for Health Policy." *Journal of Health and Social Behavior*, 51 suppl., (2010): S54–S66. https://pmc.ncbi.nlm.nih.gov/articles/PMC3150158/.

"Understanding the Connection Between Sleep and Dementia." Harvard Pilgrim Healthcare, August 2021. https://www.harvardpilgrim.org/hapiguide/understanding-the-connection-between-sleep-and-dementia/#:~:text=In%20a%20long%2Dterm%20study,to%20eight%20hours%20per%20night.

"Urinalysis." https://www.mayoclinic.org/tests-procedures/urinalysis/about/pac-20384907#:~:text=A%20urinalysis%20is%20a%20test,concentration%20and%20content%20of%20urine

USCDornsife. "Common Drug Shows Promise in Extending Lifespan" October 23, 2024. Accessed March 6, 2025. https://dornsife.usc.edu/news/stories/mifepristone-anti-aging-effects-from-increased-mitophagy/.

"Vagus Nerve." *Psychology Today*. Accessed December 14, 2024. https://www.psychologytoday.com/us/basics/vagus-nerve#:~:text=Among%20the%20many%20operations%20of,response%20to%20stress%2C%20curbing%20the.

"Vagus Nerve Stimulation (VNS) Therapy." epilepsy.com. Accessed December 14, 2024. https://www.epilepsy.com/treatment/devices/vagus-nerve-stimulation-therapy.

Vaishya, R., and A. Vaish. "Falls in Older Adults Are Serious." *Indian Journal of Orthopaedics* 54, no. 1 (2020): 69–74. https://pmc.ncbi.nlm.nih.gov/articles/PMC7093636/.

Valenzano, D. R., E. Terzibasi, T. Genade, A. Cattaneo, L. Domenici, and A. Cellerino. "Resveratrol Prolongs Lifespan and Retards the Onset of Age-Related Markers in a Short-Lived Vertebrate." *Current Biology* 16 (2006): 296–300. https://pubmed.ncbi.nlm.nih.gov/16461283/.

Veeresham, C. "Natural Products Derived from Plants as a Source of Drugs." *Journal of Advanced Pharmaceutical Technology & Research* 3, no. 4 (2012): 200–201. https://pmc.ncbi.nlm.nih.gov/articles/PMC3560124/.

Vetr, N. G., and N. R. Gay. MoTrPAC Study Group, and S. B. Montgomery. "The Impact of Exercise on Gene Regulation in Association with Complex Trait Genetics." *Nature Communications* 15 (2024): 3346. https://www.nature.com/articles/s41467-024-45966-w.

Volpi, E., R. Nazemi, and S. Fujita. "Muscle Tissue Changes with Aging." *Current Opinion in Clinical Nutrition and Metabolic Care* 7, no. 4 (2004): 405–410. https://pubmed.ncbi.nlm.nih.gov/15192443/.

von Kobbe, C. "Targeting Senescent Cells: Approaches, Opportunities, Challenges." *Aging (Albany NY)* 11, no. 24 (2019): 12844–12861. https://pubmed.ncbi.nlm.nih.gov/31789602/.

Wan, G., X. Yu, P. Chen, et al. "Metformin Therapy Associated with Survival Benefit in Lung Cancer Patients with Diabetes." *Oncotarget* 7 (2016): 35437–35445. https://pmc.ncbi.nlm.nih.gov/articles/PMC5085241/.

Wang, C., D. Jurk, M. Maddick, G. Nelson, C. Martin-Ruiz, and T. von Zglinicki. "DNA Damage Response and Cellular Senescence in Tissues of Aging Mice." *Aging Cell* 8 (2009): 311–322. https://pubmed.ncbi.nlm.nih.gov/19627270/.

Wang, W., Y. Zheng, S. Sun, et al. "A Genome-Wide CRISPR-Based Screen Identifies KAT7 as a Driver of Cellular Senescence." *Science Translational Medicine* 13, no. 575 (2021): eabd2655. https://pubmed.ncbi.nlm.nih.gov/33408182/.

Wang, X., Q. Ding, T. Li, et al. "Application of Vagus Nerve Stimulation on the Rehabilitation of Upper Limb Dysfunction After Stroke: A Systematic Review and Meta-Analysis." *Frontiers in Neurology* 14 (2023): 1189034. https://pmc.ncbi.nlm.nih.gov/articles/PMC10321132/.

Wang, X., Y. Xu, X. Li, et al. "Day-to-Day Deviations in Sleep Parameters and Biological Aging: Findings from the NHANES 2011–2014." *Sleep Health* 9, no. 6 (2023): 940–946. https://pubmed.ncbi.nlm.nih.gov/37648648/.

"Want to 3D Print a Kidney? Start by Thinking Small." *Science News*, April 13, 2022, https://www.sciencedaily.com/releases/2022/04/220413151120.htm.

Washington Post Staff, "The Post Spent the Past Year Examining U.S. Life Expectancy: Here's What We Found." *Washington Post*, October 3, 2023. https://www.washingtonpost.com/health/2023/10/02/takeaways-us-life-expectancy-crisis/.

Watts, E. "Can Being More Flexible Help People Live Longer?" *Medical News Today*, August 26, 2024, https://www.medicalnewstoday.com/articles/being-more-flexible-help-people-live-longer.

Wei, M., S. Brandhorst, M. Shelehchi, et al. "Fasting-Mimicking Diet and Markers/Risk Factors for Aging, Diabetes, Cancer, and Cardiovascular Disease." *Science Translational Medicine* 9, no. 377 (2017): eaai8700. https://pubmed.ncbi.nlm.nih.gov/28202779/.

Wei, M. L., M. Tada, A. So, and R. Torres. "Artificial Intelligence and Skin Cancer." *Frontiers in Medicine (Lausanne)* 11 (2024): 1331895. https://pubmed.ncbi.nlm.nih.gov/38566925/.

Weir, R. F., P. R. Troyk, G. A. DeMichele, D. A. Kerns, J. F. Schorsch, and H. Mass. "Implantable Myoelectric Sensors (IMESs) for Intramuscular Electromyogram Recording." *IEEE Transactions on Biomedical Engineering* 56, no. 1 (2009): 159–171. https://pmc.ncbi.nlm.nih.gov/articles/PMC3157946/.

"What Causes Cancer?" Stanfordhealthcare.org. Accessed December 12, 2024. https://stanfordhealthcare.org/medical-conditions/cancer/cancer/cancer-causes.html.

"What Is Cancer?" cancerresearchuk.org. Accessed December 10, 2024. https://www.cancerresearchuk.org/about-cancer/what-is-cancer.

"What Is FoundationOne Liquid CDX?" foundationmedicine.com. Accessed December 9, 2024. https://www.foundationmedicine.com/test/foundationone-liquid-cdx?utm_source=google&utm_medium=cpc&utm_campaign=UB+%7C+LiquidCDx+Priority&gclid=Cj0KCQiA2KitBh CIARIsAPPMEhIB0EmWi4_1jw-Yl6ZCAcUFnu2CvqKN5rTC85LTYdeH zABZFlNqdYsaAsTSEALw_wcB&gclsrc=aw.ds.

"What Is Huntington's Disease?" Huntington's Australia. Accessed December 9, 2024. https://huntingtonsaustralia.au/#:~:text=From%20the%20onset%20of%20symptoms,occasionally%20even%20later%20in%20life.

"What Is Narcolepsy?" Johns Hopkins Medicine. Accessed December 13, 2024. https://www.hopkinsmedicine.org/health/conditions-and-diseases/narcolepsy#.

"What You Need to Know About Blood Testing." MedlinePlus. Accessed December 9, 2024. https://medlineplus.gov/lab-tests/what-you-need-to-know-about-blood-testing/.

"Why We Age: Stem Cell Exhaustion." Lifespan Extension Advocacy Foundation, June 23, 2022. https://www.lifespan.io/topic/stem-cell-exhaustion/.

Wiginton, Keri. "What to Know About Over-the-Counter Sleep Medications." WebMD.com, July, 16, 2023. https://www.webmd.com/sleep-disorders/otc-sleep-medications-what-to-know.

Williams, Vivian. "Mayo Clinic Minute: Dietary Supplements Don't Reduce Dementia Risk, but 3 Tips Do." Mayo Clinic, June 11, 2019. https://newsnetwork.mayoclinic.org/discussion/mayo-clinic-minute-dietary-supplements-dont-reduce-dementia-risk-but-3-tips-do/.

Willmer, Gareth. "Helping the Body and Brain to Welcome Bionic Limbs and Implants." *Horizon*, October 12, 2022. https://projects.research-and-innovation.ec.europa.eu/en/horizon-magazine/helping-body-and-brain-welcome-bionic-limbs-and-implants.

Wilmanski, T., C. Diener, N. Rappaport, et al. "Gut Microbiome Pattern Reflects Healthy Ageing and Predicts Survival in Humans." *Nature Metabolism* 3, no. 2 (2021): 274–286. https://pubmed.ncbi.nlm.nih.gov/33619379/.

Wirth, A., B. Wolf, C.-K. Huang, et al. "Novel Aspects of Age-Protection by Spermidine Supplementation Are Associated with Preserved Telomere Length." *GeroScience* 43, no. 2 (2021): 673–690. https://pubmed.ncbi.nlm.nih.gov/33517527/.

Woolf, Stephen H., Sara M. Simon, L. Aron, E. Zimmerman, L. Dubay, and K. X. Luk. "How Are Income and Wealth Linked and Longevity." Urban.org, April 2015. https://www.urban.org/sites/default/files/publication/49116/2000178 -How-are-Income-and-Wealth-Linked-to-Health-and-Longevity.pdf.

World Stroke Organization. "Global Stroke Fact Sheet 2022." world-stroke. org. Accessed December 14, 2024. https://www.world-stroke.org/assets /downloads/WSO_Global_Stroke_Fact_Sheet.pdf.

Xie, L., H. Kang, Q. Xu, et al. "Sleep Drives Metabolite Clearance from the Adult Brain." *Science* 342 (2013): 373–377. https://pubmed.ncbi.nlm.nih .gov/24136970/.

Xu, C. H., H. Zhu, and P. Qiu. "Aging Progression of Human Gut Microbiota." *BMC Microbiology* 19, no. 1 (2019): 236. https://pubmed.ncbi.nlm.nih .gov/31660868/.

Yakupu, A., R. Aimaier, B. Yuan, et al. "The Burden of Skin and Subcutaneous Diseases: Findings from the Global Burden of Disease Study 2019." *Frontiers in Public Health* 11 (2023): 1145513. https://pubmed.ncbi.nlm.nih.gov/37139398/.

Yamanaka, S. "Strategies and New Developments in the Generation of Patient-Specific Pluripotent Stem Cells." *Cell Stem Cell* 1, no. 1 (2007): 39–49. https://pubmed.ncbi.nlm.nih.gov/18371333/.

Yaribeygi, H., Y. Panahi, H. Sahraei, T. P. Johnston, and A. Sahebkar. "The Impact of Stress on Body Function: A Review." *EXCLI Journal* 16 (2017): 1057–1072. https://pmc.ncbi.nlm.nih.gov/articles/PMC5579396/.

Yasir, M., A. Goyal, and S. Sidharth. *Corticosteroid Adverse Effects*. ncbi.nlm. nih.gov, July 3, 2023. https://www.ncbi.nlm.nih.gov/books/NBK531462 /#:~:text=%5B13%5D%20These%20adverse%20effects%20 include,of%20hair%2C%20and%20perioral%20dermatitis .&text=Glucocorticoids%20increase%20the%20risk%20of,ulcer%20 formation%2C%20and%20GI%20bleeding.

Youmshajekian, L. "Your Organs Might Be Aging at Different Rates." Scientific American, December 6, 2023. https://www.scientificamerican.com/article /your-organs-might-be-aging-at-different-rates/.

Yousefzadeh, M., C. Henpita, R. Vyas, C. Soto-Palma, P. Robbins, and L. Niedernhofer. "DNA Damage—How and Why We Age?" *eLife* 10 (2021): e62852. https://elifesciences.org/articles/62852.

Yousefzadeh, M. J., Y. Zhu, S. J. McGowan, et al. "Fisetin Is a Senotherapeutic That Extends Health and Lifespan." *eBioMedicine* 36 (2018): 18–28. https:// pubmed.ncbi.nlm.nih.gov/30279143/.

Yu, L. X., and R. F. Schwabe. "The Gut Microbiome and Liver Cancer: Mechanisms and Clinical Translation." *Nature Reviews Gastroenterology & Hepatology* 14 (2017): 527–539. https://pubmed.ncbi.nlm.nih.gov/28676707/.

Zee, Phyllis. "What Do Sleep Trackers Track?" *Northwestern Medicine*, December 2021. https://www.nm.org/healthbeat/healthy-tips/what-sleep-trackers-track#:~:text=Sleep%20trackers%20use%20an%20accelerometer,the%20quality%20of%20your%20sleep.

Zein, N. N., L. A. Hanouneh, P. D. Bishop, et al. "Three-Dimensional Print of a Liver for Preoperative Planning in Living Donor Liver Transplantation." *Liver Transplant* 19 (2013): 1304–1310. https://pubmed.ncbi.nlm.nih.gov/23959637/.

Zhang, B., D. E. Lee, A. Trapp, et al. "Multi-Omic Rejuvenation and Life Span Extension on Exposure to Youthful Circulation." *Nature Aging* 3 (2023): 948–964. https://pubmed.ncbi.nlm.nih.gov/37500973/.

Zhao, L. Y., J. X. Mei, G. Yu, et al. "Role of the Gut Microbiota in Anticancer Therapy: From Molecular Mechanisms to Clinical Applications." *Signal Transduction and Targeted Therapy* 8 (2023): 201. https://www.nature.com/articles/s41392-023-01406-7.

Zheng, C., T. Chen, J. Lu, et al. "Adjuvant Treatment and Molecular Mechanism of Probiotic Compounds in Patients with Gastric Cancer After Gastrectomy." *Food & Function* 12 (2021): 6294–6308. https://pubmed.ncbi.nlm.nih.gov/34052844/.

Zhou, L., K. Yu, L. Yang, et al. "Sleep Duration, Midday Napping, and Sleep Quality and Incident Stroke: The Dongfeng-Tongji Cohort." *Neurology* 94, no. 4 (2019): e345–e356. https://www.neurology.org/doi/10.1212/WNL.0000000000008739.

Zhu, Y., J. Ge, C. Huang, H. Liu, and H. Jiang. "Application of Mesenchymal Stem Cell Therapy for Aging Frailty: From Mechanisms to Therapeutics." *Theranostics* 11, no. 12 (2021): 5675–5685. https://pubmed.ncbi.nlm.nih.gov/33897874/.

Ziegler-Graham, K., E. J. Mackenzie, P. L. Ephraim, T. G. Travison, and R. Brookmeyer. "Estimating the Prevalence of Limb Loss in the United States: 2005 to 2050." *Archives of Physical Medicine and Rehabilitation* 89, no. 3 (2008): 422–429. https://pubmed.ncbi.nlm.nih.gov/18295618/.

Zou, Q., Y. Lai, and Z.-R. Lun. "Exploring the Association Between Oxygen Concentration and Life Expectancy in China: A Quantitative Analysis." *International Journal of Environmental Research and Public Health* 20, no. 2 (2023): 1125. https://pubmed.ncbi.nlm.nih.gov/36673882/.

About the Authors

Thomas Lobl, PhD

Dr. Lobl has over 55 years of experience in the pharmaceutical and medical device industries His experience includes immunology, inflammatory, infectious, cancer, reproductive and endocrinology disease areas. He has taken drug and device projects from conception stages through clinical trials and has presented and managed regulatory filings with the FDA and European regulatory agencies. He has participated in an Ad Hoc UCLA longevity committee that evaluated publications on longevity, stem cells and senescence scientific work. The longevity committee studied super-centenarians (people over 110 years of age) and tried to identify markers associated with their longevity. He has also studied implanted medical devices. His microbiome projects evaluated how the microbiome influenced the effectiveness of anti-cancer drugs and therapies. He has worked on Alzheimer's Disease and programs on dementia. Tom has over 76 publications and patents, co-authored 2 books and has been a scientific reviewer or editorial board member on a variety of scientific journals. Dr. Lobl has a PhD from Johns Hopkins Univ. and post-graduate work at Caltech and Rockefeller Univ and is a Fellow of the American Institute for Medical and Biological Engineering. He has worked in both big pharma and a variety of biotech start-up companies, at the Alfred Mann Found. (Emerging Technology Strategist), at the Alfred Mann Inst. at Univ. S. California (Entrepreneur in Residence) and as a consultant. He mentors several start-up companies and is a co-teacher at UCLA's Medtech class and lectures at KGI, City of Hope, USC and other academic institutions.

Stan Schatt, PhD

Dr. Schatt can be described as a futurist with a knack for identifying the future impact of innovative technology well before the general public. He spent two decades in senior management positions with some of the world's leading global technology consulting firms including Forrester Research. Schatt's more than forty books include college textbooks and technology guides for such major publishers as Simon and Schuster, Prentice-Hall, John Wiley, and McGraw-Hill. His latest book, *Still Room for Humans: Career Planning in an AI World*, was published in 2023 by Business Expert Press. A gifted speaker, he received citations for outstanding teaching from the University of Southern California, the University of Houston, and DeVry Institute of Technology. He also served as a Fulbright Professor to Japan where he taught at Tokyo University. Schatt holds a PhD in English from the University of Southern California, an MBA from the American Graduate School of International Management, and an undergraduate degree in Chemistry from Arizona State University. Schatt wrote a regular column for *ComputerWorld*. He has been quoted in dozens of major periodicals including *Fortune Magazine, Bloomberg Businessweek, The New York Times*, and *Money Magazine*, and he has been interviewed on CNBC.

Index

www.ingramcontent.com/pod-product-compliance
Lightning Source LLC
Chambersburg PA
CBHW061155220326
41599CB00025B/4493